A Country Boy From Pitkin
My Life Story

by

Curtis Francis Hoglan

authorHOUSE®

AuthorHouse™
1663 Liberty Drive, Suite 200
Bloomington, IN 47403
www.authorhouse.com
Phone: 1-800-839-8640

First published by AuthorHouse 11/16/2007

ISBN: 978-1-4343-4911-8 (sc)

Printed in the United States of America
Bloomington, Indiana

This book is printed on acid-free paper.

PREFACE

2007

Over the last few years, several people have asked me to write my memoirs. I have been privileged to live a "rich" life, full of exciting experiences, and some that could be characterized, as a Dust-Off Army Medical Helicopter Pilot said it, "hours and hours of boredom interrupted by moments of stark terror"! Obviously, it is not going to make anybody's best-seller list. I am doing it for my family, some great cousins and friends, and my special army friends and comrades. My motivation for writing it stems from several reasons:

First, and perhaps foremost, my knowledge of *my* parents' early lives is almost non-existent. They were 48 years old when I was born, and I know very little about their lives up to that point. My Mom and Dad were children in families of 10 siblings each, so I once had more than 30 aunts and uncles that I could have (should have) asked more questions about my parents. All of my aunts and uncles are deceased now. They were some of my very favorite people. My uncles spent time with me, and my aunts raised me with lots of love and hugging---I'm still a hugger today! I have also been blessed with dozens of great cousins. A few Christmases ago, I talked to one of my first cousins who made the trip from Louisiana to Texas, along with his mother, brothers and sister---the trip that started everything for me. Carroll Richmond has been one of my favorite cousins and is now deceased. He told me wonderful stories about those days. How I wish I had recorded that session and more, but I will relate what I can remember from our conversation, in the beginning of this epistle.

Second, I want my family, our children, grandchildren, their children, etc. to have a record of my experiences. Although it is *my* autobiography, it also relates some of the experiences of my wife and children to this point, in 2007. I have not kept a diary. All I will relate comes from memory, a few documents, pictures, and a lot of help from my wife, whose memory is better than mine in most respects. In particular, her memory of all my mistakes is close to that of an elephant! (I may omit a lot of these!) I surely have misquoted some dates, misspelled some names, and forgot to mention *all* of the folks who have helped me so much along my great journey. Also, I have used my Senior Citizen "entitlement" to embellish some of these stories and accounts, and I have engaged in *some* minor reconstruction. But they are basically all true. And when I remember individuals who, let us say, I did not find helpful, they shall remain nameless. It is not my intention to slam-dunk anyone, but the *story* may be necessary, or at least entertaining, so I may have included it. Anyway, when I look back over these 73 years, it's easier and much more pleasant to remember just the good times and the great people, and there were plenty of both.

I owe so much to senior military officers who gave me the opportunity to command the finest soldiers in the world---America's soldiers, and to let me have the freedom to learn how to do it. I am enormously grateful to all my junior officers and all the great soldiers that made me look good. I have a special place in my heart for Non-Commissioned Officers (NCOs). Senior NCOs *raised* me in the Army, and taught me so much. Incidentally, they also *run* the Army!

So this manuscript is dedicated to my civilian family and my army family.

CONTENTS

Chapter One

THE EARLY YEARS

ONE

Texas Adventure

In the beginning, there was a beautiful young girl, Amy Ann Thornton, the daughter of William Aaron and Amanda Elizabeth McCollough Thornton. She was the oldest of ten children with 3 brothers and 6 sisters. She was born on 1 August 1886 in Ouiska (Whisky) Chitto Creek, Vernon Parish, Louisiana. There was also a handsome young man, C. F. Hoglan, son of James F. and Mary Angeline Talbert Hoglan, also with ten siblings in the their family. He was born on 31 August 1886. These folks were married on 24 December 1915. Sorrowfully, I do not know very much about their lives until about 1934. C. F. worked in various jobs, in a sawmill, and as a merchant, operating a general merchandise and furniture store. He served 33 months in the U.S. Army, fighting in France in World War I as a medic in the 114th Field Signal Battalion, of the 39th (Dixie Delta) Infantry Division. Amy taught in a one-room country school, worked in a furniture store, ran a hamburger stand, and took in boarders.

In 1934, C. F., at age 48, decided that he wanted to go to college. They were living in Pitkin, Louisiana, a small village in central Louisiana very close to where they were born. He and his wife, Amy, together with Amy's sister, Zada, and Zada's 4 children, piled into C.F.'s old Model T Ford truck, and struck off to Nacogdoches, Texas, home of Stephen F. Austin College. The trip was an awesome adventure. The only money they had between them was $5. On day one of the trip, Zada went into the woods to "powder her nose" and *lost* the $5. They literally worked their way to Nacogdoches, Texas, picking cotton, thinning corn and doing other work for food along the way. They would just drive up to a farmhouse and ask if there was any work they could do for food. They also earned enough gas money to get to Nacogdoches (thank God gas was not $3 a gallon or else they would still be out there on the road somewhere picking cotton).

Upon arriving in Nacogdoches they kept on working. Amy was a waitress in a little café, and C.F. got a part time job in a small Post Office. C. F. enrolled in Stephen F. Austin College as a freshman in Business Administration at age 48. He graduated four years later at age 52 with a Bachelor of Arts degree in Business Administration. But I am getting ahead of myself.

In the summer of 1934, a very important event took place, extremely important to me! C. F. and Amy drove down to Austin, Texas in that old Model T truck, and entered an adoption ward of a hospital. Amy said she picked out the loudest and wettest boy in the house! And I still may be the loudest, if not the wettest boy in the house! They adopted me shortly after I was born on 20 June 1934, and I cost them the whole amount of 50 cents. Although some may disagree, I claim I am worth every penny of it!

I have no idea who my biological parents were, and have never wondered about it very much. My Mom made a trip back to Austin in 1957 and tried to find out, and get a birth certificate for me, but there were no records. With the assistance of a lawyer, she did get a birth certificate for me, dated 1957---let's see---that makes me about 50 years old in 2007, doesn't it?? They always told me that I was adopted, even before I knew what the word meant, so there was no big shock or emotional moment when I was older. One thing I *do* know. I *do* know who my *real* parents were---C.F. and Amy Hoglan! As a little girl once responded when asked what it was meant by her being adopted, she said, *"I grew in my Mommy's heart instead of her tummy!"* That is an awesome and perfect definition of the term adoption (Excuse me for choking up a little bit when I relate this story----I'm not getting emotional, it's just that my underwear is a bit too tight!). My folks never had much money---the sale of the little house they lived in for their last few years didn't even pay for their funerals, yet they were rich in so many other ways, and they gave everything they had to me. They gave me unconditional love, continuous encouragement, and a tremendous set of values that I treasure and try to live up to today.

I can remember several cousins coming by the house to say goodbye on their way back to college or wherever, and Mom giving them a five or ten dollar bill---a lot of money in those days. It is fair to say that she was a favorite aunt to all those dozens of cousins of mine. She had a well-deserved reputation for being the best lemon and coconut pie maker in the land. All her sisters were my favorite people---Aunt Etta, Aunt Bertie, Aunt Nell, Aunt Lola, Aunt Jane (Lydia), and Aunt Zada. Her three brothers were my Uncle Virgil, Uncle, Sam, and Uncle David. More about these wonderful aunts and uncles, and kinfolks on my Dad's side of the family later. My Mom was also a Saint. She loved the Lord and was only one of two people I ever met, that if she would have ever been slapped, would literally turn the other cheek, forgive the person, and pray for them. She would never, never let me get away with saying a critical remark about anyone. She was the most perfect woman I have ever met. I know that the good Lord is enjoying her company now as she sits at His right hand. The other "perfect" woman in my life was my Mother-in-Law. More about this other Saint later. I am very proud of my Dad's military service in WW I. He is still my favorite hero! I just wish I could have done more for both of them.

TWO

Home in Pitkin

We lived in Nacogdoches, Texas for four years, and then moved back to Pitkin, Louisiana, in 1938. Now, Pitkin had (and has) a population of about 200, counting people, chickens, cows, and armadillos. In case you don't know where Pitkin is, it's between Cravens and Dido--now you know! Our biggest industry was Jury duty and our heaviest industry was a 300-pound Avon lady! We lived with my Grandmother Thornton in the old Thornton place, a big, two-story farmhouse, one half mile from "downtown" Pitkin.

The two-story house had four fireplaces, screened back porch, two open verandas, kitchen with wood stove, water well at the end of the porch, several bedrooms, and no bathroom or indoor plumbing. Of course, there was no air conditioning, and heating was accomplished by the 4 fireplaces and the wood stove in the kitchen. We heated water on the wood stove and took it out to the bathhouse, and poured it into a large metal washtub, for baths. The well casing at the end of the back porch was about three square feet. After milking the cows, we would strain the milk into mason fruit jars, tie long strings around the top of the jars, and lower them into the well for cooling by the cold water, and tie off the strings to nails driven around the top of the well casing. Later we got the modern convenience of an icebox--not a refrigerator--the iceman would come about once a week and deliver a huge block of ice to put into the insulated icebox. Separate from the main house were a blacksmith shop, smokehouse, bathhouse, two barns with hayloft, corncrib, and a two-hole outhouse (WOW). In addition to a big garden, the farm consisted of about 200 acres, where we raised corn, cotton, and hay. We owned several cows, horses, chickens, pigs, at

6

least one dog, and seventeen cats. There were enough rats in the barns and corncrib to keep the cats pretty busy. We had a 1 X 10 inch board about 12 feet long laying in the back yard. I can remember Mom taking table scraps outside and spreading them on the board, and then yelling K-I-T-T-E-E-E-E, and cats would come running from all directions. We usually had a hired hand to help us with the farming. Dad began teaching Business Administration, typing, shorthand, etc. at Pitkin High School. The first year, I would cry when he left most mornings to go to school, because I wanted to go with him. So the next year, 1939, when I was barely 5 years old, he took me to school and enrolled me in the first grade. I attended school in Pitkin through the sixth grade. My Aunt Bertie and Aunt Jane taught me for two of those six years. I still have my report cards. They prove I was an average student.

Everybody in the family works when you live on a farm. Although I was quite young, I certainly got in on many chores. During the next seven years, I picked cotton, thinned corn, hauled in hay, and did some plowing in the fields. I milked cows, fed the animals, and my favorite chore was saddling up my horse, Fanny, and going across the branch (creek), up into a field and rounding up the cows and herding them back to the barn. It was not very difficult---the cows knew it was the time of day for feeding, so they pretty well herded themselves. I was not old enough to do lots of heavy work, but I did get a little experience in farming. We had no tractors or motorized machinery. All farming was done with horse-drawn implements. I remember the mowing machine, hay rake, wagon, and some plows: Georgia stock, harrow, disc, gee-whiz, turning plow, and middlebuster. The turning plow turned the dirt in one direction, either right or left. The middlebuster had two "blades" and turned the dirt both left and right. It was the hardest to control. I do remember that the main purpose of the brace between the tops of the handles on the plow stock was for jumping up and hitting me under the chin when the middlebuster plowed under a tree root. Thank goodness old Nellie, our plow horse, would stop until I regained consciousness. One chore had a *lasting* effect on me-----hog killin'. You take a 55-gallon drum; partially bury it at an angle in the ground. Heat water on a wood fire until it boils, and fill the drum. Dip the hog in it (*after* it was killed, preferably). The scalding water makes it easier to scrape off the hair of the hog. Then you hang the hog up by the hind legs, gut it and take out the entrails. Now, intestines have a smell that gets on your hands and stays for at least a week, no matter how you scrub them. But they say that there's nothing better than tree whipped chitlins!! So you have to clean them---you don't waste anything on a farm. I had a girl friend, Virginia, 9 miles down the road in Elizabeth, Louisiana, and I could not go see her for at least ten days after one of our hog killins'.

There are no days off, when working a farm. Those cows have got to come unmilked every day! And the animals must be fed every day. Although these were great experiences, I became convinced that I needed to look for a career change down the road---I was never going to make it as a farmer. But we did have great entertainment. Daddy would gather some cousins and me in his old Chevrolet, and drive the 9 miles on a usually washed out gravel road to Elizabeth, La. on most Saturday nights to the black and white shoot-em-up movies---westerns only, Lash LaRue, Tom Mix, Hopalong Cassidy, Gene Autry, Roy Rogers, Gabby Hayes, etc. We also had rat killins' down at the barn and corn crib, climbed the huge magnolia trees in the yard, had corn cob fights with the cousins, played "piggy wants a motion" down at the barnyard, rode horses, and swam at the Old Ford on six mile creek, after we threw rocks to scare off the snakes. We had our share of bruises and busts. I fell in a rut and broke my arm, playing down at the branch where the cows crossed. And my cousin, Billy Cain, and I were riding old Fanny bareback, and she spooked and jumped sideways. I was hanging on, but Billy, sitting behind me, grabbed me to keep from falling off, and pushed me to the ground, then fell on top of me! I broke my collarbone. Kept me out of school for a few days.

We moved away for four years, but when we moved back to Pitkin, I practically lived at the old Thornton place, occupied then by the Cain family, Uncle Alton and Mom's sister, Aunt Etta. So the cousins had more corncob fights. Uncle Alton was every cousin's favorite uncle. What an entertainer! He could dive in six-mile creek in 12 inches of water! Never figured out how he could do that. He kept a pet chicken snake down at the barn and would delight cousins by showing it off. He was amazing with kids. He could take a young kid that was crying tears as big as biscuits, and have him laughing his head off in 20 seconds. I wrote my first essay in college about my Uncle Alton. The Cain's had a fine family, but three of their children died early, untimely deaths. Three boys remain; Alton Jr, who later was best man at my wedding. James David is a former State Senator and a State Representative in Louisiana, and Burl is the Warden at Angola State Penitentiary. Their wives are Rene and Jonalyn. Alton Junior married Anita Hinson and they have a great family: Diann is married to Kenny Norris and they live in Pitkin. Diann has a PhD degree and teaches at LSU in Alexandria. Her daughter, Katie is married to Paul Williams. Kenny works at Angola State Penitentiary. Dena is married to Dr. Larry Parker, a medical doctor, and Dee Ann, the youngest daughter teaches school at Simpson, LA.

Uncle Joe Howard and Aunt Bertie, Mom's sister continued to live in Pitkin. Aunt Bertie was the youngest in the Thornton family and like all my aunts, was a great cook. I remember that every time I went to their house, she would have a mess of butter beans in that old iron pot, ready to be heated up. Uncle Joe took me fishing and squirrel hunting many times, and we shared some great times together. Their daughter, Gloria Jean, and I, being close to the same age, were close, and used to have to fend off the older cousins, when they would treat us like brats. Who, us?? Glo married Nathan Bray, and they have a terrific family, Nathan Jr and wife Carol, and Karen and husband Darrell Spencer. Nate was one of the classiest men I ever knew, fought cancer (with a smile on his face) for many years and passed away in 2006.

Although many of the Thornton descendents scattered far and wide, Uncle Bill Goetzmann and Aunt Nell, Mom's sister also lived in Pitkin while we were there. Among their children, Leroy was the closest to me in age, so we were good friends. He taught me all about fast cars, because *his* car was always the sportiest and fastest. I remember one earlier year when we were very young; Leroy got into Uncle Alton's car and started blowing the horn. Uncle Alton showed up in the front yard and yelled at him, "Leroy, that horn only has so many times to blow". Leroy said, "I know it, I'm countin' 'em"!

Leroy married Wilma Sue, a local Pitkin gal, and they have two fine children, Walter and Patricia. Leroy had a nephew close to my age, Roland, and we keep in touch.

Aunt Zada, Mom's sister, had 4 children: Carroll, Dilton, Otis, and Audrey. They were older than me but were some of my favorite cousins. They all made that famous trip to Texas with Mom and Dad. Carroll lived in Pitkin, and was everybody's favorite cousin. He drove the getaway car after my wedding, but that is a story I'll tell later. He married Lavelle, and their son Royce was close to my age, so we were good friends and playmates. Lavelle was the daughter of my Dad's sister, Aunt Belle, so they were my first cousins twice! Dilton went to LSU where he was a star football end and pass receiver. Most people remember the famous quarterback, Y. A. Tittle. He played at LSU, and the NY Giants, etc. Well, Moe (as Dilton was called) caught most of his passes in their successful years at LSU. Much later, I met Y. A. Tittle. We had lunch together and he told me hilarious stories about his football days, and he certainly remembered Moe. His son, Little Moe is a close cousin now. Otis and Marguerite lived in California and we did not see them often. We visited them one summer in Vallejo. I remember that Otis was so proud of his lemon tree in the back yard. Audrey married Lonnie Hoye, and they lived in New Mexico, so we did not see them very often either, although we visited them in New Mexico one summer. Lonnie was a great fisherman. When he visited Pitkin, he would wade down Six Mile and Ten Mile Creeks and catch a mess of fish and everybody knew there were no fish in those creeks.

Mom had a sister named Lydia, who died at an early age, and I did not know her. She had a beautiful daughter, Bernadine, who married Lindsey Heard and we know them very well, since they settled in DeRidder, close to Pitkin. They have a great family; daughter Lydia Jane, husband Bob and grandchildren. Lindsey is the other super fisherman in the family and teamed up with Lonnie Hoye to catch all those fish that weren't in Ten Mile and Six Mile Creeks. Lindsey took me fishing several times to a camp he had on Anacoco Lake near Leesville, La. The cabin had a tin roof and a screened porch. I did some serious sleeping on that porch during the afternoon thundershowers. Caught some bass on top water lures, too. Fun.

Aunt Lola, Mom's sister married Uncle Volney Mitchell. They had 3 daughters and lived in Leesville. Wanda has passed away, but Mary Ethelyn and Nelda Gaye remain good friends. We visited Mary Ethelyn in Texarkana once, and had lunch with Nelda in Lafayette in 2005. We usually see them at the Thornton family reunion at Christmastime.

One annual occasion for which I have the fondest memories, was the Christmas reunions on Christmas Day, at the old Thornton place. We attended many of them and had great times. The older men would pitch silver dollars (later nut/bolt washers, after inflation set in) in the front yard and the ladies would be busy cooking. In earlier days, Mom and a couple of the aunts would cook a bunch of delicious pies and set them on a big post outside the kitchen window to cool. James David Cain and I would ride up to the window on horses, and sneak a pie or two. We also "stole" watermelons from Uncle Alton's field when the Cains lived in the old house. He knew we were doing it and we could have just asked him and he would have given us all the watermelons we could eat----but they just tasted better if we snuck them out of the field at night!

After most of the aunts and uncles died, and the old place was sold outside the family, Carroll and Lavelle Richmond would host the Thornton family reunion every year on Christmas Eve. So for many years, we were able to renew friendships and enjoy our fellowship together. I can remember several reunions when there were 75 to 100 kinfolks present.

For the last several years, my first cousin, Burl Cain has been hosting the family reunion. He is the warden of Angola State Penitentiary, and has been for over 11 years, longest tenure of any warden there. You should see the looks I get when I tell people I am going to Angola Penitentiary for my family reunion. They always ask why it is being held there, so I tell them "that's where all my kinfolks are"! That's true---they are all there on the second Sunday in October. They have a prisoner rodeo conducted every Sunday in October, and Burl started inviting the family to it on one of the Sundays. We had about 75 folks show up in 2004. The next year, some hurricanes disrupted the occasion, so there were fewer participants. Burl feeds the family two meals, gives guided tours of the Penitentiary, and escorts us to the rodeo. The prisoners built the arena in about 3 months. At the rodeo, prisoners can display and sell their wares---paintings, woodworking, leather goods, etc. They make a lot of quality stuff---they have plenty of time to work on it. The average sentence for a prisoner at Angola is 88 years. You aren't sent there for running red lights. So if you are sent to Angola, you will die there. They have a large cemetery in the prison, because many of the prisoners' families will not claim the bodies. It is the largest maximum-security prison in the U.S., and encompasses 18,000 acres. The prisoner population is over 5,000. They farm and raise everything they eat, including beef cattle. There are 5 compounds where the prisoners sleep, encircled with tall fences and razor wire topping the fences. Nobody escapes. Burl has cleaned the place up. It was once a place where prisoners were treated brutally, tortured, killed. He established an outstanding museum. He has collected enough donations around the country to build a chapel in each of the five compounds, without spending one penny of taxpayers money. He does not tolerate brutality or mistreatment of prisoners. If they break the rules, privileges are withdrawn. It is amazing the respect the prisoners show him. The prisoners and the guards clearly know who is the boss. He has been interviewed by Barbara Walters twice, Diane Sawyer, and 60 minutes. Barbara Walters heard about a story involving a prisoner, and came for an interview with Burl. Parts of the interview were aired on national TV, including the following exchange. She said that she had heard that Burl held a convict's hand while he was given a lethal injection (there were 87 on death row when we visited there). She asked Burl if that was true. He said, "yes ma'am". She asked him why he did it. Burl gave her the perfect answer. He leaned into the camera and said, "Because he asked me to". He explained to her that he didn't send anybody there, or order any executions, but his job was to keep them in custody, and, unfortunately, they had to execute them if directed by proper authority. He said that he would have been privileged to hold the hand of the murderer's victim if he could have. Burl arranged to have professors from colleges and seminaries to come to Angola and teach prisoners. They can earn a degree in religion and it is surprising how many take advantage of the program. Like I said, they have plenty of time to do it. We are all very proud of Burl, but it's hard for me to realize that just the other day, it seems, he was just a little brat cousin that I was throwing corn cobs at down at the barn on the old Thornton place!

I didn't know my Grandfather Thornton. He died when I was two years old, while we were still living in Texas. But Grandmother Thornton lived with us in the farmhouse until she died in 1944. I know she was a good woman, but I must confess that she was a hard woman for me to get along with. She was always correcting me and fussing at me. For example, once she really blasted me when she caught me peeing through the screen on the back porch---whadda you do?---it was dark and too cold to go way out to the outhouse. Picky, picky, picky! But she and my Mom would give me silver dollars for participating in piano recitals. Although I never got to be an accomplished piano player, the lessons got me interested in music. Little did I know then how important this was to be for me in the future.

During several summers, Mom would take me to Forester, Arkansas to visit her brother, my Uncle David Thornton and Aunt Inez. He was a sawmill medical doctor. I really enjoyed these visits. We would ride the "Doodle Bug"---little train from Pitkin to DeRidder, then catch the Kansas City Southern train to Mena, Arkansas, then bus to Forester. Uncle David would take me fishing in some of the most beautiful hills, (mountains to me) with fast rushing rivers of clear water. I was not accustomed to that—there is no clear water in Louisiana! Only muddy water!

I also made several trips to Port Arthur, Texas, at least one by myself, to visit Uncle Virgil Thornton, Mom's brother, and Aunt Eva, and their sons, Ben and Sam. I guess Uncle Virgil came over and got me----I really do not remember how I got there, but I know Mom was not along on this one particular trip, because Aunt Eva taught me to *dance*----ssshh! We need to keep that a secret from the rest of the Thornton family, "dyed in the wool" Southern Baptists---don't believe in dancing. You know the story---Baptists don't make love standing up---they are afraid somebody will see them and think they are dancing! I loved Aunt Eva, and enjoyed these visits. Their sons, Ben and Sam are about my age and we enjoyed each other's company---I see them about once a year now. Not often enough! Their sweet wives are Shirley and Inez.

Mom had another brother, Uncle Sam Thornton. He married Aunt Bert. They had two daughters. Isabell was close to my age and we knew each other well. They lived in Boyce, Louisiana, so we did not see them as often as the Pitkin folks.

Mom, Dad, and I also attended the Baptist Encampment in Dry Creek, Louisiana for ten days for several summers. We took a tent and pitched it, and slept on cots. We were there when WW II ended, and I remember the announcement----it was a joyous occasion. The main revival service was held in a large outdoor (although covered) "tabernacle". There were classes, church services and many recreational activities to enjoy. Neither one of us knew it, but a young girl named Katherine Elliott also attended at least one encampment when we were there. We never met then.

I do not know nearly as much about Dad's family. Most were older and died when I was very young. But I remember visiting the old Hoglan place down on Six Mile Creek. I remember at that time, Aunt Nettie, Aunt Rosa, Aunt Martha, and Aunt Lizzie lived there. I do not remember Grandpa and Grandma Hoglan. My Aunt Lola, Dad's sister married a Beeson and had several children. They lived in Baton Rouge. Their daughter, Mary Angeline and I were close to the same age, and I was sweet on her. When she visited Pitkin, cousin Carroll would take us swimming in Six Mile Creek. She is still a sweetheart, but we seldom see each other.

When I was about nine years old, I became a Christian, and joined the Pitkin Baptist Church. It was quite natural since my folks had raised me in a Christian home, going to church regularly. Our pastor at this time was Rev. Tommy Vernell Owens, a young dynamic preacher who everybody loved. He had a profound influence on me. He gave me an old cornet, taught me enough to play duets (hymns) with him. After many years passed, I found him and he presided at my marriage to Katherine, in the Harmony Baptist Church in Glenmora, La. My piano lessons helped me to read music. With the cornet, I only had to read one note at a time, not whole chords as with the piano. So reading music came easy for me.

My experience in joining the church **was** probably more of an emotional event than anything else. I believed in God and Heaven, but didn't have a clue as to the true meaning of being a Christian. I didn't realize that becoming a Christian was not just one event, at least for me. It didn't happen in an instant. It has been a process over many years of learning and experiencing God. I guess this a good place to explain my philosophy on religion. There is no doubt whatsoever that there is a God. Although I cannot empirically *prove* His existence to anyone else, I know beyond any doubt whatsoever, there is a God and that He cares about me. He is my Savior. I think what proves it to me, is there are events in my life that I could not possibly survive or even explain without the intervention of God. "Luck" could not possibly have had anything to do with it. Not even close! Literally, miracles that defy logic, even descriptions. I am fascinated by the current ruckus about "Intelligent Design". Any fool with no sense at all can look at the human body, animals, the earth, sun, moon, other planets and how they interact with each other, and butterflies, and know that there is intelligent design. It all came from a big bang? You've got to be kidding! This "intelligent design" is not new-----it is also called creation and has been around since the beginning of time. But if it was a big bang, and if we evolved from apes, that is the way God decided to do it. But why do we still have apes? Hmm!

I am a little resentful at being sarcastically categorized in a demeaning manner, as an evangelical, or on the Christian Right, by my friends, the liberals. Can't I just be a Christian? I am also upset that there are people trying diligently to remove any trace of God in our society. Our great country was founded on Christian-Judeo principles. Virtually every document our founding fathers produced referred to a strong belief in God---not Budda or Allah. We do not persecute Budda or Allah worshipers. So don't move here and try to take away *my* right to believe in and worship God. If you don't like the way we worship, leave---Delta is ready when you are! The founding fathers did not want the state to establish one single, denominational church, as it had been done in England. They certainly did not mean that we must erase all references to God----quite the contrary. OK, sorry I got on my soapbox, but I feel very strongly about this subject and I want my kids, grandkids, their kids, etc to know how I feel and why. This gets worse, because later I may explain my "politics and ideology"! I've been told that I am about 10 degrees to the right of Attila the Hun! Soap box time again----then.

We moved away from Pitkin (the first time) in 1945 to the Acadia Baptist Academy, a parochial high school near Eunice, Louisiana. We lived on the Academy grounds and my Dad taught school there. I attended 7th grade in a nearby little town of Richard (pronounced Ree-shard for all you gringos). This was our first, but not last adventure into cajun country. At the end of the year, Dad was recruited to be the President of a Business College, way up north in yankee land, Monroe, Louisiana. So crank up the U-haul (actually Carroll Richmond's truck). We moved again.

THREE

High School

We moved to Monroe, Louisiana in the summer of 1946, and took up residence with another family and paid them rent. I entered the 8th Grade in Ouachita Parish High School, in Monroe. It was a large high school, especially by my standards and experience. I joined the beginning band, my first. With trumpet in hand, I was on my way. After six months Dad decided that the Business College was not for him, and we moved to Kinder, Louisiana, back in Cajun country. For the last half of the 8th Grade, I transferred to Kinder High School and continued there through the 9th and 10th Grades. We lived with an old Syrian lady, Mrs. Khouri, and paid her rent for a little apartment. She was a nice lady and taught me how to crochet potholders! I joined the Kinder High School Band, and took private trumpet lessons from the band director, Mr. Howard Smith. He lived in Oakdale, La and was the band director there, but drove to Kinder two or three days a week to be our director also. Mr. Smith was a very good band director and an outstanding teacher. He got me into the music festival business, playing classical trumpet solos around the state in a competitive environment. He would demonstrate how the solo should sound by playing it on a baritone---then he would accompany me on the piano. He was a terrific musician. I won several "Superior" ratings in regional and state festivals and recitals. He was the very best music teacher I ever had. In my sophomore year, I was a band member, boys glee club member, and member of the mixed chorus. I was voted the most attractive boy in the sophomore class (just to show you what a sense of humor the class had)! My girlfriend, Lois was named most attractive girl (hey, as you will see later on, I don't take up wid no dawgs)!!!   If nothing else, I've got good taste and judgment.

At the end of my sophomore year, we moved back to Pitkin. It was still in our blood, and it is still in my blood today.   Well, Pitkin (population of 200) was still a small school and did not have a band. Had I stayed and graduated from Pitkin High School, my graduating class would have had 9 students. The school only had 5 typewriters, so the senior class had to draw names to see who could take typing. Did I say I was from the country?? But they didn't have a band, and I was too far into trumpet playing to quit now. The closest high school that had a band was in Glenmora, Louisiana, 24 miles from Pitkin. So, for the next two years, I would drive my 1932 Ford Coupe B-Model (with a '38 Ford motor—for all you car buffs out there---wish I still had it) 9 miles on a gravel road to a country road intersection, and park it in a farmers yard. I would then catch the school bus, and ride the other 15 miles to school at Glenmora High School and back home to Pitkin after school each day.

Now, I would *like* to say that going to school in Glenmora was a brilliant, calculated move on my part, but the best part was, I guess, plain old luck. Rather early in my junior year, I fell head over heels in love with one of the band majorettes. We now have been married 53 years (not including common law-----just kidding).   I put the habeas grabus on her, one Katherine Evelyn Elliott, and never let her escape. Glenmora School had never had a yearbook until our senior year. Katherine was the Assistant Editor of the "GHS Gems", the first one ever. I was the Advertising Manager. Katherine was a majorette in the band, President of the 4-H Club, Vice President of the BETA Club, Social Chairman of the Senior Class, and Valedictorian of the Senior Class. She was voted "Prettiest Girl" in the Senior Class, and, "Prettiest Girl" in the entire High School. (You remember what I said about no dawgs?) She excels at everything she tries, always has, and I have always been so very proud of her-----more accolades and honors for her to come in College. I stumbled along, just trying to keep up! I was Captain of the band, President of the Glee Club, Vice President of the Senior Class, and was voted "Most Popular Boy" in the Senior Class. Although I was in the Glenmora High School Band, I continued to drive to Oakdale a couple of times a week, to take private trumpet lessons from

Mr. Howard Smith. We continued to participate in competitive music festivals and I was fortunate enough to win several "Superior" ratings at State level.

I was on the high school softball team and in my senior year, we won second place at the State Tournament. I remember only too well one game on our home field. We were playing against Lecompte, and I was the shortstop. Before the game, one of my teammates produced a large package of chewing tobacco and passed it around. Every player cut off a plug, and when it got to me, I really didn't want it, but all the other players had a plug, and peer pressure being as strong as it is, I reluctantly cut off a chew. After a couple of innings, I was feeling a little puny. Then, in the third inning a hot ground ball was hit to me at shortstop. As I tried to catch it, the ball bounced over my glove, not surprisingly, and hit me square in the sternum. It was hard hit, and it hurt, but that was not my biggest problem. I swallowed the whole cud of tobacco! After about two more innings, we came to bat, and my typing teacher, Ms Wilkie, called me over to the backstop and asked why I was as green as a gourd. After the game, I drove my 32 Ford out into the woods, puked my guts out, and slept for the rest of the afternoon. Ended my chewing tobacco "habit"! We had some good classmates at GHS. Bennie Monroe and his wife Bobbye currently own a printing company in Lake Charles, Louisiana. Bennie has done more than anyone to try to keep our classmates in contact with one another. For our Fortieth and Fiftieth Reunions (1991 & 2001), he contacted all our classmates, urged everyone to attend these reunions and produced two outstanding, professional booklets for those occasions. The school has a reunion annually and I was asked to be the guest speaker in 1995.

I need to say a few words about the Elliott family. From the very start, Katherine's Mother, Mrs. Leola Elliott treated me as if I were her own son. No one could have been as kind, nice, sweet, and considerate to me, especially since I was in the process of stealing her daughter! But she understood that she was not going to lose a daughter, she was just going to gain a son that loved her with all his heart. She was that *other* saint that I mentioned earlier. Until her last days, she drove her car 6 miles into town, and worked all day as Manager in her son's hardware store. She was a 1930 graduate of Glenmora High School, an active member of the Glenmora Alumni Association, and the Glenmora Home

Demonstration Club. She was Past Matron and a 50-year member of the Jewel Chapter #100 Order of the Eastern Star of Glenmora. She was a member of the Glenmora Baptist Church. To illustrate just one of the many ways she was a saint, I want to relate her accomplishments as the Secretary of her Sunday School Class. She was the class Secretary for over 30 years. Recently we found her meticulous records for 27 years. She bought cards and stamps and sent 7,454 birthday, get well, sympathy, etc cards to her class members. That averages more than 1 card every other day for 27 years! Every card and addressee was neatly logged in her records. She was an amazing woman. She was hospitalized for a short time in 2001. We drove to Rapides Parish Hospital in Alexandria, Louisiana to visit her and while we were there, she passed away. Katherine was at her side. She was not in pain and she did not suffer---that was not just a coincidence----God was not going to let a Saint like her suffer. He loaned her to the world for 90 years, then quietly took her to join with His Angels.

Katherine's Dad, Mr. Landis Elliott, was one of the hardest working men I ever knew. He was more skilled at his job than men with Masters' and PHD degrees, yet he never attended college. He was a forester, working in the woods all his life. A Master Forester. And all those PhDs with any common sense came to him for advice and to learn. He worked for several large timber companies, and even after he retired, they would consult him and ask him do things, inspect fire lanes, check timber growth, etc. He died in April 1994 at age 86, after spending several years in a nursing home. No wonder Katherine was and is so outstanding------she came from such outstanding stock!!

Katherine has one brother, Harold "Happy" Elliott. He is outstanding in his own right.

I want to tell you about him, because you future nieces and nephews need to know about your Uncle Happy! Two years behind us in school, Happy graduated in 1953 and entered L.S.U. Guess what he majored in? How did you know?---Forestry. He amazes me. He can walk in the woods and identify every tree and bush, tell you how old they are, and whether they should be thinned out, harvested, burned, or what. He is the best, except for one man, of course, his Daddy. While at L.S.U., he was Vice President of The College of Agriculture and President of the Agriculture Fair Association. He was a member of the Student

Senate and Agriculture Council, and Vice President of the Society of American Foresters. After college, he served his country in the Army for two years, including 16 months overseas, in Germany and in Lebanon during that crisis. He has been elected School Board Member for his District, Town Council Member and Mayor Pro-Tem for Glenmora, La. He has been President of the Southern Forestry Heritage Museum & Research Center (the site in Longleaf, La of an old sawmill, complete with wood burning locomotives). Happy has always been very active in the Masons. He is a Shriner, deeply involved in their work of building and supporting childrens' hospitals. He serves on the board of the children's hospital in Shreveport, La. He is the Past Worshipful Master of the Masonic Lodge, and was the President of the Mid-State Shrine Club in Louisiana. For several years he has owned Glenmora Hardware store. And besides all that, he is the best brother-in-law in the world.

I need to say one more word about this family. You would think, that with all the achievements and honors accorded to this family, they must have been born into great wealth and influence. How else can you achieve so much without wealth, and high societal, influential friends? Maybe you can't anymore. So how did they do it? Hard Work! Katherine and her best girl friend in high school, Mary Rollins, discussed what their future would be after high school. Katherine would like to go to college, but she reasoned that her folks could not afford two kids in college at the same time. She thought that it was more important for her brother to be able to go to college and she knew he wanted to go to L.S.U., *The* State University, but it was relatively expensive. So she had accepted that she should not burden her folks with the expense of a college education, and just maybe, she would take a short secretarial course somewhere. Such is her character and consideration for her folks. BUT, I intervened! I'm not sure she credits me, today, with talking her into coming with me, with her parent's permission, to Northwestern State College in Natchitoches, Louisiana, but I'm claiming credit for it anyway! My folks didn't have any money either! But Northwestern was a State College with inexpensive tuition and I told her and her folks that we could work our way through college with minimal financial help from our parents. I sold it! We did it! We graduated from Glenmora High School in 1951, and then went on to Northwestern State College (now, Northwestern State University of Louisiana). It only got better!!

FOUR

College & Marriage to Katherine

Katherine Evelyn Elliott, a country girl from Glenmora, and Curtis Francis Hoglan, a country boy from Pitkin, started summer school at Northwestern State College of Louisiana, home of the "Demons", in Natchitoches, Louisiana, in the summer of 1951. Katherine lived in Agnes Morris dormitory, and I lived in A-Frame dormitory on the other side of the campus. What Katherine's major was going to be was never in doubt. She was a whiz at sewing and cooking, taught by her Mother. She majored in Home Economics. It was not so easy for me. When they asked me what I was going to major in, I didn't have a clue. The only thing I could do was play the trumpet, so I asked if I could major in that. They listed me in Music Education. I got a half-time scholarship, paying one half my tuition and meals, working in the Band Director's Office. I filed music, retrieved music from the files at the direction of the band director and placed it in each band member's music folder, and did other office jobs. Katherine got a half-time scholarship working in the college library. My supervisor did not require me to keep time cards on the hours I worked. He really didn't care about time, as long as the job got done. Katherine's library job wasn't that way. They kept strict hours on all the students working there. I hardly ever saw her---she was working all the time not spent in class. She made 21 cents per hour! I worked in the office for the first full year I was in college, including 2 summers. Katherine worked in the library for the *entire 3 years* until she graduated, including summers. She got her Bachelors Degree and teachers certificate in 3 years and 3 summers. She wasn't Valedictorian of her high school class just because she was pretty!

At the beginning of my sophomore year, I auditioned for the official college Dance Band, the Demonaires, was selected and received a half-time scholarship for that one year. For my junior and senior years, the band members elected me Leader of the Demonaires. That gave me a *full- time scholarship* that paid my full tuition and all meals for my last 2 years in college. Remember I said we could work our way through college. We did! I even made extra money, because to fulfill the requirements of the scholarships, we only had to play one "all-college dance" per month, free to all students. We also played for the gymnastics team during their routines. We even went to New Orleans and played while they did their routines and won the Southern AAU championship. At other times we were free to play dances for fraternities, sororities, military Officer and NCO clubs in the State, etc., and *got paid* for them ($5 per as I recall---WOW!). Even in high school, I knew about the Demonaires. They were pretty famous in the State, and it was my earliest ambition to someday play in that band. It was a 15-piece band: 5 saxophones, 3 trombones, 3 trumpets, piano, bass, and drums and female vocalist. It was patterned after the big bands of the day: Harry James, Ray Anthony, Tommy Dorsey, Artie Shaw, Billy May, Stan Kenton, Buddy Morrow, but *not* Lawrence Welk. He was much too, as we kool kats called it, ricky tick (square)! When some of the bands above would visit our college and play a concert, some would give us a few of their old arrangements. The Demonaires were a great band. Frank Pasqua was the Leader and 1st trumpet player while I was in high school, and for my first year in college. He was my idol, and still is. Sadly, Frank passed away in October 2006. When I joined the Demonaires, these were my best days. Frank graduated after my freshman year. Hardy Rose became the Demonaires Leader for my sophomore year, my first year in the Demonaires. He was (is) a great musician, played tenor sax and clarinet like Pete Fountain, and we didn't know it then, but we were to cross paths many times in the future. I need to mention that I was a great friend with several other members of the Demonaires. Our friendship continues today. Gordon Young, Gerald Carter (trumpets), Jerry Payne, Jim Thomasee (sax), Ben Singletary (trombone), Dean Clark (piano), Kamal "Arab" Kathey and Gardner Vaughn (drums). I already mentioned Hardy Rose. These were my heroes in college. Fine, fun loving musicians, that I respect, admire, and certainly treasure their friendship. Maybe more about the fun loving part later, when, hopefully, they will still be my good friends. I wish I had recorded the band. They were great. This was my first love and I *almost* felt guilty that I was getting a scholarship and getting paid for this!

Back to our freshman year. Of course, as a new freshman, my hair was all shaved off, as was the custom at our college. I wore a dumb looking cap and answered to the name 'Dog' Hoglan. Thankfully, they didn't treat the girls this way! Katherine was invited and joined Alpha Sigma Alpha Sorority, a great group of gals. I joined Sigma Tau Gamma Fraternity with a great group of guys. I will never forget my fraternity initiation. Initially, I lived in A-Frame, an *old* wooden building with my buddy, Johnny Derrick, who later married another friend, Joy Fields---I was in the wedding.

Before Christmas, that first year in college, I bought Katherine an engagement ring. Her Mother's family always held a Christmas Eve reunion at her Grandmother and Grandfather Martin's house in Glenmora, and we were all there for Christmas Eve, 1951. Now, Katherine's Mom was always my buddy. I knew she would support me, but I was a little anxious about her Dad. So I chose a moment when Mother was on the back porch, and we walked up to her, and I held out Katherine's hand, with that '*big*' *ole* diamond on her finger. Without saying a word, and with not a second's hesitation, she dumped her full glass of iced tea and ice cubes on Katherine's hand! Well, I almost had a heart attack! This certainly was not the reaction I was expecting or desired. All I could think about was, if *Mother* had this kind of reaction, her Dad would probably kill me! So I chickened out and we never, never told him we were engaged. But after we were married and had two kids, I think he figured it out. When Mother *regained consciousness,* and my heart started beating again, she explained that she thought that meant we were going to quit college and get married right away. We assured her that we were going to wait to get married until much later, and that we were committed to finishing college. Everything was A-OK. Dodged a bullet! Whew!

The plan was to try to finish college in three years by going to summer school each summer. Katherine did. I realized that I could not, because I was enrolled in ROTC and it was a four-year program.

I went to summer school anyway, for two reasons: I wanted to be close to Katherine, and I was having too much fun being leader of the Demonaires. I didn't want to take the chance that someone else may ace me out of being leader, while I wasn't there. The other band members elected the leader each year. Consequently, I graduated in four years, with a total of about 160 hours, instead of the required 130 or so. In my senior year, I took the least number of credit hours possible to still be listed as a full time student. Goofed off, in other words.

Very early in college, I took Katherine over to Pitkin to meet some more of the kinfolks. One couple I was close to was Alton Cain, Jr. and his wife, Anita. We had grown up together in Pitkin. Junior and Anita took us for a ride in his pick-up truck, on a dirt road, down through the woods on the edge of a field. An armadillo ambled across the road in front of us. Junior stopped the truck. The girls were busy talking and not paying any attention to what we were doing, as usual. We chased down the armadillo, snuck around behind the truck, and came up on the passenger side. I opened the door to the cab, and Junior threw the armadillo in on the floor of the truck, and I closed the door. Well, there was a lot of excitement in that truck for the next few minutes! The armadillo was scratching around, making weird noises, trying to get out, the girls were screaming, and when we finally opened the door, I swear the girls were on top of the seat back!! I immediately began to wonder if taking Katherine over to Pitkin to meet more cousins was such a good idea after all! We all survived that experience, including the armadillo. Speaking of armadillos, I know that Katherine's Mom killed hundreds of armadillos over the years. They would tear up her garden at night, so Pa Pa would hold the flashlight and Mother would shoot them right between the eyes with a 22 rifle. Dead shot.

Back to college. Katherine and I finished our second years, 1952 and 1953, still enjoying the college experience. Our small college did have some outstanding athletic teams. For example, our Gymnastics team, under the coaching of John Piscopo, was really outstanding. We took on the University of Texas, Texas A & M, L.S.U., and Kansas State, and beat them all!! Our team won the Gulf AAU championship, the Southwest AAU title, and the Mid-South Intercollegiate, all for the second time, and captured its sixth consecutive Southern AAU crown. Our swimming team was also very good, beating Vanderbilt and Texas

Tech, under coach John Piscopo. Maybe the college should have made him the football (we don't need to go there) coach!

The Demonaires played for some of the gymnastics events. "String of Pearls" and "In The Mood" seemed to help the athletes get motivated in their routines. I could (should) write a book about our Demonaires' adventures. Names would have to be changed to protect the guilty. I will just relate a few.

I had my Dad's old, 1948, Dodge sedan for my last two years at Northwestern. I can well remember loading 5 guys in the car, and the blonde colored bass fiddle on top of the seats, and driving almost as fast as it could go, to "gigs" all over the state. Two other guys would take their cars, with 5 people each, one with the music stands and music in the trunk, the other with the set of drums in the trunk. Once, we got all the way across the state and discovered at the last minute that all the music had been left behind. Now, a little 4 or 5 piece combo can jam a whole dance, without music, but a 15-piece orchestra? We all just took turns jammin', and I don't think the crowd knew the difference.

On our way back from a gig at the 40 & 8 Club in Shreveport, we stopped at a liquor store, just to look around of course. After "shopping" awhile, we left the store. The owner came out to the car, and asked, "Would the guy that took a bottle of wine, return it to the store?" I told him that I didn't know what he was talking about---and I didn't. About that time, he pulled out the biggest pistol I had ever seen and said, "Please?" I got out of the car and announced that we were not going anywhere until the bottle of wine had been "found" and returned to the store. A trombone player, who shall remain nameless, "found" the bottle, got out and returned it to the store, and we departed!

On another occasion, we arrived at a gig, and while I was in a room, changing into our "Uniform"---Navy Blue Blazers, Charcoal Grey Slacks, white dress shirts and ties, and, of course, blue suede shoes, the guys were in other rooms, changing. When I came out into the ballroom, here is my band, all on the bandstand, and all in their *ROTC uniforms!* I was petrified. They changed back; it was just a little drill to get my attention and add to my stress. Found out later it was Carter's (trumpet section) idea. I should not have been surprised. He was a joker!

After a local gig in Natchitoches, and at other times also, some of us would gather down at Mr. Maggios beer parlor and liquor emporium

 25

about two blocks off campus. It was the "high brow" place to go. It seems he always had a special on beer in quart bottles. I don't really know about that, but that's what the big boys told me! Anyway, there was an old guy, a favorite of ours that hung around there. He was a man hired by the college to pick up trash around the campus. He had a big sack, hung around his neck, and a broom handle with a nail in the bottom end of it, to help him pick up papers, trash, dixie cups, etc. He was affectionately known as "the sack man". How can I delicately explain what his answer would be when we asked him if he loved *it*? Well, we won't go there. But he would eat a razor blade for a dime!! And he would eat a light bulb for a quarter!! I don't know how he did it, but I *saw* it! This was the entertainment down at Mr. Maggios. Mr. Maggios' son, PhD Dr. Chris Maggio is now the alumni director for the University. He did a magnificent job orchestrating our 50th graduation reunions at the University, and other events I will explain later.

Back to year three. Katherine and I started year three in the fall of 1953. Because I had taken so many hours in the first two years and summers, I was classified as a senior when I was 18 years old, but it would be another two years before I would graduate, for reasons previously noted. I graduated when I was 20, and my ROTC buddies, when I was about to be commissioned as a Lieutenant in the Army, told me not to worry, "my Mom would sign for me"!! This would be Katherine's senior year in college. At some point I moved out of A-Frame dorm into the Brick Shack, a two-story dorm for more senior students. Steve Westbrook was my roommate and great friend. Our house Mother, Mama Rhodes was the greatest! Katherine moved into Varnado Hall, for women senior students. There were *no* coed dorms, Heaven forbid. Men were not even allowed into women's' dorms, except in the foyer to pick up your date for an early movie, etc., and you had to sign in. And we always had curfew. We had the ugliest and meanest Dean of Women on the planet Earth! I think she only lasted one year. I can remember harassing her, on a rainy day, when I was coming from the science building to the dining hall, I would enter the nearest door and run the entire length of Varnado Hall, yelling, "man in the hall, man in the hall"! The coeds loved it, and one day the Dean stepped out into the hall and I almost ran over her---luckily she did not recognize me.

School year '53--'54 was a very special year, for several reasons. Katherine and I were married at mid-semester of this year, on 29 January 1954, in Harmony Baptist Church in Glenmora, Louisiana. I previously mentioned that I found out where the Rev. Tommy Owens was located and asked him to perform the ceremony.

Did I mention that Katherine was an outstanding seamstress?? She *made from scratch*, her beautiful wedding gown, and the three bridesmaids gowns, their headpieces, veils, etc. Of course, I made the ushers' suits (just kidding). The wedding took place between semesters, so we had all of 3 days for a honeymoon to Natchez, Mississippi. On our wedding day, my cousins took me quail hunting, and my cousin, Junior Cain kept me out so late, I was late for my own wedding, although he probably won't admit it!! At least Katherine surely thought I was late. Junior was my Best Man in the wedding! A tradition in the Thornton family was to find the wedding getaway car and "decorate" it. Now in most families, this consists of writing, with soap, on the back car window, Just Married, etc., and tying a string of tin cans behind the car as it leaves the wedding. Not so with the Thornton family, and I'm not sure when this got started. But there are cases where the "getaway" car was completely disabled, for example: car jacked up, wheels removed and secured by ropes in a tree, car hidden where the wedding couple could not find it, or shrimp placed in the hubcaps. Once, Irish potatoes were stuffed into the tail pipe---didn't work---Junior Cain's truck just blew them out, and treated the wedding party to French Fries!! Now, historically, our first cousin, Carroll Richmond, had been the one ordained (I don't know when or by whom) to get the wedding couple from the church to wherever the getaway car was hidden, which turned out to be the biggest mystery of the wedding. Carroll's car was off limits. Carroll told me that he would do it for me, and then he was retiring. He should have been a racecar driver. After the wedding and reception, he took us through one of the most harrowing driving experiences of our lives. The whole doggone wedding party of cousins was racing behind us, trying to catch up. Carroll did his usual bob and weave stuff at high speed and back roads, and eventually left them in a cloud of dust on the way from the church in Glenmora to Pitkin. After the dust settled, and all the cousins had given up, Carroll took us to the old 1948 Dodge, our getaway car, which had been hidden in his chicken house in Pitkin! My folks were already home from the wedding, and we stopped by to visit them for a little while, and my best man, Junior Cain, showed up---he said, "not to worry", and he did not give our location away.

After our short visit, Katherine and I drove to Alexandria, Louisiana, where we stayed the first night in Strubes Motor Court. I guess we had a good time, because Katherine left her nightgown tangled in the bed sheets when we left the next morning—never recovered it! We have had a lot of conversations about Strubes. We spent the next couple of days on our *short* honeymoon in Natchez, Mississippi.

When we immediately returned to college, we rented a one-room apartment above a small garage, one block from the campus. Sadly, for the first month's rent, I had to use the 35 silver dollars that my Mother and Grandmother had given to me over the years for participation in music recitals and festivals early in life. I wish I had them now! We continued to live there until Katherine's graduation in June of that year.

She finished in Home Economics with a Bachelors Degree and Teachers Certificate. Of course, she graduated with honors, magna cum laude. (I graduated, Lordy, Lordy have mercy, the next year). She was also a member of Alpha Sigma Alpha Sorority, member of the Baptist Student Union Freshman Council, Secretary of the Euthenics Club—'52, 53, Dormitory Council---'52, Chaplain of Alpha Sigma Alpha---'52, 53, and President of Alpha Sigma Alpha ---'53, 54.

Toward the end of her senior year she got a job teaching Home Economics in the little town of Montgomery, Louisiana, about 25 miles from Natchitoches and the college. As soon as she secured the job, and long before she got her first paycheck, I went over to the town of Many, La. and *bought* a brand new car---a 1954 Plymouth Belvedere (top of the line, no less). It was a 4-door, blue with a black top. The price tag was $2,095 dollars---that's right folks---Two thousand---not twenty thousand. I told the dealer that I did not have any money, but he let me drive the car home!! He knew my roommate, Steve Westbrook, from Many, and trusted his folks, I guess. Katherine was a little more than perturbed that I had bought the car without her knowledge, and didn't even give her a choice of cars, model, colors, or anything. I just thought she would trust my tastes. I learned my first serious lesson of married life----you better keep Mama informed, even better, ask her in advance, and no surprises! After I got the car, I went to Oakdale, Louisiana, about half way between Pitkin and Glenmora and went into the Bank there (Pitkin and Glenmora had no banks). I inquired about taking out a loan---they did not know me---I needed $300. I think that was the down payment on the car. They asked if I had ever had an account with them. I said no. They asked me if I had a job. I said no. They asked if I knew how I was going to repay the loan. I said no. Well, it began to look pretty bleak for my loan. Then they asked who my parents were. I told them C.F. and Amy Hoglan in Pitkin, and my in-laws were Landis and Leola Elliott in Glenmora. This was the magic key that opened the cash drawer. The President of the bank said he knew both families and their credit was always good. He personally knew them to be honest, hard working folks, who had *always* paid their (few) debts on time (or early). He loaned us the money, and once again, I had escaped a slow and painful death!

In the summer of 1954, between my junior and senior years, I went to Fort Bliss, Texas for ROTC summer camp. I never dreamed that 30 years later, I would be Commanding General in charge of a ROTC summer camp. Those six weeks were spent studying basic soldier skills, with lots of physical training (PT), and field duty. In the field there was a lot of beach, but no water, until a hard rain brought flash flooding in the desert and interrupted the camping out! I decided early on that I would not trade my Louisiana tall pine trees and green grass for desert sand.

The school board member that had approved hiring Katherine as their High School Home Economics teacher in Montgomery, La, insisted that she live in Montgomery. He said that he would find us a place to live---and he did---with Ms. M., a sweet lady that welcomed us into her home. We became *her chirren!* It was church twice on Sundays---- Mondays and Tuesdays, bible study at the church. Wednesday was prayer meeting, Thursday, choir practice, Fri, something else--it just was not working out. So, after a few months, I was talking with my Aunt Nell in Pitkin about the situation. She owned a house trailer close to Fort Polk that had been rented to GIs. It was now vacant, and she suggested that we pull it up to Montgomery and use it for the year. We did. There was a vacant lot right next to the high school, owned by a nice couple that lived across the street. I rented the vacant lot and paid the rent by teaching their two sons trumpet lessons. I parked the house trailer in the middle of the vacant lot under a very large pine tree. For water, we ran a garden hose (with extensions) to a water main nearby.. I dug a septic tank, using two 55-gallon drums, buried at the appropriate depth. This pine tree had a bunch of vines climbing on it, so, in the early fall, in my swim suit, I pulled all these vines out of the tree-----I soon found out, it was Poison Ivy. I spent several weeks in agony. This trailer was all of 32 feet long, and we did not have air conditioning!

Katherine was very successful in teaching Home Economics her first year, naturally. As her first year was ending, the school board superintendent offered me the opportunity to be the band director of any band in the Parish, and a combination of any of them if I desired. Since I had applied for immediate entry into the active duty army, to fulfill my ROTC obligation, I declined. Katherine's first year of teaching was interesting. I was driving back and forth every day, to Northwestern for my senior year, and they informed Katherine, at the last possible minute, that by the way, she would be the girls' high school basketball coach! It went with the job! Katherine had never played a game of basketball in her life! So, *I* became the girls' basketball coach. I don't want to brag, but it was the first season in a long time that Montgomery had a winning girls' basketball season.

I continued my senior year, driving to and from Montgomery and Natchitoches each day, and still having a ball leading the Demonaires. I remember that Gordon Young (trumpet player in the Demonaires) and I had to take Music History in our senior year. It was the most boring subject on the planet Earth. Our teacher, Ms McCook, bless her heart, would tell us about all the old classical masters, and she would get so excited just pronouncing the names: Guiseppe Verdi, and Goethe. We drove her crazy. Gordon and I still refer to each other in E-mails as Guiesssepeeeee and Goeeeetheeeeee. When we told her that Guiseppe Verdi just meant ole Joe Green she would croak!

None of our college experiences would be complete without mentioning Doc Marx, now deceased. He was in the Athletic Department, and he taught me my first freshman class. I remember more of what he taught me, than any other class in college----it was practical stuff. He taught us how to preserve shoes! Polish was the answer, and shoetrees. He could stand in front of his desk and jump, flat-footed to the top of his desk. He taught us how to take baths, holding on to the end of the towel that we wiped the private parts with, in one hand, so we wouldn't forget! Our yearbook in 1954 was dedicated to him. He was a jewel and a favorite teacher on the campus. Among other things, Doc Marx was a trainer for the football team. I have mentioned that during my 4 years in college, our football team had some tough losses—we only beat our chief rival, La. Tech, one time. I knew most of the football players---we were a small college, about 1,500 enrollments---everybody knew everybody.

One of my favorite football players was Earl Haynes. Earl and I had a couple of things in common-----*not* in athleticism. I *did* make the swimming team but could not stay on it---their practice coincided with band practice every day. Earl was a great football player, and one of my idols. We were in ROTC together and we were sweet on the same girl! Gene Jensen was a college Beauty---not just in our opinion--- high priced judges selected her and her picture is in the 1952 college yearbook as a Beauty. Now, only two things stood between Gene and I getting together. First, there was Earl. Being smarter than the average bear, he put the habeas grabus on Gene and got engaged to her when they entered college. He took no chances. Then there was my first (and only) love, Katherine, who had me handcuffed as a junior in high school. I actually handcuffed her—I didn't want to take any chances either. So I never even got to date Gene. Third problem---she probably did not know I even existed---I was just a secret admirer. We have visited with them the last three years during NSU Homecoming weekends. Earl is still one of my idols and Gene is still a beauty. Good friends.

I finished my senior year, graduating in early June 1955. My lil' track record was: Band, 51-55; Vice President, 54-55; Orchestra, 51-55; Chorus, 51-52; College Singers, 53-54; Baptist Student Union Freshman Council, 51-52; Sigma Tau Gamma Fraternity, 51-55, Secretary, 51-53, Vice President,54-55; Phi Mu Alpha Fraternity, 52-55; ROTC, 51-55; Demonaires Dance Band, 52-55, Leader, 53-55. Upon graduation, I was commissioned a Second Lieutenant of Artillery in the U.S. Army. I had applied for immediate active duty, because, although I had enjoyed ROTC, I wanted to serve my 2 year obligation on active duty as soon as possible and then become the best high school band director in the land. These last four years were some of the very best years of our lives.

31

C.F. & Amy Hoglan

Curt at age 1

Curt at age 12

Curt in High School

Katherine Elliott, HS Band Majorette

Curt, Grad, Glenmora HS   *Curt, HS grad & 32 Ford "B" Model*

Curt, Demonaires Dance Band Leader

NSU Demonaires Dance Band

Curt & Katherine, Wedding

Chapter Two

MY ARMY BEGINNING
THE COMPANY GRADE YEARS

ONE

*AAA Officers' Course, Fort Bliss, Texas
Operation Sagebrush, Louisiana, Platoon Leader,
C Battery, 82nd AAA Battalion
Fort Lewis, Washington, Platoon Leader, C Btry, 82nd
AAA Bn*

I was commissioned a Second Lieutenant of Artillery in the United States Army on 31 May 1955. Prior to my commissioning, my Professor of Military Science and Tactics (PMS&T) at the college, Lieutenant Colonel Orlando Greening, called me in and said that he wanted to designate me a Distinguished Military Graduate (DMG). It sounded good and I was flattered but I did not understand what that meant. He told me that I had done very well in my four years in ROTC, and this designation would mean that I would receive a Regular Army (RA) Commission instead of a Reserve Commission. At that time in the Army, most officers had reserve commissions, although they were serving on active duty---very few had RA commissions. He explained to me that a Regular Army commission was a better guarantee of tenure in the Army. He said that in the event of a Reduction in Force (RIF), which was fairly popular at that time, when the Army was shrinking and needed fewer officers, RA officers would be the last to go. A RA commission would virtually keep you in for a career if you met or exceeded standards, etc. I was OK with this, until he mentioned that accepting a RA commission would obligate me for an initial tour of three years, instead of the two years I was prepared to serve. Although I was looking forward to serving on active duty, I was not looking to serve more than the two-year obligation I would have as a Reserve

Officer on active duty. Remember, I wanted to get started being the best high school band director in the land. So I thanked the PMS profusely, but declined the RA commission. Later, I met officers who would have given limbs of their body for a RA commission and they thought I was crazy. I had enjoyed ROTC, but I realized that ROTC was not the Army, and I didn't realize what it would be like, or how much I would take to it!

I received orders to report to Fort Bliss, Texas on 24 July 1955, to attend the Anti-Aircraft Artillery (AAA) Officers Basic Course (OBC). So we loaded up the Plymouth with everything we owned (clothes and a black & white TV) and set out for Fort Bliss. We arrived in El Paso and rented a small apartment near Fort Bliss. The OBC (14 weeks) consisted of studying basic officer leadership, AAA tactics, basic electronics, military map reading, and lots of time out on the ranges, firing all the AAA weapons of the day: 40mm cannons, quad .50 caliber machine guns, 75mm, 90mm, and 120mm guns. Normally the aerial targets used were a metallic mesh, rectangular 'sleeve', towed by a cable attached to a B-25 bomber furnished and flown by the Air Force. One day we were at Oro Grande range in the desert, firing 90mm guns. The gun control radar acquired the target, and we began firing. The ammunition had a time fuse that was set to explode the rounds, hopefully at the same range as the target. Well, the target tracking radar crept up the metal cable and a few rounds exploded, with the attendant big puff of smoke, just *ahead* of the aircraft! The pilot immediately cut the cable loose, and radioed down to the range,---"Hey, tell those gun bunnies, I'm pulling the target, not pushing it! I'm going to 'happy hour'!" We enjoyed our stay at Fort Bliss, visited Juarez, Mexico (just across the border), saw bull fights (one was enough), and had good steak dinners (on bull-fight days)! One evening at a Mexican restaurant in Juarez, just before I ordered a meal, I saw a waiter deliver a delicious looking dish to a gentleman at the table next to ours, and I asked our waiter what it was, and if I could order it. He said, "Si Senor, that is a special delicacy, the testicles of the bull, from the bull fight today, but, of course, there is only one order available today. Would you like to reserve it for next Sunday, the day of our next bull fight?" I replied that I would. The next Sunday we arrived at the restaurant and I ordered the dish.

When our waiter delivered it, I noticed that the serving was much smaller than the one I had observed the previous Sunday, and when I questioned him about this, he said, "Si Senor, sometimes the bull wins!" OK, it's an old E-mail joke, but I couldn't resist. It fits here.

Operation Sagebrush, Louisiana, Platoon Leader, C Btry, 82ⁿᵈ AAA Bn

Toward the end of the course, the class received orders, assigning us to our first units in the Army. Nine of us received orders for the 82ⁿᵈ AAA Battalion, 2ⁿᵈ Infantry Division stationed at Fort Lewis, Washington. We graduated on 2 November. On 3 November, we joined the 82ⁿᵈ right there at Fort Bliss. The Battalion had convoyed with all the wheeled vehicles from Fort Lewis in Washington State, down to San Diego and across to El Paso, on the way to Louisiana for Operation Sagebrush, the largest maneuvers since the 1941 maneuvers in Louisiana. Katherine rode back to Louisiana with a couple of our classmates. I crawled into my jeep and took a little five-day excursion across Texas to Operation Sagebrush in Louisiana. The battalion had shipped, by rail, all of the tracked vehicles, from Fort Lewis to a railhead near Many, La. Our first task was to unload all the tracks, service them, etc. The tracks consisted of M42's, a full track vehicle (some civilians would call it a tank) with twin 40mm cannons in an open turret, and M16's, a halftrack (I know I am dating myself) with quad .50 caliber machine guns mounted in the rear.

I was assigned as the Assistant Platoon Leader, of the Second Platoon in Charlie Battery. During the first week of the maneuver, a snake bit my Platoon Leader, Lieutenant Rutledge. He yelled for me and I ran over and sliced his leg with a *bayonet*, and tried to suck the poison from his leg, just above his boot. The Platoon Sergeant and I put him in the ¾ ton and took him to the Battalion Aid Station. The Battalion surgeon, Doc Reynolds examined him and shipped him off to the hospital. He said he thought he would be OK, if he didn't bleed to death----my surgery was a little ---shall we say---sloppy. I was pretty excited and the Doc wasn't sure *I* would be OK! I never saw Lt. Rutledge again, but I heard that he recovered and was OK. He did not rejoin our unit, so now I am the Platoon Leader. Within a week, we had another soldier in the platoon bitten by a snake. I treated him; he recovered OK, but I began to wonder if the snake Gods were picking on me for some reason. Operation Sagebrush lasted about one month. I was a local hero because I think I was the only platoon leader in the battalion that never got lost. I was pretty good at military map reading and I had squirrel hunted in most of the woods that we occupied.

I had the best jeep driver in the Army, one PFC Chico Torres. Late one dark night, my battery commander called me on the radio and asked me to meet him pronto at a specific location. Chico and I headed out to the place, on a gravel road, naturally. We came upon a convoy of military vehicles. I called the battery commander and told him we had encountered a convoy that was moving rather slow. He told me to pass the convoy and get to his location as soon as possible. The last vehicle in the convoy was a jeep, and I told Chico to pass it. As we got along side, the jeep swerved toward us, almost hitting us, and ran us completely off the road, and followed us through a shallow ditch almost into the woods. I was infuriated. After we stopped, I jumped out of my jeep. The other jeep was now behind us with it's lights right in my eyes, almost blinding me. A guy got out of the other jeep. His back was to the lights, so I could not see anything but a silhouette. I began to read the riot act to him. This was my first opportunity in the Army at butt-chewing, and I was going to make it good. I was really giving him hell for nearly causing an accident, and as I ranted, he just turned slowly until I began to see him in the lights and recognize some of his features. I then looked up at his cap, and saw two of the biggest silver stars I have ever seen. I guess I began to salute with both hands, and guess what? He was not impressed! And he had no sense of humor at all about being chewed out by a 2nd Lieutenant! He told me to get back in my @$#%^&* jeep, get back on the #$%^&#$ road, go in the opposite #$^@$#% direction, and *never, never* come back! I called my battery commander on the radio and told him there had been a change of plans and that I would see him in the morning. Later I began to worry that I had not covered up my nametag on my field jacket. I was thoroughly relieved when I remembered that I had borrowed Lt. Rutledge's field jacket with his nametag on it!

Our unit's mission during Sagebrush was to provide ground and air defense for a new unit in the Army: a 280mm "Atomic Cannon" battalion. My platoon had the mission of protecting one of these new artillery weapons. The cannon, in its march order (traveling) position, looked like a huge telephone pole with a truck on either end of it. It was unique in one respect. At that time, the technology was such that the smallest projectile that could be packaged to carry an atomic weapon was 280mm. So the gun was literally designed around the projectile, instead of the other way around. Later, nukes were developed for weapons as small as 8 inch and 155mm howitzers. So this new 280mm atomic cannon was hot stuff. All the Generals wanted to see how it faired during the maneuver, hence the 2-star I *ran into* in the convoy.

During the Sagebrush maneuver, my college, Northwestern held its homecoming football game. Katherine was living with her folks in Glenmora, and I called and told her that I thought I could sneak off and meet her at the campus in Natchitoches. Chico and I bailed out and drove to the game. I met Katherine and we were enjoying the game, in our combat gear, when Chico and I saw in the distance, soldiers of the 82nd Airborne Division parachuting close to the area where the bridge over the Red River stood. I knew that the Division was acting as the aggressor force during the maneuver. I also knew we were on the wrong side of the river! I told Chico we had better saddle up the jeep and split. We made it across the river just before the aggressors took control of the bridge. It would have been more than an embarrassment if we had been captured, particularly since we were just slightly AWOL! At least we were not where we were supposed to be.

While Katherine was living with her folks, and I was in the woods treating people for snakebite, Katherine acquired a beautiful, snow-white kitten. Naturally, we named him Sagebrush. When the maneuver ended around the middle of December, I took a couple of weeks leave, and we spent Christmas with our parents. The day after Christmas, we again loaded up the Plymouth with all our worldly possessions, now including the cat, and headed for Fort Lewis, Washington. We did a little sightseeing along the way. For many years the only way we could afford to travel was between duty stations, using Uncle Sam's travel allowance. We spent New Year's Eve with one of my OBC classmates in Las Vegas. We visited the Grand Canyon, and had to sneak Sagebrush into the lodge.

Fort Lewis, Washington, Platoon Leader,
C Btry, 82nd AAA Bn

After our first experience driving in snow, in Oregon and Washington, we rolled into Tacoma, Washington, home of Fort Lewis. We got a motel for the night, and I checked in to my unit, C Battery, 82nd AAA Battalion the next morning. When I left early that morning, I gave Katherine a "mission-type order". This is an important military term and I need to take some time here to explain it. In the Army, commanders almost always gave "mission-type orders". That means the commander would tell subordinate commanders what the particular mission was and the desired outcome, if it weren't already obvious. They almost *never* tried to tell you how to accomplish it! I loved that about the Army. It encouraged initiative, creative thinking, and showed confidence in the junior commander by the senior commander. If the junior commander needed more guidance, he would ask for it. I always used the example of the greatest "mission-type order" I ever heard. It was when the President of the United States told General Eisenhower, "Invade the Continent of Europe"! Wow, could I work with an order like that! He did not tell him when to do it, where to do it, or how to do it.

So that first morning, in Tacoma, Washington, I gave Katherine a "mission-type order". I told her to find a place for us to live. I didn't tell her where, when or how. She was in a strange land, at the motel without a car, and could hardly even speak the language. When I came home that evening from my first day at work, there was a note at the motel, that I should come to an address on the grounds of the beautiful Tacoma Golf and Country Club to see our new rented house! When I went through the front gate, I thought surely this must not be the correct location. I couldn't afford even to be the grass man in this place! I found the address, and it was a beautiful split-level house, called the Tepee house, right on American Lake. It was owned by U.S. Senator Cain (no relation to my cousins, etc.) from Washington State. It seems they were just waiting for the right tenants-----and it seemed that a pore' 2nd Lt and his bride fit the bill. Wow. I made a mental note to give Katherine more mission-type orders in the future! Steve Pawlik and several of my Army buddies always told me that I rode Katherine's coattails to a successful Army career! Lots of people had told us that we might not like the Fort Lewis area because it rained a lot. Heck, after living in Louisiana all of our lives, this was a *dry* (well, semi-dry) climate.

My unit was located on north fort, and all of the administrative buildings and troop barracks were the OLD WW II construction. It was here for the next six months that I learned so much about the Army, and I liked it. We had good, well-motivated soldiers, with few exceptions, and a great group of senior Non-Commissioned Officers (NCOs), who taught me so well. The only credit I can claim is that I was *willing to learn!* That is important. Not all 2nd LTs are willing to learn from NCOs—some think "well, I outrank this guy so he can't teach me anything"—those LTs were doomed---more war stories about that later. I also had a tough, but good Battery Commander that taught me things I never forgot: Captain Bill Connors. He was a Korean vet, spent several years as an enlisted man through Sergeant, and was now a Captain. He retired as a LTC and has passed away, but his widow, Mavis ("Mike") lives in Homosassa, FL. and is our good friend—we visit her when we go south---she is a sweet lady.

I well remember one of the first *hard* lessons I learned from Capt. Connors. I was in the motor pool one day, supervising(?) vehicle maintenance and Capt. Connors came up to me and asked me to take care of a task. Several hours later he saw me and asked me if I had taken care of the task. I was a little embarrassed, and told him that I had asked Sgt So-and-so to do it, but I would take care of it. He just turned around and left without saying a word. Later, he came up to me and asked if I had taken care of the task----now I was really "put out" about this and told him that I would jack up Sgt So-and-so, and tell him *again to do it!* At this point, Capt Connors stood me at attention, got right in my face and said, and I quote verbatim, because I never forgot a word of it, "LT, let me tell you something; 10% of your job is telling somebody to do something; 90% of your job is to make damn sure it gets done. Now you are doing a great job on the 10%, but you're not doing doodly squat on the 90%"!

We occasionally went over to Yakima, Washington to maneuver and fire our weapons. It was in the desert. I didn't know that Washington State had a desert, but they do! I was the Platoon Leader, 2nd Platoon and my Platoon Sergeant was Sergeant First Class (SFC) Henry L. Bell. As I recall, his formal education ended at the third grade, but don't let that fool anybody----he was smart, and taught me much. At Yakima, our platoon had the mission to set up a perimeter defense of a notional target against an air attack. My platoon Sgt said, "Sir why don't you go over to the east side of the perimeter, take 4 tracks (AAA weapons---40mms and quad .50 cals) with you and set up that side of the perimeter, and I'll go over to the west side and set it up". I said, OK. He said, "good decision, LT.". (You can see where this is going, can't you??). I took the 4 Section Chiefs of the 4 tracks with me and set up my side of the perimeter, and then met my Platoon Sgt at the Platoon CP, a ¾ ton truck. He looked it over and said, "good job, LT.". He told me that a couple of our Section Chiefs, may be a little lazy and did not want to set up their camouflage nets over the vehicles, so they set up their weapons under a thick tree, where they could not possibly fire at an airplane! He suggested that *he* would go over to the weapons section chiefs in my sector and get them positioned away from under the tree, so that they could fire at hostile aircraft, without firing through the tree top. I agreed. He said, "good decision, LT.". Now the next sequences are very important! Important enough to spend some time explaining it. But, pay attention!

At the outset, I did not know what I was doing! I knew that, and that was important. My Platoon Sergeant, SFC Henry L. Bell, understood that I did not know what I was doing! And that was even more important. I *knew* that he knew that I didn't know what I was doing. Even more important, I *knew* that he *knew,* that I *knew,* that he *knew,* that I didn't know what I was doing! Saved me!

From our Battalion area, we had a spectacular view of Mount Rainer. One weekend, we traveled up there for our first attempt at skiing! I got a quick lesson, and was told that when you needed to turn, just face the way you wanted to turn and the skis would do the rest. They lie! When I was coming down the mountain fast, and needed to turn right, I twisted my body to the right, and guess what? The skis kept going straight until I encountered yonder big, pine tree. Injured my knee--- missed two Division parades. More about our assignment at Fort Lewis, Washington. We enjoyed the Northwest, and were surprised about leaving, 6 months later. While at Fort Lewis, we thought we would be there for the remainder of my two-year obligation of service on active duty. Well, one day, our Battalion Personnel Warrant Officer, Ray Bonner, came by the orderly room, and told me "Congratulations, your Indefinite Category has been approved", to which I replied, "Say what"?! I had *not* applied for an Indefinite Category, and when I inquired as to what that meant, he said that it was a good deal, and incidentally, obligated me for an extra year on active duty! I was beginning to get the message-----Uncle Sam wanted *ME*!! *FOREVER*!! I was never quite sure about how I got this Indefinite Category designation. The only reason I could come up with was, back at the Basic Course, I had applied for Airborne (parachute) School at Fort Benning, GA. I received an answer back that since I was being assigned to the unit at Fort Lewis, I should just wait until after I joined the unit and go to Airborne Training on the 2nd Infantry Division's quota. Somehow that got garbled and I received the Indefinite Category. At the time, I didn't have any idea of just how *indefinite* it was going to be.

My unit, the 82nd AAA Battalion had been selected to participate in Operation Gyroscope. This was a trial of a new concept in unit replacement vs individual replacement. Two Battalions at Fort Lewis were chosen to participate. They were to replace two Battalions at Fort Richardson, Alaska. I didn't pay much attention to it, because I did not have enough time left on my 2-year obligation to make the cut off and go to Alaska. Now, after CWO Bonner's little visit with me, and I was obligated for one more year, I was eligible to go with the unit. Several of my Lieutenant buddies were getting permanent change of station (PCS) orders for Korea. At that time, it was an 18 month unaccompanied tour of duty. The thought of being away from Katherine for 18 months made it an easy decision. I ran over to the S-1 Personnel Office and quickly volunteered to go with the unit to Alaska in the summer.

Gyroscope was a very interesting concept, and it worked well in the beginning. After much planning, an advanced party journeyed to Fort Richardson to prepare for the unit's arrival. The Battalion was loaded on busses and driven to the docks in Tacoma-----all the soldiers, Officers, NCOs, their families, pets, etc. We were scheduled to board a troop ship that day. However, our troop ship was rammed by another ship in the Strait of Juan de Fuca. So we were put up in hotels for a couple of days, while another troop ship, the U.S. Morton was taken out of moth balls and put into service. Our Battalion Commander was senior to the other Battalion Commander, so he named the staff. The other Battalion's officers got the not-so-good jobs, like Troop Compartment Commanders. I was the Special Services Officer and my main job was to pass out hundreds of decks of cards to the troop compartments. It was not a fancy cruise, but Katherine and I had a private 'stateroom'. We sailed the inland passage (same route that the cruise ships take today), had nice weather, saw our first whale, and pulled into the docks in Anchorage, Alaska.

TWO

Fort Richardson, Alaska, Platoon Leader 82nd AAA Bn, 867th AAA Bn, 96th Gun Bn

The first things we saw as our ship was docking in the Anchorage harbor, were two battalions of uniformed soldiers, on the dock, in formation, and all the families, pets, etc. We were all in our uniforms, and we marched our troops off the ship and they marched on. We were then bussed to the battalion area they had just vacated, where we occupied their buildings, mostly Quonset huts, motor pools, troop barracks, weapons, equipment, etc. Their advanced party was already at Fort Lewis in our old area, preparing for their arrival. So entire battalions of @ 500 soldiers each, with families, pets, etc. just swapped places. It went amazingly well, considering the magnitude of the operation. It was the summer of 1956. We had certainly experienced many things in our first year in the Army! And now I had two more years (remember I had been extended 1 year) to have fun. When we got to Alaska, Katherine taught school at Elmendorf Air Force Base, next door to Fort Richardson.

My Platoon Sergeant, SFC Henry L. Bell, was still with me. And the C Battery First Sergeant, one First Sergeant Billy C. Sommerville was the best First Sergeant I ever had. I was in awe of him, if not a little afraid of him. He was an old soldier from the "old" school. He taught me so much. First Sergeants had a collective reputation---you didn't screw around with the First Sergeant—no matter if you were an Officer, an NCO, and particularly if you were a soldier. Why should I be in awe of him? For starters, he joined the Army the month and year I was born!! That was enough. When we first got to Alaska, I went into the Orderly Room (the first sergeants domain) and asked where my office was. The first sergeant handed me a clipboard, and said, "here it is" LT. You are the motor officer. I expect you will be spending most of your time over there, in the motor pool. He was an "old school" senior NCO. When I would come in every morning to check my in-box (I didn't tarry), I would speak and say, "good morning First Sergeant". He would say, "good morning Sir, how is the Lieutenant this morning?"--- Always in the third person. He was always very respectful, particularly if there was anybody else in the orderly room. Sometimes when we were in the orderly room alone with just the battery clerk present, he would send the clerk over to the mess hall for coffee---when the 1st Sgt and I were alone, he would say, "come here Junior. That damn Motor Sgt is blowing smoke up your skirt. Now, you go over to the Motor Pool and grab him by the stacking swivel, and tell him you want those damn tracks off deadline. Got it'?" To which I replied, "Yes First Sergeant"!

B Battery also had a great First Sergeant, Melvin Tyra. He was tough, but had not been in the Army quite as long as First Sergeant Sommerville. He would walk into our Orderly Room, and say to our First Sergeant Sommerville, "hello, you old, worn out, crusty SOB". My First Sergeant would respond, "I'm fine, you raw ass recruit---I've spent more time in the chow line than you have on active duty!" The first time I heard that, I thought they were going to fight, but it was just their way of showing a *lot* of *respect* for each other. B Battery had a 2nd LT that was arrogant and would not listen and learn from the first sergeant or any NCOs. One day the B Battery Commander went over on main Post for a while and the LT came in the orderly room and asked the 1st Sgt where the troops were. 1st Sgt Tyra told him they were in the motor pool, maintaining equipment, according to the training schedule. The LT told him to assemble the troops back up in the Battery area. The 1st Sgt balked a little at this and asked the LT why he wanted a troop formation. The LT said, "I am the Battery Commander right now, and I want to talk to the troops". 1st Sgt Tyra looked at him and said, "screw it LT, you can be the 1st Sgt too", and walked out. When the real Battery Commander returned, he just about killed the LT. B Battery had another LT—a very good one. One day, in our orderly room, I overheard a conversation between these two 1st

Sgts. They did not know I was in earshot of them. Tyra said that he had the best LT in the Battalion. Sommerville said, "no way. My LT can run circles around yours---I know---I trained him myself. He is by far, the best LT in the Battalion". After a little bit, I realized that 1st Sgt Sommerville was talking about me. That may be the greatest compliment I ever received!

The Army had been reorganized into Battle Groups vs Brigades. A Battle Group was commanded by an Infantry Colonel, and had several battalions of Infantry, Artillery and Engineer support, and logistics units. Our unit, C Battery, 82nd AAA Bn was assigned to support one of these Battle Groups. The Battle Group Commander's attitude was, since there was a good chance that we may have to fight in this rather hostile arctic environment, we would train in it. And train we did. We practically lived in the field. During Operation Willow, one of the many field-training exercises we participated in, my Platoon was supporting one of the Infantry Battalions. The Battalion Commander and I had a good relationship, realized through habitual association----we normally supported the same unit. He and I were discussing maneuvering toward an objective which involved crossing what looked like a field, with not much vegetation. I told him that I thought it was muskeg, a frozen-over bog, quite common in the tundra. Now, it will support dismounted Infantry, but my heavy tracks were a whole different ball game. He thought we could make it, and ordered us to charge. Well my third track in line, started sinking in the muskeg, causing the following track to have to stop, and it began sinking. We called a wrecker to the scene, and spent all day getting those tracks out of the bog. The Infantry Battalion Commander breathed a sigh of relief, along with me. He had told me that he would assume full responsibility if something like this happened. There are stories about bulldozers being sunk in that stuff and had to be abandoned in the winter, and dug out after the thaw in the summer.

I was promoted to first Lieutenant and attended the Arctic Warfare School for 3 weeks, at Fort Greely, Alaska, up north. This was quite an experience for an ole country boy from Pitkin, Louisiana. When we were at Base Camp, we lived in Quonset huts, barely heated by one gasoline stove. We lived in the field most of the time. Once when we were in the field for 4 days, it was 56 degrees *below* Zero-----I still have my "50 below card". But we followed the training schedule, which called for spending the first night in 10 man tents with a small gasoline heater, the second night in 2-man snow caves that we had built, and the third night in a squad lean-to, made from trees we were to cut down. The first night went OK. We had to be careful and place the gas stove/heater on layers of cardboard from C-Ration boxes. The tents had no floors, and there was a danger that the heater would melt the snow and tip over, and burn the tent (and occupants) in about 20 seconds. We had one fireguard that had to be awake and clothed to keep watch on the heater at all times---this was standard operating procedure (SOP) throughout Alaska. The next day, the cadre took away our tents and gas heaters. They had demonstrated how to construct small, 2-man snow caves, and that worked pretty well. It used a candle to do two things, one; glaze over the snow inside until it formed a fairly rigid "dome", and two; the candle was the only heat source in the little cave. It was critical to have a vent in the top for ventilation, and these were inspected by the cadre. Of course we had air mattresses and arctic sleeping bags. The third day/night was a disaster. They issued to us wood saws and axes, and gave us *all day* to cut down trees and limbs to construct lean-to's to sleep in that night. First, you *do* know what all day at Fort Greely, Alaska consists of in the wintertime. The sun comes up about 1130 in the morning and sets about 1300 (1 PM) in the afternoon. A little further north, the sun does not rise at all in the middle of the winter, and in the summer it does not set---it just dips toward the horizon and goes back up. We discovered another phenomenon. Trying to cut down a tree when it is 56 degrees below zero is like trying to chop down the Washington monument. The trees are frozen solid! We were told that this was the first time it had been this cold in the field since the school began. After 20% of the cadre got frostbite, they gave us our tents and gas stoves back. So we did not get to experience the fun of lean-to living.

The most enjoyable part of the school was the skiing. We did lots of cross-country skiing and that was fun. We also were taught ski-joring. A long rope was hitched up to the back of an Otter or Weasel (rather light weight full track vehicles that were very capable on snow). An entire squad of 9 or 10 soldiers would space themselves at intervals holding onto the rope and be pulled by the tracks. It was a good way to move a rather large number of troops without wearing them out---cross-country skiing can be tiresome, depending on the terrain.

We wore arctic parkas, with fur around the face hood, and a wire that allowed you to pinch it down so there was a small slit for vision, and your body (breathing) would keep your face frostbite free. We used the buddy system; every 15 minutes or so, you and your buddy would open up each others' face mask to check for frostbite. Frostbite is serious. We were shown movies where guys with severe frostbite had their toes removed by pinching them off with a pair of pliers. Got *my* attention!

We also wore 'Mickey Mouse' boots, heavily insulated, or snow Pacs, knee length, fur-lined footwear. Everybody has heard stories about kids trying to lick pipes, hand railings or other metal objects when it is very cold and the metal is frosty. We had that happen---the hand railings at the back steps to our apartments were painted, metal pipes, and occasionally a kid would try to lick off the frost and his tongue would stick. Very painful.

This next story is a little *delicate*. I am still at the arctic warfare school in "cool" Fort Greely. I know this is a family show, but I feel like I must tell this story, for this epistle to be complete and honest. You will know that I couldn't make this up! At temperatures hovering around 50 below, some of the normal body functions become a challenge---think about it---at that temperature, *any exposed skin* will get frostbite in several seconds. Now the arctic parkas pretty well protected your face, helped by the buddy system in place. But in some other *areas,* you were own your own. While on the ski slopes, there comes a time when nature calls. Now, the standard procedure was when the need got sufficient enough, you were to stop, turn perpendicular to the ski trail, stick your metal ski poles in the snow on either side of you, un-zip, and er, uh, *whiz*! (*quickly!*) One day, this older Captain felt the need, and he stopped and followed this procedure. Now, it was very cold, and his metal ski poles were very frosty. While he was er, uh, *whizzing*, one of the metal ski poles fell over against his er, uh *whizzer*, **and stuck!** While it may be funny now, it was very serious then, at least to the Captain!

Meanwhile, back at the ranch, the Army was transitioning the Artillery from Anti-Aircraft Artillery guns to Air Defense Artillery Missiles. After about one year, in the summer of 1957, the 82nd AAA

Bn was deactivated. Sad. I thoroughly enjoyed my time in the 82nd. One more "war story"---. Our unit had the extra mission of guarding the "tank farm", a number of large petroleum tanks near the port of Anchorage. It was kind of desolate countryside, and bears and other critters visited the area often. The guards were armed with live ammunition. When I was the Officer of the Day, and checked the guard, especially at night, I made sure that the guard knew I was there, gave the correct password, etc. It was a spooky place on the side of a mountain, and I didn't want to screw around with young soldiers that had a full clip of live ammo. Our Group (Brigade) Commander was an adventuresome sort, and enjoyed playing games with the guards, when he would check them. On one occasion he had his driver turn off the jeep headlights. He dismounted and walked through the darkness, until challenged by the guard. The guard yelled, "Halt!" The Colonel thought, OK that is correct---let's see if he continues to know what to do, so he keep walking toward the guard, where upon the guard yelled, "I said Halt!" So far so good. The Colonel kept walking until he heard the guard chamber a round. The Colonel halted. He was adventuresome, not stupid! OK, still good---the guard was on his toes and following his general orders, perfectly. They exchanged passwords and the guard said, "advance and be recognized." Then the Colonel complimented the guard, but asked one more, final question. What would the guard have done if the Colonel had not halted the last time? Without hesitation, the guard said he would call the Sergeant of the Guard, back at the guardhouse----the Colonel couldn't believe his ears. He asked, irately, what the hell would he call the Sergeant of the guard for?? The guard said, "Sir, I would call to tell him to come up here and haul your dead ass off my mountain!!"

Before I left the 82nd, my Battery Commander had been bugging me to apply for a Regular Army Commission----you remember, the one I had turned down before. Well, I had a buddy that applied for a RA Commission while on active duty----he finished his active service, was a deputy sheriff in Louisiana long enough to realize it wasn't for him---he spent all his time shaking hands and politikin' for the parish (county) sheriff. After all this time, he received an approval for his RA Commission, and came back on active duty. This seemed a good idea to me---Department of the Army (DA) was taking a long time---

months and months to act on these applications. It would, at least, get my Battery and Battalion Commanders off my back about "going RA". Well, in just a few months, the Battalion Commander called me in to his office. He congratulated me---my approval for a RA commission had been approved. Oh me! I asked what this changed in my obligatory tour in the Army. He seemed surprised at the question but said it would obligate me for a minimum of one more year! Have we been here before?? So you see, I never woke up one morning and said,; Wow! This is for me—I want to stay in the Army forever-----it was more like I kept being extended, and never bothered to do all the paperwork to get out----there's much more paperwork involved in getting out, that getting in!!

In June I was transferred to the 867th AAA Bn, (75mm gun). I was assigned to A Battery as a Gunnery Officer/Platoon Leader. The 75mm gun was an interesting weapon. It had an 'automatic loader' with a high rate of fire---unusual for a cannon with that large of a projectile. The loader was made by the Singer Sewing Machine Co. I enjoyed firing it on the firing range.

On 16 July 1957, one of the most important events of our lives occurred! Our precious daughter, Sonja Lynne Hoglan, was born at the Air Force Hospital on Elmendorf, AFB. I was so excited that I called the Brigade Commander (full colonel) at 3 in the morning to tell him about it. I don't think he was as impressed about it as I was. She was delivered by an Army Doctor that was on duty that night at the Air Force Hospital. When Sonja was one year old, Katherine flew with her to Louisiana to visit our folks.

I decided after they were in Louisiana that I would also go back for a visit, and I *hitchhiked* on military aircraft from Elmendorf AFB, Alaska to England AFB in Louisiana. During these various flights, I would check into Base Operations to see what was available, and if any flights were going in the general direction that I was headed. On one flight, I signed on as escort officer for some dead bodies. The caskets were inside large wooden crates, and the only place I had to lay down was on top of one of the boxes. Didn't sleep too well. One flight I boarded left Travis AFB in California going to Lackland AFB in Texas. I signed on as a courier officer for 2,000 pounds of top-secret cargo, locked in heavy canvas bags. The flight surgeon on board told me it would be a long flight, and offered me his bunk. I took him up on his kind offer and had a pretty good night's sleep. When I awoke early the next morning, we were flying over a large city---I asked if that was San Antonio. The co-pilot said no, it was Omaha, Nebraska! Say what? Did I get on the wrong flight? I told them that I thought we were going to San Antonio. The crew laughed and said, "we are, eventually."

Returning to Alaska was just as adventuresome. I flew from England AFB, Louisiana to Albuquerque, New Mexico in an old B-25 bomber. An Air Force Major was the only other passenger, other than the crew. When we crawled into the *waist gunners' seats (I think)*, he looked at me and asked if I had ever flown in this airplane before. I told him that I had not. He pulled out a big ball of cotton, handed it to me and told me to stuff as much as I could in my ears. He said it was the loudest aircraft in the Air Force and we were seated right behind one of the engines. Two weeks later in Alaska, I could still hear those engines turning!

Three of us, including a sailor and an Army Warrant Officer ended up in Moses Lake, in eastern Washington State. Boeing had a facility there where their aircraft were taken for installation of the electronics, etc. When they had no flights to McCord AFB in Settle, at the recommendation of the Personnel Manager at the Boeing plant, the three of us chartered a small plane to fly us to Seattle. Since it was a civilian plane, it couldn't land at McCord. The pilot landed on a *grass airstrip* near the little town of Tillicum (close to McCord). From there we hitched a ride in the back of a farmer's truck hauling hay. He dropped us off at the gate to the Air Base, and we finally made it back to Alaska.

In September of that same year, the 867th was deactivated. I was transferred to the 96th Gun Bn (120mm gun). I was assigned to B Battery, out in a very picturesque wilderness area, with a stream running through the Battery area, which was really beautiful in the winter. The 120mm guns were the largest cannons in the Anti Aircraft Artillery, and we fired them on a range close to Anchorage, out over the water. In March of the next year, 1958, the 96th Gun Bn was deactivated. I began to wonder if I was a jinx to these units----seems like every one I touched, disappeared. I was then transferred to the 500th AAA Operations Detachment, stationed at Elmendorf Air Force Base, next door to Fort Richardson. We were the Army Air Defense Command

Post (AADCP) for what was left of the Air Defense Artillery in that area. The name changed to 12th Detachment, 62nd Artillery, and then to HQ, 4th Missile Bn, 43rd Artillery, when the Nike Hercules Missile Battalion arrived in the area, but our mission in the AADCP did not change. Our detachment was located in the Elmendorf War Room, where all aircraft picked up by radar was displayed and tracked (plotted) on a big plexiglass board. The officers worked 8 hour shifts--days (0800 to 1600 hrs), swings (1600 to midnight) and midnights (midnight to 0800). Every 5 weeks or so, we would take turns going out to Fire Island via Air Force helicopter, and spending 2 weeks at the site out there.

I should take the time to explain the Officers Evaluation Report, called by various names (some are unprintable!), over the 30 years I was on active duty. Although the form changed several times over the years, it typically consisted of a Rater's portion, your 1st boss's cut at you, with numerical ratings in various categories as well as an important comments section. The second part, and equally important, was the Indorser's portion, virtually the same as far as numerical categories and a comments section. This Indorser would typically be your boss's boss. Then your boss's, boss's boss, the third guy in your chain of command had to sign the report, as the Reviewer. He would only sign the report, signaling that he generally agreed with the report, and it was filled out properly. I did not take these things seriously!

Maybe I should have! Although the overwhelming majority of my bosses over the 30 years I served on active duty were top notch officers that I had the most respect and admiration for (and I have tried to mention them by name in this book), I also worked for several losers—that's not atypical---I'm sure every Army officer could relate a similar story. During my Lieutenant years in Alaska, and even later, you notice that I did not comment on the bosses that I considered less professional. It is not my intention to slam-dunk anybody by name— and thank goodness, they were few, but I had some. Back in those days, we had a lot of officers that were retiring as Captains and Majors, who had served with enlisted time and were finishing up their service of 20 years. I had a couple of Captains and one Major that I had really worked hard for, and, I thought, I had performed exceptionally well. I was a little surprised when they showed me my OER, and gave me a mediocre report and (what is known in the trade as) damned me with faint praise—used words like satisfactory and excellent, when superior and outstanding were the words of choice for an above average report. But, again I didn't care! Maybe somebody should have pulled me over and said, "hey this is important, and if you don't think the OER is a fair evaluation, you can and should contest it". But I didn't.

The most flagrant abuse of the OER for me, and the funniest to me, was when a Battalion Executive Officer, my number two boss (the Indorser) mistook me for another officer in the Battalion and wrote in his portion of my OER that I was "a short, quiet, reticent officer, who seldom expresses himself and gives the initial impression of coldness". I remember it verbatim (and have a copy)! I have had many laughs about this one over the years. Later, I met officers who told me I was crazy—that I could easily have contested that one and had it thrown out. But it was too funny to get rid of. It was very obvious that the report did not refer to me. Since I graduated from college and was commissioned as a 2nd Lieutenant, I was never short (unless you consider 6 foot 2 inches, short. And I have never been accused of being quiet, reticent, or cold! Later I learned those kind of things were to hinder me somewhat. Incidentally, the few times I visited this battalion executive officer in the battalion headquarters, he was either reading Playboy Magazine or had his head down on his desk, sound asleep! More about these impediments to progress, later.

One of the things I enjoyed most about our tour in Alaska was the great fishing. I well remember driving up to Palmer for some lake fishing. Capt. Connors and I would be in one fishing boat, and when we looked behind us, there were our wives, Mavis and Katherine in a boat with Sergeant First Class (SFC) Clegg, our Battery supply sergeant. One would be paddling the boat, and the other would be baiting his hook with salmon eggs, or getting him a beer out of the cooler. SFC Clegg had it made. Incidentally, he was a great supply sergeant.

My next battery commander was Cal Wilson and he loved to fish also. We had traded in our Plymouth for a used ford station wagon, so our little fishing boat would slide in the rear of the wagon. Hunting and fishing were official, recognized recreational activities for soldiers stationed in Alaska. We had hunting rifles and shotguns in the arms room, and a supply room full of fishing rods and reels. We could use the Army ¾ ton trucks on the weekends for fishing trips. This was back when the area was still pretty wild and had not been fished out. We almost always caught the limit, whether it was Rainbow Trout, Steelhead, Salmon, or Arctic Grayling. Cal and I would get to a lake and fish all night long—why not?—it never got dark. The only down side, was the mosquitoes! I heard two of them talking one evening---one said to the other, shall we eat him here, or hide him so the big ones won't take him away from us!

The Air Force maintained a great fishing camp at Nek Nek in the Valley of Ten Thousand Smokes. It was on a river where it exited a large lake. We would fly from Elmendorf on a large Air Force plane south to an airport somewhere, then transfer to a 4-passenger floatplane, for ferrying to the camp. The camp capacity was 22 guests (fishermen) at one time (plus staff). So you and a buddy would sign up for the trip. The staff cooked and served all meals, great food, including the fish you caught that day. Every morning your 2-man boat would be cleaned, gassed, and ready to go. Your fish would be cleaned by the staff. It was all *first class!* All ranks were treated like VIPs. I caught some huge rainbow trout and have the pictures to prove it.

On one of the trips, I met an aircrew that flew refueling missions out of Elmendorf AFB. They flew KC 47 aircraft, a propeller driven tanker. They invited me to go with them on a refueling mission. I went, and it was very interesting. I went over to Elmendorf AFB after dark one night. We were briefed on the mission. They did not tell me where we were to meet up with the B-47 we were to refuel, but I know it was west of Attu on the Aleutian Chain. When we were close to our rendezvous point, the aircraft commander directed me to the rear of the aircraft to the boom operator's post. The boom operator has just enough room to lay down, and to observe the procedure, I had to lay down on top of the boom operator (sorta glad no-one took pictures of that!). The boom operator literally flies the boom (it has little wings) and positions it near the fuel intake, lighted by a circle of lights in the nose of the B-47. When he gets the position just right, he pulls a trigger and the boom extends into the fuel intake "hole". Now, the KC 97 is an old prop job, and the B-47, although old, is a jet bomber, so during the entire refueling operation, we had to fly at max speed and slightly "downhill" to prevent the B-47 from eating our lunch. I guess he was at idle speed. Nowadays, the refueling is done by a KC 135 (Boeing 707 with extra fuel tanks). I flew in those too, but more about that later. At Elmendorf, I also flew in a B-57 Canberra Bomber. It is subsonic but we got right up to the sound barrier and I felt the vibration-----close enough for me.

We also did a little big game hunting. Three members of the "*Fab 5*" (see 2nd para below) went caribou hunting one day. We killed two very large caribou and drug them about 1 mile to the road through deep snow. We were wearing snowshoes and used Akios (200lb sleds) to get them to the road, with great difficulty! We gave one away there; field dressed the other one and brought it to my back yard on Post. We finished dressing and skinning it, cut it up and put it in a cooler (several were provided by the Post). It was actually a *'warmer'*, since it was about 58 degrees inside and about 10 below outside. We left it in the 'cooler' for about 10 days as I recall. When we took the packages out, we had to cut the mold off the corners. I learned about curing meat----you want fish fresh, but not beef, deer, or wild game. It needs to be aged. We ate caribou, moose, and bear in Alaska that was absolutely terrible, because people did not know how to cure it! Sam Myers was our expert in this. He and another friend did a lot of hunting in Alaska----much more than the other "Fab 5" guys.

In April 1959, I finished my tour in Alaska and returned to the states, to Fort Sill, Oklahoma. I don't mean to minimize our cat, Sagebrush's importance to our family. He grew to full size, long hair, and blended into the snow perfectly. Since we were going to take our time, traveling back to Fort Sill, we shipped ole Sage from Alaska to Katherine's folks home in Louisiana, by air, train, and bus. He retired in the country, and lived until he was @ 16 years old. We flew from Anchorage to Tacoma and picked up our car, which we had shipped. We had a great drive down the west coast to San Diego, visiting Army friends in the Imperial Valley in California.

I need to explain "the Fab 5". I'm going to chase that rabbit here and now. There were 5 couples that were stationed in Alaska at the same time. Some of us lived in the same building on Post. We became great friends. The guys were all new Lieutenants, and we had so much in common----mainly *poverty!* All five guys were ROTC graduates and all 5 *intended* to get out of the Army as soon as we had served our obligated tour of duty. Well, we all served on active duty at least 20 years, some 25, and I served just over 30 years. After we left Alaska, some us of served together again, some did not, but we kept in close contact. We did this for several years by what the ladies called the "Round Robin". Katherine would write a letter, send it to Doris, who would write a letter, send them both to Jackie, who would write a letter and send all three to Lynn, etc. When the 'Robin' got back to Katherine, she would pull out her old letter, write a new one and then mail them, etc. It was a great way to keep in contact and share the news of what everybody was doing. We lost track of one couple, the Lowerys. Several years after we had all retired, Sam and Lynn Myers, from Mississippi, were traveling through Maine and remembered that Carl Lowery had graduated from the University of Maine. They stopped in Orono at the University and asked the registrar if they had a current address for the Lowerys. They did, but because of privacy concerns, they would not give their address or phone number. But the office said they would contact the Lowerys and ask them to get in contact with the Myers. They did! After Carl retired from the Army, he taught school in Anniston, Alabama, and retired again. Then they moved to Santa Rosa Beach, Florida and were building a new home *20 minutes from Niceville where we were building a new home!* Amazing!

They had been coming to this area for vacations for many years, and so had we (40+), and we never bumped into them. About 7 years ago, we started having annual reunions. We held one reunion at the Myers home in Hazelhurst, Mississippi. Sam built this home, himself, with very little help from anybody, out in the country. It was originally going to be just a rustic cabin in the woods. When Sam finished it, the house was huge and spectacular. At our reunion there, each of the 5 couples had a private bedroom. We had a great time, as we always do, telling lies about, "the older we get, the better we used to be!!" We had a reunion in Branson, Missouri, took in the shows, etc. Another reunion took place at Opryland in Nashville, Tennessee. The hotel is spectacular and the Country Music Hall of Fame and Museum were really enjoyable. We held one reunion here at our house in Niceville, FL, and one was a Caribbean Cruise out of Mobile, Alabama. We have held two reunions by invitation of the Lowerys---Carl and Loretta, at their cabin on East Grand Lake in upstate Maine. This is probably our favorite place to visit during the summer. The cabin is a large 2-story house; every couple had private bedrooms, with the lake 20 feet from the back of house. The scenery is unbelievable---East Grand Lake is a huge lake and is the border between the U.S. (Maine) and New Brunswick, Canada. The house had been handed down from Carl's Granddad, to his Father, and now is owned by Carl and his brother. The Lowerys have 3 boats at the lake, an aluminum fishing boat, a great 1966 Lone Star runabout, and my favorite, an original Old Town Canoe that they recently had refurbished. It is beautiful. Carl took us on many boat trips on the lake, including boat trips into Canada. All 5 couples made it to the first Maine reunion, and 4 of the 5 to the second one, in 2005. I named the guys, "The Fab 5" (Fabulous Five Lieutenants). It stuck! All five are still married to the same women that were our brides, 50 years ago in Alaska---That's gotta be a record of some sort. I think it's a testament to the good taste and judgment of the 5 guys, although I guess some credit is due the ladies! Like a lot!

I could write another book about the great times we have enjoyed at the lake. The first time, Katherine and I flew to Boston, rented a car and drove to the lake and we stayed a week. This last time we drove all the way from FL and back (1 month), visiting ole Army buddies along the way and renewing friendships. After we got close to Maine, we started eating fresh lobster 2 meals a day (at least). We stayed 10 days at the lake. Driving, stopping, eating, and sightseeing on U.S. 1 (stay off the interstate), "down east" in Maine is wonderful. We always stay in Kennebunkport, Boothbay Harbor, and Bar Harbor (for all you southerners, it is pronounced *(Bah Hah Bah)*! The Fab 5 group is very compatible---very close. We have been together for 50 years! They are Doris and Ron Coffman from Kentucky, Lynn and Sam Myers from Mississippi, Loretta and Carl Lowery from Santa Rosa Beach, FL, Jackie and Ken Burgoon from Kansas, and the Hoglans.

I have digressed, but I think chasing that rabbit at this time was necessary. It was also fun, just to reminisce about all the great times with these close friends over the years. Let's see, we were leaving Alaska on the way to our new duty station, Fort Sill, Oklahoma.

THREE

Fort Sill, Oklahoma, FA Battery Officers' Course
Btry Commander, Hq & Svc Brty, 2/80ᵗʰ FA Missile Bn
(Corporal) Artillery Officers' Advanced Course
Warner Robins Air Force Base, Georgia, Battalion S-3
and A Battery Commander, 4/61ˢᵗ Missile Battalion
(Nike Hercules)

We arrived at Fort Sill, Oklahoma in May of 1959. I was assigned to the 2ⁿᵈ Battalion, 80ᵗʰ Field Artillery (Corporal), with Temporary Duty (TDY) to the FA school for attendance at the Associate Field Artillery Battery Officers' Course. I started the 18 weeks course on 3 June 1959. I had attended several Air Defense Artillery schools and had experience in several ADA units, but this was my first experience with the Field Artillery. The gunnery problem and solution is quite different, obviously, when you consider that in ADA you are shooting at a moving aerial target, and in FA you are shooting at a stationary ground target. That was the reason for this transition course.

We rented a little apartment in Lawton, Oklahoma, near the Post. Now, Oklahoma has *critters*. We had to teach Sonja (quickly) how to run to us and say *'dirty bug. dirty bug'* when she found a scorpion in her bed or a tarantula spider in the yard, or a 'thousand leg' about 1 foot long. We lived in the apartment until October 1959.

Then we bought our very first house, in Country Club Estates. It was almost finished, but Katherine was able to select the inside hardware, cabinet pulls, interior paint colors, etc. It was an all brick, 3 bedroom, 1 & ½ bath, with attached garage, in an "up scale neighborhood." A very nice house! As they say in the TV sitcom, we were "movin on up"!

But the price was really humongous ---the total cost of the house was $ 14,150, including the lot! The house payment was $97 per month. It scared me to death. My housing allowance from Uncle Sam was $85 per month, but why should I worry---my salary was a whopping $218 per month, before taxes!

I enjoyed the Field Artillery course. I did not realize it then, but with only one exception, I was to spend the rest of my career in the Field Artillery. Redleg! King of Battle! Last Argument of Kings! We put the balls (Cannon Balls) where the Queen (of Battle, the Infantry) wants them! Hooaah!

Not All are Privileged to be Field Artillerymen!

Battery Commander, Hq & Svc Battery 2/80 FA Missile Bn(Corporal)

After the Battery Officers' Course, I reported to the 2nd Battalion, 80th FA and was assigned by the Battalion Commander to command Headquarters and Service Battery of the Battalion. Some explanation of this outfit is required. The Corporal missile was one of the very first generation of surface-to-surface missiles for use by the Army. I think it was designed by *'Rube Goldberg'!* The missile was a liquid propelled missile designed for surface targets only. I commanded the battery that was responsible for assembling the missile, fueling it, and delivering it to the firing battery for firing. The two liquid propellants used to fuel the missile were red fuming nitric acid and aniline! Now, these ingredients were hypergolic---meaning they did not need a spark to ignite them. Even if the fumes got together, you had made your last public appearance! My "refuelers" looked like space men in their refueling suits. The follow-on surface-to-surface missile was the 'Sergeant' missile. It had solid propellant and was much more stable. Then, I heard there was even a follow-on missile after that—it was named the "Civil Servant". But it wouldn't work and you couldn't fire it!!! Oh, sorry 'bout dat!

It was while I was in the 2/80th, that I applied for Jungle Warfare School (4 weeks TDY) at the Jungle Warfare Center, Fort Sherman, Panama Canal Zone. I don't know why I did it. When my request was approved, I decided to go to the embarkation point, Charleston Air

Force Base, South Carolina by train. It had been a long time since I had ridden a train, and I didn't realize how far backward we had come in rail travel! I was on the train to New Orleans, schedule in hand, and I noticed that we were getting close to the time for changing trains in New Orleans, but we were nowhere close to N.O. I kept asking the conductor about it, and he kept saying, "No problem, we'll be there in time". When the transfer time came and we were nowhere near New Orleans, I asked the conductor one more time, and he said that we were *not* going to make it, but he said that the train from New Orleans to Charleston was coming out of N.O. toward us, and they would drop me off at a point and I could flag the other train, to which I said, "say what??" He was serious. So they stopped the train at what I thought would be a train station. I got off the train and looked around. It was very dark by this time, and there was no train station! There was a single light on a pole, and a park bench! It was in the middle of thick woods and spooky! After a time I saw a train light coming toward me. When it was about ½ mile away, I got out on the tracks and *flagged down the train. Fortunately, it stopped. Unfortunately, it was the wrong train! The engineer was* **not impressed.** I began to think that I must be on "Candid Camera". Surely somebody had set me up for this, but…I looked around…no camera.

I flagged down the next train; luckily it was the correct train, and I settled in for what I thought would be a boring ride to Charleston. Wrong! We came upon a train wreck and were delayed at least half a day. Fortunately I had started my journey a couple of days early. I met another Lieutenant, Gil Altom, on this train, who was on his way to Jungle Warfare School also. Finally, we made it to Charleston AFB, and the Air Force flew us to the Panama Canal Zone. I retired from train rides.

The Jungle school was very interesting, but not what I expected. I thought that the training area would have been relatively cleared of a lot of underbrush, etc. Not so. It was virgin jungle---they would use different training areas, and the last one would be overgrown in no time. Some of the toughest events were the day and night compass courses. We were divided into squads consisting of a point man (big ugly dude that could swing a machete---ME!), a compass man to tell the point man which direction to go, a pacer to count the distance between legs (tie a knot in a long string for each 25 meters, etc.), a machine gunner, ammo carrier, and remaining squad members. I was surprised at how rugged the terrain was. I expected to see Tarzan running barefoot on relatively flat land! We encountered all kinds of obstacles. Cliffs, waterfalls, etc. that could not be traversed, had to be circumvented, which required shooting offsets by compass readings, and hopefully you got back on track after a little scenic detour.

They fed us snakes, iguana, tapir, and monkey. Once they gave us live chickens and you should have seen the city boys struggle with that! Heck, I just wrung that chicken's neck, like I had seen my Mamma do a hundred times, plucked it, and our squad had a good meal. Snake meat was the worst---the more I chewed a bite, the bigger it got and it tasted awful. Monkey was too tough; tapir (wild boar-like animal) was OK. Iguana, the big, *ugly*, lizard was the best. Thank goodness we did not have to eat this stuff every day. We usually carried C-Rations. An interesting exercise one day was rappelling down the face of a big waterfall. One student got turned upside down (not difficult to do) and I thought he was going to drown before they got him down. We had to build individual rafts and float our clothes, rifle, and gear across the Chagres River. They said there were piranhas in the river, so we set some speed records in swimming across. We also did the "slide for life" down a cable, and dropped off in the river close to the other bank.

We had some very interesting classes about surviving in the jungle. They taught us which plants were safe to eat and which were poisonous. There are quite a lot of snakes in the jungle, some poisonous and some not. A large, poisonous snake was the Bushmaster. It has hemo-toxin, like a rattlesnake---lots of it! Hemo-toxin works through the blood system. Coral snakes have neuro-toxin, and it works on the nervous system----very bad! There is no known positive anti-toxin that is guaranteed to combat this. Then there is my all time favorite---the Fer-de-Lance. The Fer-de-Lance has a mixture of hemo-toxin and neuro-toxin, and is a very aggressive snake. A new litter comes out hungry and mean. There are other Eyelash Vipers, Sea Snakes, etc. The largest snake we encountered was the Boa Constrictor. It is non-poisonous, and squeezes its prey. The school Commandant, Colonel Goldoni asked us to be on the lookout for Boa's and bring them back to his Zoo. That was the snake they gave us to eat, and his stock was usually running low. One day on patrol through the jungle, a squad found a large Boa and several of the squad members captured it. One guy held the snake tightly just behind his head (they are not poisonous, but can still bite) and draped it around his body, and another student helped him hold the remainder of it. They came out of the jungle to the base camp, grinning, so proud of their accomplishment, and looked up the Commandant. The Commandant took one look at the snake, and said, "don't move, that's not a Boa Constrictor—that's a Bushmaster!" One of the senior NCOs on the cadre began instructing the guys how to unwind the snake from around themselves and toss the snake to their front. The student holding the snake's head couldn't speak a word—he just stood there shaking his head '*No'*, squeezing that snake's head so hard I thought the snake's eyes were going to pop out. Several cadre members were now assisting in this wrestling match, and they had to finally cut off the snake's head and pry the student's hand loose from it. Obviously the boy wasn't paying close enough attention during our 'snake recognition' class!

During some of the field exercises, we had an aggressor force, supplied by soldiers stationed there. On one occasion, I lugged the .30 caliber machine gun for three days and three nights, and when we got to the objective, the doggone thing had rusted so badly, it wouldn't fire. On our side of the Canal Zone, the average annual rainfall was over 150 inches a year. Wet! They told us to stay off the roads, but we learned that we could walk the roads at night, and when the point man encountered the aggressor force setting up an ambush, he would signal and our entire squad would run down the road, putting a little distance between us and the aggressors, then we would turn right or left and jump as far off the road as we could, into the jungle. *And hope we didn't jump off a cliff or land in **wait-a-minute grass!*** Then just lie very still and they could never find you---the vegetation was that thick.

The school was a real 4-week adventure. Most all the courses and events were graded, and LT. Altom and I were awarded the Jungle Expert Badge. We served together later at Ft. Benning. Since I learned at the Arctic Warfare School in Alaska that I would never want to fight in that environment, now I had found another environment to add to that list. As you can see though, it did provide for lots of war stories. And looking backward at it, it was not so gruesome.

Artillery Officers' Advanced Course

Meanwhile, back at the ranch, I had been selected to attend the Artillery Officers' Advanced Course, starting at Fort Sill. I left the 2/80th and reported for class on 26 August 1960. The course was 10 & ½ months long, 7 months at Fort Sill, 3 months at Fort Bliss, Texas, then back to Fort Sill for 2 weeks and graduation.

On 26 September 1960, the third major event in my life took place. The first major event was my marriage to Katherine; the second was the birth of our daughter, Sonja. It was now time for Steven Landis Hoglan to make the scene. Steve was born at the Fort Sill, Oklahoma Hospital. So now we had an 'Eskimo' and an 'Okie'! Throughout Katherine's pregnancy with Steve she had been seeing one particular doctor that was familiar with her case. She has negative blood type and sometimes there can be a potential problem. When the time approached, the Doctor (Captain Arlie Westfall) told me that there would be a qualified doctor on duty at night in the hospital. However, he told me that he had a personal interest in this one, so even if it happened in the middle of the night, I was to call him and he would go to the hospital and deliver the baby. Sure enough, @ 2AM on 26 September, Katherine woke me up and said it's time. I called Arlie, then dressed in 17 seconds and drove Katherine to the hospital. I left her in Arlie's good hands, and since we didn't know how long it would be before the birth, he convinced me there was nothing I could do there, so I left the hospital and drove over to my old unit, 2/80th and had a cup of coffee with the Charge of Quarters (CQ). I called the hospital as soon as I arrived. Arlie came on the line, and said that I should come back to the hospital and see our new son! Wow! While Katherine and Steve were being cleaned up, Arlie and I talked about hunting and fishing in Alaska. Arlie is now deceased. His wife, Betty is a sweetheart and lives in Lumberton, North Carolina, and is a dear friend. Each year, on the 26th of September I tell her that Arlie would have been so proud of Steve.

By the way, the reason that we stopped populating the Earth, after having just 2 kids, was back then, I read an article that said that every third baby born in the world was Chinese, and I just didn't want to take a chance!! (No offense to my Chinese friends!)

I enjoyed the Advanced Course---two members of our car pool were Captains Don Campbell and Max Bunyard. Don retired as a Colonel and Max eked it out to Lieutenant General (3 stars), but Don was the smartest one in our car pool and had to teach the rest of us gunnery. They are both married to dolls! Janet Campbell is a beauty and is an accomplished artist into oil paintings. We visited the Campbells in Austin, Texas recently, in their beautiful home overlooking Lake Travis, and they came to see us here in paradise. Celia is a beautiful gal and no doubt stays busy supervising Max. We just recently got back in contact with them and look forward to seeing them in the future. I was promoted to Captain on 21 March 1961 and graduated from the Advanced Course in July 1961.

Warner Robins Air Force Base, Georgia, Bn S-3 and A Battery Commander, 4/61ˢᵗ Missile Battalion (Nike Hercules)

In August 1961, I was assigned to the 4ᵗʰ Missile Bn, 61ˢᵗ Air Defense Artillery (ADA), and we moved to Warner Robins, Georgia. We lived in government leased housing in a nice civilian neighborhood. The Battalion Headquarters was located on Warner Robins Air Force Base, adjacent to the town. I was initially given the job of Assistant S-3 (Operations Officer), in the Battalion HQ. My main job was to bring on board a new fire control system, the Battery Integrated Radar Display Equipment (BIRDIE). Raytheon was the prime contractor and (thankfully) stationed one of their best technical representatives, Jim Osborne at the Battalion. We got the system operational, and when my boss, the Battalion S-3 departed, I was designated the S-3.

The Bn HQ was located on the Air Base, and the 2 firing batteries were several miles out, on either side of the Base. As the S-3 (Operations Officer), I was responsible for the training and testing of people and systems to insure that we could successfully accomplish our mission of defending the Air Base against air attack. The battalion was activated there when the Air Force dispersed their Strategic Air Command (SAC) assets (mainly B-52 Bombers) to other than just a few SAC Bases. Our battalion was a two-battery, above ground site. At permanent sites around cities, etc. the Nike Hercules battalions were four-battery, below ground sites. Besides the numbers, the main difference was that the above ground sites had missiles in the launching area that were on launchers, covered by air inflatable shelters (tents with air pumps) that could be uncovered in a matter of seconds. The below ground sites had launchers under ground with elevators to bring the launchers up for missile launching. In addition to the Launching Area, about ½ mile away, each firing battery had an Integrated Fire Control (IFC) area where the radars were located, along with the battery HQ, barracks, mess hall, etc. The Launching Platoon area had a Military Police unit, with guard dogs assigned to the Battery.

As the Bn S-3, I would conduct, 15 minute crew drills in the firing batteries---just show up at the gate, walk into the Fire Control van and command "Blazing Skies," training lingo for "Battle Stations". The requirement was for the crew on duty to simulate launching a missile inside of 15 minutes. We were often inspected by an Army Air Defense Command (ARADCOM) (national) team. We also were subjected to Technical Proficiency Inspections (TPIs). These were 'biggies'— involving the assembly of a *training* nuclear warhead to a missile. Failing one of those inspections would ruin your whole day, and your career! We were also subjected to Short Notice Annual Practice (SNAP) shoots. An ARADCOM team would show up, unannounced of course, at one of the firing batteries, conduct a 15 minute drill and then declare the unit would execute a SNAP drill. The unit would have 48 hours to load into an Air Force airplane (already pre-positioned), and fly to White Sands Missile Range, New Mexico, and, (1) Assemble a missile (mate a high explosive warhead to a missile), and, (2) then fire a missile at a simulated aerial target.

Our A Battery was called upon to execute a SNAP shoot, went to White Sands, and *failed!* Unfortunately, the Battery Commander was personally involved in one of the major mistakes. There were twin brothers in the Battery. They were experienced E-5s and one was the Target Acquisition Radar Operator in the Fire Control Van, seated next to the Battery Commander (BC). The evaluators would put fake targets into the radar system, which made it sporting just to select the *real* target.

But Specialist Reid was very good at his job and would not be fooled. He designated the correct target! The BC did not agree. Spec

Reid held his ground as long as he could, but the argument was short lived. The BC stated that *he* was the commander, and *ordered* Spec Reid to designate what he (the BC) thought was the target. It was not the target, but it *was* one of his last orders to anybody. The Battery Commander was relieved of command by the Battalion Commander. He called me into his office, and said, "Curt, do you know what I called you in for?" I told him that I *hoped* I knew. He said, "Yes, I want you to go out and command A Battery". I smiled and saluted smartly and immediately launched out to Jeffersonville, Georgia, about 15 or 20 miles east of the Air Base. A Battery was located near the town. Now, if anybody wanted to *think* that the Battery was there to protect the Air Base, that's OK, but the good citizens of Jeffersonville *knew* that the Battery was there to keep the Russians out of Jeffersonville. They adopted us. I got to be very good friends with Mayor Califf, Mr. Rozier, owner of the only service station, other folks, and County Sheriff Earl Hamrick. The sheriff made me a special deputy, badge and all. He would invite some of the battery officers and NCOs to dove hunts. One day he dropped me off at the end of several rows of corn in a field, and told me that at 2PM the doves would really be flying. I asked him if he would join us, and he said, "heck no, that's a baited field" (slightly against the law)!

I took command of A Battery when the morale was pretty low. They had just failed the most important test an Air Defense unit can fail------an actual firing of a Nike Hercules missile, down at White Sands Missile Range, New Mexico. The failure was accentuated by the fact that both areas of the unit failed their parts of the exercise. I have just iterated how the Integrated Fire Control (IFC) Platoon failed (they fired at the wrong target)! Well, the Launching Platoon failed also---they made too many mistakes in assembling the missile. I should point out that expert evaluators are present and *will not under any circumstances,* allow the missile to be fired if the assembly was not perfect. All mistakes are corrected before the missile is fired! But the Battery failed! I don't guess you can fail good, but they failed BAD! And I had to find out why, since I was now the "Daddy Rabbit"! And I damn sure didn't intend to fail anything!! After checking everything I could possibly check, I decided I had some really great soldiers, and the problems were attributable to a *very few* people, thankfully. For the next 25 or so days, my radars were down for maintenance/parts, and other problems, so I did not get to run a complete 15-minute crew drill, as I wanted to do. Surprise, surprise, A Battery got another SNAP shoot notification, 28 days after the Battery went to White Sands and failed! My Battalion Commander almost had a heart attack, but I was confident (easy for me to say now!). I never told my Battalion Commander that I had never ran a complete 15-minute crew drill with my Battery, because of the radar maintenance problems.

Now, my Battalion Commander, LTC Marshall P. Kean, and I were tight. We had a lot of confidence in each other. Strangely, we were the only 2 officers in the entire Battalion that were RA Officers, vs Reserve Officers---didn't mean a thing to me (or I think to him). When we got the call to go to SNAP, he came out to see me, and asked whom I was taking as the leaders of the crews. I told him that I was not going to take Warrant Officer (shall we say) Dip Stick, the Launching area tech, who had failed the missile assembly less than a month before. We had a brand new Launching area Warrant Officer (WO) Mike Feely. I called him in and asked him if he could assemble one of these missiles. He said, 'yes, sir, I can!' The Battalion Commander thought I was making a mistake—he stated that WO Dip Stick had the experience under his belt and he *strongly* suggested that I should take him. I disagreed and told him that I wouldn't take a loser----I had rather take my new Warrant Officer. He let me know that I was taking a big chance and that I would take responsibility for that decision. I told him that I accepted that when I assumed command of the Battery, but that I did not want to rely on a proven loser! This is called, *you bet your bars, big time!*

Also, the rule was, at the White Sands missile shoot, if the Battery Commander had been in command for less than 30 days, the IFC Platoon Leader would fire the missile, instead of the Battery Commander. I had been in command for 28 days!! No way! I was the Battery Commander and I was not going to wimp out and hide behind some arbitrary rule and not fire the missile. To make a long story shorter, when we were in the IFC van for the shoot, Spec. Reid identified the real target on the radarscope to me, and I didn't hesitate. I designated it to the Target Tracking Radar (TTR)---The other Specialist Reid acquired the target------we scored a direct hit. The Launching Area had already maxed the course under the supervision of WO Mike Feely. When I walked (floated) down the stairs from the IFC van, the Battalion Commander was at the foot of the stairs, grinning like a Cheshire cat, and hugged me! All of a sudden, my bold decisions were golden! The Battery received a rating of "Honor Battery", which required a total score of above 95% on everything! It was not awarded very often. We were all heroes! Newspaper articles, pictures, autographs, pay raises (just kidding!).

I know I was lucky. I take some credit, that of knowing my people, and trusting them to do their jobs, etc., but in those days, we (the Air Defense Artillery) ate our young. Young, quality officers were sacrificed, as an example, when the electronic magnatron cooked off in the radar van at the wrong time during a crew drill. The standard procedure was to relieve the battery commander and *then,* investigate what went wrong!

One of the more interesting events took place while I commanded A Battery. I went to work early one morning, and didn't come home until one week later. We were placed on 15 minute alert around the clock. It was called the Cuban Missile Crisis. The Russians were threatening war if we blockaded their ships from delivering missiles to Cuba. They eventually backed off. Some of my troopers were a little disappointed that they didn't get a chance to blow a few Russian bombers out of the sky! Such is the warrior ethic! Ain't all bad!

I enjoyed lots of good fishing during this tour of duty in Georgia. Lt. Billy Garrett, in my Battery, took me up in the north Georgia hills for trout fishing in streams. He warned me, that if we came upon a scene in the woods, with barrels, pipes, plumbing, etc.----------just keep on walking and do not even look at the stuff. Moonshiners didn't take to revenuers lightly! Four of us went to a small lake in central Georgia. Billy Garrett and I were in one boat, and Major Hinson and CWO Bulger were in another boat. They finished fishing before us and were in the tent going to sleep. Billy and I stayed out quite late. I hung a monstrous bass. We looked for the net and realized we had left it on shore. Billy got the flashlight on him, and said, "never mind, he won't fit in the net anyway." I played him for a while and got him in the boat. He weighed almost 9 pounds (I still have his head mounted in my shop). Later, Katherine cooked him and invited the fishermen over for dinner. Four of us took 2 flat bottom river boats to Fargo, Georgia, where the Suwannee River comes out of the Okefenokee Swamp, and took a great 2 day float down the Suwannee River, ending our journey at White Springs, Florida. The river and the sand bars were beautiful----wilderness. We fished along the way---caught enough for our meals. The river is not muddy, but is burgundy wine colored, because of the tanic acid in the swamp. So ends the chapter about our first assignment to Georgia, but.........we shall return!

In the early days, the Air Defense Artillery ate their young. The ADA Battery Commanders were constantly in jeopardy. I agree that the commander is always responsible for what his unit does or fails to do, but for awhile, Battery Commanders were being relieved because of temperamental electronic failure and other things completely out of their control.

The Nike Hercules Batteries were bombarded with inspections, some of which were a little overly nick picky, probably because of the nuclear capability of these units. In recognition of these stringent, even unreasonable inspectors, I posted the following sign in my office (it may have made the evaluators tougher on me---I was lucky):

NOTICE TO EVALUATORS

"If any pilgrim Monk come from distant parts and wish, as a guest, to dwell within the Monastery, and be content with the customs which he finds, he shall be received for as long as he desires. If indeed, he find fault with anything, or expose it, reasonably, and with the humility of charity, the Abbott shall discuss it with him prudently lest perchance God has sent him for this very thing. But, if he is found to be gossipy and unreasonable in his sojourn as a guest, let it be said honestly, that he must depart. If he does not go, let two stout Monks, in the name of God, explain the matter to him."

(Excerpt from the rules of St Benedict---480-543 AD)

FOUR

Korea, G-3 Plans Officer, HQ, 8ᵗʰ Army

In early summer, 1961, I received Permanent Change of Station (PCS) orders for The Republic of Korea. It was a 13 month unaccompanied (without family) assignment, and I did not look forward to being away from my family for 13 months. But I always knew it was coming somewhere down the line. I was thankful that I had been on active duty for 6 years and I had been with my family, except for short separations, Temporary Duty (TDY) etc. I flew to Korea on old prop jobs, mainly C-121 Constellations (old enough to vote---twice!). I logged over 35 hours in the air, with refueling stops in California, Hawaii, Guam, Wake Island, Tachikawa, Japan, then into Kimpo AFB, Korea. On the longest leg, the air circulating system on the aircraft malfunctioned, so it was a miserable flight, courtesy of the U.S. Navy!

I had orders to be assigned to a Hawk Air Defense Artillery unit on top of a mountain somewhere in Korea. But, when I arrived at the replacement center, the personnel officer told me that my records had been pulled for a possible assignment in Seoul. He told me that a new Major General (2 star) was being assigned to head the Military Assistance Advisory Group (MAAG) in Seoul, and he was looking for an Aide-de-camp. I asked why me? He said they had pulled the records of 3 Captains that had "outstanding" records, and they were going to send us over to the MAAG headquarters in Seoul for interviews as soon as the General arrived, which was several weeks in the future. I was not impressed. I was tired from all the flights, delays, etc, and asked if they could just send me on to my missile outfit. The personnel officer pulled me aside and told me, and I paraphrase, "Captain, be patient! If there is even a remote chance that you can be stationed in Seoul, instead of some leaky tent outfit on top of a desolate mountain somewhere in this God-forsaken country, you should wait and see what develops---in the meantime, go get some sleep!" Turned out to be good advice. After a couple of days at the replacement center, I was temporarily assigned to Headquarters, 8th U.S Army in Seoul. LTC (asst. G-1) Rice interviewed me and said he was assigning me to G-3. The G-3 was one of my favorite bosses to work for---not that I worked directly for him---there were at least 2 people in my chain of command between he and I, but he was super. He was Brigadier General Ralph Foster. In addition to the General, there were about 5 full colonels, 10 Lt Cols, 10 majors, and only 4 Captains in the G-3 section. That is important---more about that later.

When I reported in to General Foster, the G-3, he welcomed me, and assigned me to the Nuclear Weapons Division (one Full Colonel and ME!). He knew the story that I was going to be interviewed for the Aide-de camp job in the future, and I would going to the leaky tent missile job if I was not selected, so he knew I was short lived in the G-3 section. Now, I must stop here and chase another rabbit!

During the first week I was stationed in Yongsan Compound, 8th Army HQ, I went into the mess hall, excuse me, the dining facility, to have breakfast. I looked up and could not believe my eyes! Sure as shootin', there sat Hardy Rose, U.S. Naval Aviator, eating his grits! Remember, Hardy was the leader of the Northwestern State University Demonaires Dance Band my sophomore year, and had graduated 2 years ahead of me and joined the Navy! Hardy was always a good friend and one of the best musicians I have ever known. Well, we had a great reunion, and during the conversation, I asked if he had brought his clarinet. He sorta hemmed and hawed, and said he wasn't real sure, but it may be packed away somewhere. He asked if I had brought my trumpet. I said I would have to unpack and see! Well, that very night we went down town to the U.S. Army District Engineers Officers Club, where a band was playing. Mr. Lee's band. You no doubt have heard of them. Hardy and I unpacked our horns and walked up on the stage---I thought Mr. Lee was going to have a heart attack. We could not speak a word of Korean, and they could not speak a word of English---we looked at each other, thinking the worst, of course. Then it came to me, and I looked over and said "Saints go Marchin' In"??? (the ultimate, absolute universal language!). Well the house fell in! We took in the piano player, drummer, bass player and the trombone player (Mr. Lee, Mr. Lee, Mr. Lee, and Mr. Lee) and taught them to play Dixieland---it was brutal at first, but after awhile, we began to "cook"! Our reputation grew, (rather than famous, we were probably infamous) and we played around for various gigs. This is not the end of this story!

Meanwhile, back at the ranch, I fell in love with the General's wife, ordinarily not the smartest thing to do. Sybil Foster was a real sweetheart. On holidays, such as Thanksgiving, Christmas, etc. she decided she could not entertain with a full meal, etc, all the Officers in the G-3, (although I am sure that she had every single member over for some occasion). But for the special occasions for full meals, entertainment, etc, she decided not to invite the most senior officers, the 5 full colonels, but just to invite the 4 junior Captains over! Wow. That made a real impression on me, so I proposed------love! When I came through the receiving line at receptions where they were the hosts, the General would greet me and say, "OK Hoglan, swords or pistols"? I would always give him the choice! Then I would give a great big hug to Sybil, and tell her I loved her, to the amazement of all the full colonels in line to greet them. General Foster later became the Director of the Army Staff (3 star) and is now deceased and I need to try to find out about Sybil.

The day came when the new MAAG Chief came to town and I was called over (with the other 2 Captains) for interview for the Aide-de camp job. I reported to him and we had a nice chat, but kind of short (short in more ways than one). He thanked me profusely and I left. A couple of days later, I got a call from G-1 and was told that I did fine in the interview, but I was not selected. He told me that I was too tall! Say what?? He said that the General was about 5 foot 6 inches (I had noticed) and I was 6 feet 2 inches. I asked why that would make a difference----we didn't have to dance with each other, did we?? He explained that the General and I would be standing in a lot of receiving lines and formations, and *he* needed to be the "big guy". OK. First job I never got because I was too tall.

So I reported back to the G-3, General Foster, whom I was told had my next assignment (I assumed the leaky tent Hawk missile unit on top of the mountain somewhere). He told me that he did not want me screwing up some missile unit and that he had told G-1 to permanently assign me to G-3, so he could keep an eye on me. I hugged him. I had grown accustomed to the area, and especially since I had met Hardy Rose there. Hardy had also recently been assigned to the Joint Staff, J-2, Intelligence, so we were together for a whole year, terrorizing bands all over, including Japan!

Hardy and I went to Tokyo over the New Years weekend, and stayed at the Sano Hotel, where all the Americans stayed. We did our trick again. On New Years Eve, we went down to the ballroom where a Japanese band was playing. At some point, we just walked on stage with our axes (horns). Of course, the band members spoke no English and of course, Hardy and I could speak no Japanese. The band members were dumbfounded. Not to worry. After a few awkward moments, I remembered, and said, "Saints Go Marchin' In ??". They grinned in unison, and replied, "Ah so, Ah so!" We cooked. Thankfully, this was not the last assignment that Hardy and I had together. More about that later.

I finished my 13 months in Korea without seeing my family, and was anxious to be back with them. While I was in Korea, Katherine and the kids stayed with her folks in Louisiana. Sonja attended the first grade in the same school, Glenmora, where Katherine had attended first grade, 100 years, uh, excuse me, several years earlier!! She taught school out in the country at Plainview, Louisiana the year I was in Korea. I received PCS orders for an assignment to Fort Benning, Georgia, to be an Artillery Instructor in the Infantry School. We looked forward to it, by the way, as we did with all of our assignments. We met folks who made up their minds in advance, that they were not going to like an assignment, and, sure enough, they didn't. But we adopted the idea that they were all going to be good, maybe some better than others, and surprise, surprise, they were! On to Fort Benning, Georgia.

The Grandma Rule: "You can get more with a kind word and a revolver, than you can get with a kind word alone.......or with a revolver alone!"

2ⁿᵈ Lieutenant Hoglan

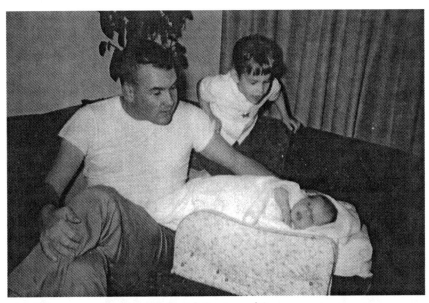

Curt with Sonja and Steve

Captain Hoglan & Bn Cdr, Col Kean

Sonja & Steve in Korean dress

Chapter Three

THE MAJOR YEARS

ONE

Fort Benning, Georgia, Instructor, Infantry School
Fort Leavenworth, Kansas, Command &
General Staff College

We arrived at Fort Benning, Georgia in the summer of 1964. We initially lived off post in Benning Hills subdivision, close to Ft. Benning. Soon afterwards, we moved on post to 111B, Butts Street in Custer Terrace. I checked in to the Infantry School, and was assigned, not surprisingly, to the Artillery Committee, Combat Support Group, Brigade & Battalion Operations Department (BBOD). I really enjoyed being an instructor! In the Army you are always instructing somebody. During all those years I was commanding soldiers, I was a teacher, trainer, and coach----I loved it. I particularly enjoyed taking the young Infantry Officers out to Concord Observation Post (OP), and conducting live shoots with the students directing Artillery fire and calling in corrections, etc. We were supported by the only Artillery Battalion at Fort Benning. Later I was to discover what was my best assignment in the Army in thirty years, when I came back to Fort Benning and commanded this Battalion-----but I'm getting ahead of myself.

We had terrific Field Artillery Officers assigned to the Artillery Committee. Captain/Major Dwight "Tex" Wilson was one of my favorite officers. I loved his sweet wife Ann, which didn't hurt! Tex was (is) smart, articulate, and one of the best soldiers with whom I had the privilege to serve. He retired as a Major (2 star) General. They are good friends today, and we visit them in Boerne, near San Antonio, Texas. Some of the other super officers on the Artillery Committee included Captains Ross Farquharsen (& Joan), Dick Brown (& Shirley), Ira Ashley (& Jenny), Paul Buckley (and Helen).

I had some great bosses; LTC Dan Clark, COL Oliver P Tjossem, Col J.P. Mabry, Col Tom Ferguson, Col Herb Wolfe. Major (later Colonel) Charley Weeks was in the Combat Support Group and with sweet wife, Betty, are now our great friends and neighbors here in Niceville.

After LTC Clark departed, I became the Chairman of the Artillery Committee for a while. I had the greatest secretary in the world----- Mrs. Iva Lee Brown. Iva Lee and I would often go down to the cafeteria in Infantry Hall for coffee, with Diane, the secretary of the Nuclear Weapons Committee next door to our office---more about Diane later. Some would say, if they did *not know* Iva Lee, that she was rather severely crippled in that one of her legs was significantly shorter than her other leg, and she wore a special shoe and brace on that foot, and limped rather badly. BUT, don't feel sorry for her or ever think or say that she was handicapped! She wasn't! People that got to know her, never even noticed it! She was a beautiful woman in every respect. She was a terrific secretary, and had a great personality and sense of humor, so I think I can tell this story and get away with it! She had a beautiful face. This gets a little delicate---I don't really know how to tell this without sounding crass, or whatever. Let's just say that she had a figure above the waist that 99% of all women would covet! OK? Now, on one occasion, I was, clumsily I'm sure, trying my best to compliment her about her figure, and she just smiled sweetly and said, "Gee boss, I'm glad you're not a leg man"---quite possibly the greatest one-liner I have ever heard!! She is special!

Diane was the secretary in the office next door. She was (is) a sweetheart. A young Infantry Captain, who was a student in the Infantry Officers' Advanced Course, Captain Mike Spigelmire, began dating her. I wasn't *too* jealous. I taught Mike and the other Infantry students Artillery subjects. He retired several years ago as a Lieutenant General (3 stars), and is one of my best friends in the entire world. He and Diane live close by, and as a matter-of-fact, they are going to dinner with us tonight, 29 January 2006, celebrating our 52nd wedding anniversary! All four of us moved here about the same time, 10 years ago, and Mike and I served in the Coast Guard Auxiliary together for 8 years. More about this later.

I became good friends with two Infantry Captains. They were in the same department with me, and they taught Infantry Tactics. We did a lot of team teaching. One on them would present to the class, the Infantry tactics for a given situation, and I would come in and give the Artillery support package. These exercises would last for several days on occasion. The three of us (3 Amigos) would serve together on several occasions in future years. The two Infantry Captains were Colin Powell and Steve Pawlik. Colin and Alma were neighbors of ours on Butts Street in Custer Terrace. We were later classmates at the Command and General Staff College (C&GSC) at Fort Leavenworth, Kansas, and we served in the Pentagon later on. Steve (with sweet wife, Louise) and I commanded Battalions in the 197th Infantry Brigade on a subsequent assignment to Fort Benning. Steve and I commented on several occasions that Colin Powell would be Chief of Staff of the Army one day. Well, can you imagine our disappointment, when he never made it?! I told him as much! He just leap frogged over that job, and became the Chairman of the Joint Chiefs of Staff! AND then, Secretary of State! Captain Ron Watts was another good buddy in the Brigade and Battalion Operations Department. He later commanded VII Corps as a Lieutenant General. I was promoted to Major on 22 December 1965.

Two other great friends that I met during this tour of duty were Lieutenant Colonel P.X. Kelly, the senior Marine instructor at the Infantry School and an Air Force instructor, Major Randy Wood. P.X. Kelly would become the Commandant of the Marine Corps as a 4-Star General. More about General Kelly later.

In the Artillery Committee, we had a tape recording of an old soldier, Lieutenant General Rueben Jenkins, (Ret), a Corps Commander during the Korean War. He said some very good things about the Artillery and we used this as an attention getter for some of our classes. The tape was practically worn out, so I did a little research and found out that General Jenkins still lived in the area. I called him and invited him out to the Post for lunch. We had a great visit. I loved to listen to his "war stories", and I think he enjoyed talking about his Army experiences. It had probably been several years since anyone had asked him about it. He told me about one of his Division Commanders (2 star), which he referred to as a young whippersnapper! He said that the division mounted an attack that did not have a very good outcome, because this young whopper-snapper did not know how to properly use his artillery. I learned many things that day. I re-taped some of his comments for use in our classes, and I thoroughly enjoyed his visit. One comment that he made has always stuck with me; "You don't *discipline* ignorance, you *educate* it!"

This three-year assignment, as an instructor at the Infantry School, was one of the very best tours of duty we had in 30 years. During this tour, Katherine taught for one year in a Junior High School in Columbus. Steve attended Patch for Kindergarten and Wilbur School for 1st Grade. Sonja attended 2nd Grade at Benning Hills, then 3rd and 4th Grades at Wilbur. We love Fort Benning. And it was not all *work!* I joined a lil' group, heh, heh. I became the leader of the Modernaires (not Demonaires—that was back in college). It was a 5-piece combo, and we played jobs around town, but our 'steady gig' was 3 to 4 nights a week at the Supper Club (Officers' Club on Post). John Beecher was our trombone player and musical arranger---a very talented guy. Rich Buchbinder, piano, Jim Stillwell, bass, and Tom Gaudiello, drums, were fine musicians assigned to the Army band at Fort Benning. We had so many great times, I should write another book! We used to look at each other on the bandstand with disbelief that they were actually *paying* us to do this. Of course, as with most small combos, we could play a 4 hour dance with no written music, but with John Beecher, we had an added dimension---he wrote enough arrangements that we could play a 4 hour dance using his written music arrangements. I have several tapes of this combo---the music is good, but the taping environment was not so good. Rather than being in a decent sound studio, I just hung a cheap microphone in the shrubbery on the bandstand, so it picked up all sorts of sounds, some of which shall remain anonymous! (or classified!)

I also started an "Artillery Committee Band". I had several Mexican rhythm instruments: claves, ouita, maracas, bongos, conga drum, etc, to which I added kazoos, comb, etc. We acquired a salvaged bass fiddle (from the army band); LTC Dan Clark painted it "fire engine Artillery red", complete with gold cross-cannons (Artillery insignia) on it. I would play the melody on my trumpet. We played for our first Artillery class to each group that we taught in the Infantry school, and it became "a legend in it's own time". Some of the Infantrymen actually thought we were musicians (no offense to my Infantry friends!). The Marines in the class never caught on! (Uh oh.)

Ordinarily, I am just average in remembering jokes, but, when you are an instructor, you tie jokes, in some way, to your class or subject matter, so I can remember all those jokes I told in my classes. I had a reputation as a pretty good story (joke) teller, but the official policy at the Infantry school was pretty strict about off-color jokes, not that any of mine *were*, but my number two boss, a full Colonel would sit in the back of my class and warn me if any school official would come in the classroom. That's what you call support from your boss.

One year we sponsored an exchange student officer from Spain, one Captain Manuel Gordo, in the Spanish Army. He attended the Infantry Officers Advanced Course. We invited him to our house often, and he entertained our kids by playing the piano. They loved it. He was at Fort Benning for 9 months without his family, and he really missed them. We saw lots of pictures of his family and he had a beautiful wife and four great looking kids. Our kids were the same age as some of his, so he enjoyed Sonja and Steve. We took Manuel on several little local trips and tried to show him a good time. We have maintained contact with him over the years, mainly at Christmas time, and later when we were stationed in Germany, we made a trip to Spain and visited with Manuel and his family. More about that great trip later.

During this first tour at Fort Benning, we discovered that the Fort had a recreation center at Destin, Florida, on Choctawhatchee Bay so we tried it out, and fell in love. Since then, we have enjoyed over 40 vacations at the Fort Benning Destin Recreation Center. It clearly is the reason we are retired in this area today! We have visited all over the world, but we still choose this area as our favorite place to live. More about the Benning Recreation Center in Destin later.

Fort Leavenworth Kansas, Command & General Staff College

Time to chase a rabbit here! Steve Pawlik attended the C&GSC one year before Colin Powell and I did. I was junior enough in rank that we would not be eligible for quarters on Post. Our son, Steve, had severe asthma, so the doctor at Fort Benning wrote a letter to the CG, Fort Leavenworth requesting on post quarters for us, so that Steve could be close to the doctors there. At Fort Benning, occasionally, we would be required to take him to the emergency room, for shots when his asthma flared up. We were verbally told and *led* to believe that this request would be approved, so we did not go early to look for off-post quarters. At the last minute, the request was disapproved. The problem now was that most all the off-post quarters were booked by the other junior officers. Colin was one of those junior officers that had secured off-post housing. He offered us his quarters, until he arrived later, and gave us time to look for a place to live. Katherine likes to tell this story----shows what kind of guy Colin is! In the meantime, Steve Pawlik, who was graduating before we arrived for the next class, was out looking for quarters for us. One day, he turned a corner and there was a man out in his front yard, putting up a "for rent" sign. Steve stopped and told the man "take down that sign, this place is *rented!!*" Nice to have two really good guys working for you!

So we moved into 1001 Kickapoo Street, Leavenworth, Kansas, in the summer of 1967, a couple of blocks from the Fort. Our landlords were Merle and Gladys Cooper. Merle was a guard at the federal penitentiary in Leavenworth, and they had moved out into the country. They were great folks and shared their homemade wine with us!

We enjoyed our year in Leavenworth, learned a lot and made some more dear friends. I don't really know why, but I remember especially one excursion they took the male students on was to Kansas City for a Victoria's Secret fashion show, ostensibly to give us ideas on what to get our wives for Christmas! Wow, did we get ideas---we won't go there!

I nicknamed the Commanding General, "Daddy Rabbit", and the Assistant Commandant, "Deputy Dawg", and it stuck. Thank goodness they had a sense of humor.

While I attended the Command and General Staff College, Sonja attended 5th Grade at Immaculate Conception, a Catholic School close to our house in Leavenworth, and Steve attended 2nd Grade at North Broadway School.

T W O

Dong Ha Combat Base, Viet Nam,
Battalion Executive Officer

From the Command & General Staff College, at Fort Leavenworth, Kansas, I received orders, for Viet Nam in the summer of 1968.

Katherine and the kids went back to the house we still owned in Lawton, Oklahoma, in Country Club Estates, to live while I served my year in Viet Nam. It was a tough year, but when I think about the 50,000 American soldiers that gave their lives in Viet Nam, and their families and suffering that they went through, and still go through, I feel inadequate to express my feeling for the admiration and respect they truly deserve! It is one thing to fight a "popular war". WW I, which my Dad fought in was a "'popular war". WW II was clearly a "popular" war, meaning that the American people, our Congress, etc. supported the war effort. I fought in an "unpopular war"! The U.S. Military *did not lose that war!!!* But America *did lose the war!!* What we have been involved in since then is an unpopular war, largely fought in the media, and amongst legislators who have never ever looked down the barrel of an Ak-47! I resent it!! The soldiers today are no less dedicated, to the preservation of our freedom than those of 100 years ago! Sorry, another soapbox item. More to follow.

I was assigned, initially, to the first Infantry Division, down south in Viet Nam. I had gotten a letter from the Division Commander and he hyped me up, telling me to sew on my shoulder insignia, big red one patch—which I did. But when I arrived in country, near Saigon, I was told that the Big Red One was full up on Majors and that I was being reassigned to the 108th Field Artillery Group, in northern South

Viet Nam. I literally had to "fight" my way to northern I Corps to get to my unit. Every time I landed at a processing base, they would see where my final destination was going to be and the first question would be, "do you have a will"??!! No one seemed in a hurry to get me to my unit, so I hitchhiked, catching hops here and there, and spent several days en route.

I will never forget the last leg into Dong Ha Combat Base, from Da Nang, in a C-130 Air Force aircraft. We were loaded into the rear of the aircraft like cattle, but with much less room. The pilot, an Air Force Lieutenant Colonel came on the intercom and said, "OK folks, we are approaching Dong Ha "International". Please grab on to something or somebody, because when I touch down on the grass (PSP) runway, I'm going to throw on the speed brakes, reverse the engines, and come to a s-c-r-e-e-c-h-i-n-g halt. Then I'm going to lower the tailgate, and I want you to *run, do not walk,* off my airplane, because if you are still on my airplane for more than 2 minutes, you will be going back to Da Nang with me! Hokay?" We were in plain sight of North Viet Nam. The demarcation line between North and South Viet Nam (DMZ) was the Ben Hai River quite close by, and it seems that every time an airplane landed at Dong Ha, the airstrip took incoming artillery. Nobody likes that, in particular, the Air Force guys. We *ran* off his airplane and a Sergeant herded us into an underground bunker. After awhile, no incoming this time, we emerged and I looked around and thought, Lordy, Lordy, Mrs Hoglan, what has your boy got himself into this time?

Dong Ha Combat Base was the northern most combat base in South Viet Nam. It was the Headquarters of the 3rd Marine Division, and had a very large ammunition storage area. There were firebases a little closer to the DMZ, most of which our gun batteries occupied from time to time. Our battalion, the 8th Battalion, 4th Field Artillery was assigned the mission of supporting the units of the 3rd Marine Division and other units with artillery support. It was a split artillery battalion with both 8-inch howitzers, and 175mm guns. These were self-propelled weapons, full track, but with exposed gun crews---not like a tank. It was heavy artillery—as an example, the 175mm gun could fire a 150-pound projectile, 33,000 meters (20 miles). So we were very far to the north, and fired about 95% of our projectiles into North Viet

Nam. Unfortunately, as I learned very quickly, we were close enough to the North, that they could fire back!

Our battalion headquarters was located on the edge of the Dong Ha Combat Base perimeter, which made me very nervous, since my "hootch" (living quarters) was on the very edge! The Field Grade hootch", a very austere South East Asia (SEA) wooden building, with a tin roof, was the home-away-from-home for the battalion commander (LTC), the Executive Officer (XO, me, second in command) and the Operations Officer (S-3), the three field grade officers in the battalion. It was pretty well sand bagged around the outside, but would not withstand a direct hit. When we were alerted that incoming rockets, mortars, or artillery were on the way (sometimes belatedly), we would evacuate the hootch to the Fire Direction Center (FDC) underground bunker next door. The 'field grade outhouse' was located about 50 yards from the hootch, and it was really on the edge of our perimeter. Don't remember how many times we had incoming artillery, rockets, or mortars, and I would run from the field grade latrine to the FDC bunker with my pants down around my knees!!

When I arrived, the battalion commander, LTC Harry Brown, was glad to see me. Among other things, he put me in charge of improving our perimeter defense. That suited me fine, since it looked pretty porous to me. I traded some steaks and some North Vietnamese Army (NVA) flags to the Construction Battalion (SeaBees--Navy) for some heavy timbers and culvert materials for construction of "bunker-towers". I designed these bunker-towers with an above ground bunker, heavily sand bagged, a ladder, completely enclosed inside a heavy metal culvert to a second story tower. The guard in the downstairs bunker would have a machine gun, grenades, etc. The guard in the tower would have night vision equipment as well as self-protection gear. I required all of our troopers to wear body armor ('flack vests') and helmets. In addition, I had claymore mines set up all around the perimeter, and trip flares, that could be set off by trip wires. We had trenches dug connecting all the perimeter defense positions, bunker towers, etc.

Immediately upon arriving in our unit, I asked several of the "seasoned" troops how one could tell which artillery was outgoing and which was incoming, because the noise was deafening. They just smiled and said, "you'll know"! WOW, did I?? The guns were extremely loud, especially when they fired directly over my hooch, but the incoming had a certain, but loud, distinctive thud that I will never forget. The ammo dump got zapped several times—4th of July fireworks, but no fun!

After about 1 week, I went to our Battalion Surgeon, Doc (Capt) Saia, and asked if there was any case in medical history, where anyone had died from lack of sleep? He smiled and said, not to worry; I would be sleeping in about 2 more days. Every night the FDC would fire missions (175mm gun) right over the top of my hooch. The blast from the 175 is unbelievable. It would literally raise me about 6 inches out of my bunk and slam me back down, with plenty of sand coming through the roof. I was sure I was going to make medical history! Then about 2 days later, I slept like a baby, all night long. The next morning, I immediately went down into the FDC bunker and thanked them for not firing any missions. They laughed and said they fired missions right over my hooch all night long!

After that, I would sleep soundly through all the artillery fire missions, bouncing all over my bunk—and never waking up. BUT, if one rifle shot was fired on our perimeter, I would sit straight up in the bed, and say, what was that? It is literally amazing what the human body can become accustomed to.

As the battalion XO, I thought that my most important job was to visit the troops in the firing batteries, spread out across the DMZ. At various times, we had firing batteries located at Con Tien, Gio Lin, Alpha 1, Alpha 2, Alpha 4, the Rockpile, Ka Sahn, Vandergriff, and even had one battery down south near Da Nang, supporting the First Marine Division. I logged over 9,000 miles on my jeep on highway 9, (graveled and dirt) across the DMG. The roads changed "ownership" every day. We owned them during the day, the North Vietnam Army (NVA) owned them at night---it was almost like we had a change of command every day. Every morning early, the Marine mine sweep team would sweep the roads for mines. One morning, they found 44 mines planted in the road from Dong Ha to our A Battery at Alpha 2. They did *not* find two---a 2&1/2 ton truck found one and a tracked vehicle (M-42) found the other. A jeep was blown up in a convoy just ahead of us----it was barely recognizable as a former jeep. The bad guys would plant 500 pound bombs, etc, whatever they could get their hand on as mines in the road. The Marines had a convoy about 2 times a week from Dong Ha to Vandergriff or other points west---there were ambushes at least once every 2 weeks---we called it ambush alley---we managed to get out---either drive through it or back up, etc.

It's time that I gave credit to the *other best* jeep driver in the world (you remember Chico Torres from 1955). Well, this guy undoubtedly saved my life on several occasions, one Spec. 4 "Spoon" Thompson. He logged those 9,000+miles, driving me. He had sand bags in the floor of the jeep---I don't know why---that would have only blown sand up our you-know-what! I would always tell Spoon to make sure he hit all the mines on his side of the jeep. When we hit the road, I had my .45 cal auto pistol, but I took his M-16 rifle, and a M-79 grenade launcher, and laid them across my lap----I actually practiced with the grenade launcher and was pretty accurate, but with a High Explosive projectile you don't have to be precisely accurate.

We had an outstanding battalion operations officer (S-3), Major Noel D. Gregg, from Tennessee. We were together in the battalion for our first 6 months in Viet Nam. Then he was transferred to a staff job in Saigon. He was smart, and was a field artillery gunnery whiz, as well as being a fine soldier. He also visited the firing batteries often. I sure missed him when he left. On one occasion, we bought $5 Viet Nam guitars and learned enough chords, with the help of our S-2 officer, to compose a few "diddies", among them, "The Dong Ha Blues". We even got to perform it for the Group Commander, Col Lee and his boss, Brigadier General Alan G. Pixton! I have the tape somewhere, hidden in a very secret place, no doubt, so secret that I couldn't find it! Noel and I also had a mustache growing contest---you can see how hard up we were for entertainment---we each gave the battalion commander $20 and asked him to award the 40 bucks to the winner at the end of the contest. I don't remember exactly how long we set the contest for, but the criteria for winning, was, the guy who had the longest handlebar mustache! Well, I claim I won it hands down, but the battalion commander, not wanting to make waves with his two field grade officers, wimped out, and called it a tie, and gave each of us our $20 back!

Our Battalion Commander, LTC Harry Brown also departed after my first 6 months. Our Group Commander, Colonel R.V. Lee, Jr, had a policy that all majors in the group of several battalions, would serve in a battalion for 6 months (either as Bn S-3 or XO) and then on the group staff for the other 6 months. The Group Commander, Col Lee, called me in and told me that he wanted me to command the battalion, after LTC Brown left, but they would probably send in a LTC. I took command for a very short time, a couple of weeks or so.

Col Lee and I were close! I did not cultivate it, but it seems like every time I was out visiting our batteries, in my jeep, he would wing in on his helicopter and see me there. One quick rabbit chase here----his Father, Major General R.V. Lee, Sr, who I never knew, signed my orders into active duty in 1955, as the Adjutant General of the Army.

We welcomed a new battalion commander, LTC Mike Kulik, one of my all time favorite bosses. He reported in to the 108th Group, and Colonel Lee briefed him. When he arrived in the battalion, he and I were talking, and he asked me what I *had* on the Group Commander? I was puzzled. He told me that the Group commander told him that he had the best XO in any of the battalions in the Group, and if he were smart, he would let the XO (me) run the battalion and he would just be free to visit the troops------Of course, I was appropriately embarrassed, and I'm sure pleased!

I explained that I knew that I was *not* the Bn Cdr and that I would do whatever he wanted me to do---he said, just keep doing what you have been doing! I did! One thing that I will always remember and appreciate, is that Colonel Lee called me after I had been the Bn XO for 6 months, and asked me if I would like to come up to the Group staff for my last 6 months in country. I requested that I be allowed to stay with my troops in our battalion as XO, and he approved it-----to my knowledge, the only exception he gave to any Major in the Group.

A little after mid-term of my assignment, I took the authorized R & R week in Hawaii and met Katherine. It was fantastic! Although I had told her that I grew a mustache (on a bet), *but that I had shaved it off*, she, nevertheless, told me that if I had not shaved it off, she would just by-pass me at the airport and grab the next clean shaven guy that got off the airplane! She *don't* like moustaches!!

We thoroughly enjoyed our week in Hawaii, staying at the Hilton Hawaiian Village on Waikiki Beach.

I thought that I had gotten a great tan in Viet Nam, until I took my first *real shower* in Hawaii----it all washed off!!

We arrived on Saturday. Charlie and Betty Weeks loaned us their car for the entire week. That night we went to the Tripler Army Hospital Officers' Club up on top of the mountain, and had a great meal, accompanied by Charlie and Betty, and Ann Wilson (Tex was in Viet Nam).

Every morning we enjoyed a Kona breakfast. On Sunday we visited Diamond Head, the Fort DeRussy PX, and in the afternoon enjoyed the Trummy Young Dixieland Combo at the Hilton Hawaiian Village, and attended a Luau. On Monday, we relaxed on Waikiki Beach, visited the Ala Moana Shopping Center, and had lunch at The Golden Dragon. On Tuesday, we visited the International Trade Mart, and had lunch at the Top of the Wai, then took the Pearl Harbor tour. The tour of the Arizona Memorial was very moving, especially when you know that over 1,000 U.S. sailors are still down there. The battleship still leaks a little oil to the surface every day, just to remind us all that they are still there!! We went to the top of the Illikai, a Japanese owned hotel on the beach with spectacular views. It seems that the Japanese could not take Hawaii by force in WW II, so they are now buying it! Wednesday we attended the Kodak Hula Show, probably the longest running show on the planet Earth. We then drove all around the island, stopping at all the tourist spots, had lunch at the Crouching Lion, and dinner at the Officers' Club. Thursday, beach, shopping, sightseeing, etc.

Friday, back to the war! We thoroughly enjoyed our R & R in Hawaii. We did not know then that we would return for a two-year tour in Hawaii in 1976-78.

After being in "paradise" for a week, it was difficult to go back to "rural, hostile living". I could not help comparing the bath facilities in Hawaii to what we had in Dong Ha. In Dong Ha, we built a "shower" at the end of the Field Grade Hooch----4 plywood walls with a cradle on top that would hold a 55-gallon drum of water. We used a mermite can heater, and the junior Major would have the duty to light the fire for showers-----I made the rule, since I was always the senior Major. I don't think I mentioned that the first time I visited Da Nang, after being assigned to Dong Ha for several months, I went to the Officers' Club---they had indoor plumbing----I went into the restroom and just stood there flushing the toilet, marveling at this modern convenience, until somebody pulled me away and threatened to send me to the Doc! It is amazing how the little things we take for granted become so important when you don't have them! Our S-3, my buddy, Major Noel D. Gregg wrote to his wife and told her about our austere conditions, and she sent each of us an ingenious device---an electric "coil" that you could plug into a socket and put the other end into a cup, that would heat coffee, tea, but most importantly, shaving water for the morning shaves---so after that, I got to shave in warm water---amazing!! And much appreciated!

Yes, we did have electric power, after awhile. I assigned an Assistant S-4, one Captain Roy Lunsford, to the duty of being "assigned" down in Da Nan as our "Materials Expediter"-----unofficially, our Battalion Scrounge!! All Viet Nam vets will know exactly what I am talking about. The "official supply line" did not work too well. I have already mentioned that we traded steaks and North Viet Nam Army flags (that some old Momma-son probably made locally) to the CBs (Navy Construction Battalion) guys for all kinds of construction materials. Well, we needed a lot of things that were "available" down in Da Nan. A generator to power the Battalion Headquarters was a big priority. I told Roy to get us a 600? KW generator and bring it north---I don't know how he did it but he did it. It powered the entire Battalion Headquarters. I should also mention our Battalion S-1, Captain Art Mulligan, a great staff officer and soldier. We had a lot of fine officers and NCOs in this battalion! One of the reasons that I could visit the firing battery troops so often, was the fact that I had such great battalion staff officers, it allowed me to shy away from staff supervision (my official job) and visit the troops, which was my first love. I knew that the battalion staff would continue to perform well!

An additional disadvantage to being so far north was that we got virtually no USO or other entertainment shows. I complained loudly to the Special Services folks down in Da Nang about this, and it paid off. They scheduled several entertainment groups to come to Dong Ha. On two occasions, I had to give up my hooch to a couple of good-looking gals, but the troops really appreciated it. I even joined in with one group with my trumpet (don't ever go anywhere without your axe (horn)! On one occasion, we had a visit from "The Moustache and Us"---a trio. The moustache was a guy who had a handlebar moustache at least 8 inches long. More importantly for the troops, he had two gals, who could not only sing, but looked liked Miss Americas! I took them up to the DMZ, to one of our "far" north battery positions—an 8-inch howitzer battery---they were fully briefed and volunteered to go---they knew the risk. Well, we set up the group on a gun platform, with their elaborate and complete set of speakers and drums. Why me, Lord, but I asked why did we have to have a fire mission right in the middle of the show, but we did. We took the "group" down into a below ground bunker, and, of course, heard the guns firing above our bunker. After the mission, we all emerged. Surprise, surprise, the guns had blown out a complete set of speakers and drums, about $2,000 worth. The show ended with just the gals signing autographs. I arranged to have the group paid more and it paid for some of their losses, but they never complained---they knew what they were there for, and they considered it an honor to entertain the troops. My kind of folks!

I cannot leave this chapter without telling the story of one of my favorite activities during my tour as Battalion X.O. Each week, we would select a small Viet Namese village to visit for our Medical Civil Action Program (MEDCAP). Our battalion surgeon, Captain (Doc) Saia would gather several of his medical personnel, with supplies and medicine, and I would assemble a security force, and we would visit a village to treat the sick, injured, whatever the village people needed, mainly the older folks, because they had virtually no medical care. The security force would consist of a couple of machine guns, and perimeter personnel with rifles, grenade launchers, etc. We would set up a perimeter defense around the village. These had to be unannounced for security reasons. On one of the first MEDCAPs, I fell in love. I even wrote to Katherine and confessed that I had fallen in love with a Vietnamese girl. She was beautiful, and so sweet, and I know she loved me too. Her name was Mai Lan, and she was 7 years old, about the same age as my precious daughter, Sonja. I asked Katherine, and she and Sonja would send me clothes, etc. for Mai Lan and all the other kids in the village. I think they got the church involved. I would really enjoy handing out clothes, soap, candy, etc to all the village kids. I learned that kids are kids, the same all over the world. I have many pictures to remind me of those occasions.

I received PCS orders for the Foreign Liaison Office in the Pentagon. They told me that I would need every military dress uniform made, so I took another little 4 day R & R to Taipei and got fitted for all those dress uniforms that I did not have, which was most of them. Much more about this exciting tour of duty, just around the corner!

About one month before I was scheduled to leave Viet Nam, I was promoted to Lieutenant Colonel. I had been on the promotion list for quite some time, which is normal, but the timing was a pleasant surprise to me. The Brigade Commander, Colonel R. V. Lee, asked me to come up to the Brigade staff for my last month, but I asked him to let me stay in the battalion---I told him that I thought the battalion could stand two Lieutenant Colonels for that short time. He approved it.

About one week before my departure from Viet Nam, my battalion commander, LTC Mike Kulik, called me in to his office, and told me that my jeep was badly in need of maintenance, and he was deadlining it. He said, "I know you want to visit the firing batteries and tell them goodbye, but you will have to use my helicopter." I laughed and told him that he knew that my jeep was the best maintained jeep in the battalion, by the best jeep driver in the battalion, Spoon Thompson. Well, he won the argument---I knew what was happening. There were many stories of how a soldier got blown away, by road mines, just days away from rotating home. So.........I visited all the batteries that last week, using the Commander's helicopter. I appreciated his concern for my safety, but I had already logged over 9.000 miles in "Indian Country" with "Spoon" and my jeep, named "Deputy Dawg".

One of my last visits was to C Battery, to tell my all time favorite NCO goodbye. Here, I must tell you about Sergeant First Class (SFC) Pearce! He was the Mess Sergeant of the battery, *not the* dining facility manager. *He was the mess sergeant!!* Old fashioned NCO. When he had less than 30 days to serve in Viet Nam, his re-enlistment came up. Now, with a re-enlistment, a soldier got a 30-day re-enlistment leave, maybe mandatory, as I recall. And SFC Pearce had a new granddaughter he had never seen, so he took his re-enlistment leave. The department of the Army contacted him and told him that since he had less than 30 days left on his Viet Nam tour, he would not return to Viet Nam after his re-enlistment leave. He said. "No, you don't understand. I have soldiers that depend on me to feed them. If I cannot return to my soldiers, and finish my tour, I won't re-enlist!!" He was the most outstanding Mess Sergeant I ever knew. When everybody else was serving cold C-Rations, he *always* served hot chow---even on the move in a convoy, he would heat C-Rats in mermite cans and serve them hot-----what a difference!! His soldiers *loved him.* They built him a mess hall and sand bagged it all around. The Department of the Army gave in, and SFC Pearce went back to the unit in Viet Nam, for his last few weeks. He was one of the last soldiers I said goodbye to in Viet Nam. About one week after I returned to the States, I got a message from the S-1. SFC Pearce and the battery's new first sergeant had been killed in a rocket attack---one rocket had a direct hit on the mess hall. I cried! He would never see his granddaughter again! I visited the Viet Nam memorial in Washington, D.C. and ran my hand over his name on the wall. He is whom I think of when I remember all of our fallen comrades on Memorial Day!! He clearly is one of my heroes!

A VETERAN
Whether on active duty, retired, national guard of reserve, is someone who, at one point in his life, wrote a blank check made payable to "The United States of America", for an amount of "up to and including my life." That is honor, and there are way too many people in this country who no longer understand it.

Author Unknown

Artillery Committee Band, Ft. Benning

Major Hoglan & his "horse", Viet Nam

The Maj. and a Huey, Viet Nam

Curt on MEDCAP & Mai Lan

175mm Gun, Viet Nam

Chapter Four

THE LIEUTENANT COLONEL YEARS

ONE

Department of the Army General Staff, ACSI, The Pentagon

When I returned to the States, we had a wonderful family reunion of our little family. Although I had been with Katherine for a week in Hawaii, I had not seen my children in a year. And I had not seen any of my family for the 13 months I spent in Korea. So this time was precious. After a few days to refresh, we took off for Washington, D.C. to look for a place to live for my tour in the Pentagon. We stayed for about 2 weeks with our great friends, Ken and Jackie Burgoon---(see the notes in the previous "Alaska Chapter" that describes the "Fab 5")! We found and bought a new, nice split-level two-story house on Andrea Ave, in Annandale, Virginia. I could drive from our house to the Pentagon in 11 minutes at 3 AM in the morning---no red lights--- BUT, in rush hour, it took an average of one hour to work and 1&1/2 hours to get home. I *never* got accustomed to the traffic—(remember, I am a country boy!). On either end of the journey I was ready to kill somebody! Luckily, Katherine understood and never stood in the cross hairs. The kids went to school at Canterbury Woods and Frost. The area we lived in was named Canterbury Woods, and we adopted a dog—a full-blooded, registered beagle pup, that was the light of our lives! We named him, "Senator Beagle of Canterbury Woods"! Remember, we already had "Goldwater", a beautiful gold kitty. They got along great---sort of gives a hint to my political beliefs, doesn't it? Senator and Goldwater?

I was assigned to the Foreign Liaison Office, in the Office of the Assistant Chief of Staff for Intelligence, (ACSI) on the Army Staff in the Pentagon. My boss was Colonel John Deaver, another one of my super bosses. He was so smart, could speak Spanish and Portugese like a native, and was a terrific gentleman, ably complimented by his sweet wife, Pauline! We really enjoyed this assignment, and it's a good thing—it was one of our few 3-year assignments. The Foreign Liaison Office consisted of about 10 officers, and we were charged with taking care of about 140 Foreign Military Attaches and Assistant Attaches assigned to 64 Embassies in Washington. We would approve their visits to U.S. military posts and bases, as well as furnishing unclassified information to them as requested. We also administered the Chief of Staff invitational visits for his counterparts. Of course it required much coordination with our military installations, protocol offices, etc. Another major duty was approving and arranging for groups of military officers from the foreign countries to visit our military installations. These requests would come from the particular country, through the country's military attaché office in Washington, to our office. We also arranged for foreign military students to visit. These visits would include a reception in Washington, hosted by a U.S. Lieutenant General (3-star), ably assisted by one of our officers. I attended many of these, standing in the receiving line with the General and his wife, acting as his adjutant. I would brief the General on the receiving line drill and to just make a stab at pronouncing names, and don't worry about it. The secret was in mumbling! When the foreign officer introduced himself to me, (and most of the time the name was un-pronounceable), I would turn to the General, and say, Captain brezzlefrassin (mumble) and the General would greet him and say, hello Captain erjhgwendfbbn (mumble), and then introduce Captain hdgebvcjsnnsz (mumble) to his wife.

We were also the "experts" on foreign protocol, and received many questions from our installations and others on how to seat people at formal dinners, and how to render honors to dignitaries. We used a State Department protocol guide for some of this stuff, but I would *often* get questions for which there were no known answers, so I just made up an answer, based on common sense, and who was going to argue with the "Department of the Army Foreign Protocol Officer?!!" I just invoked "rule 14", which says, "When you are in charge, *take charge*!"

For about the last half of my tour, I was given the job of administering the Army Chief of Staff VIP tours program. General Westmoreland was the Chief of Staff, and he would invite, based on our recommendation, a foreign counterpart, his wife, and two officers of his choosing to visit military installations in the U.S. for a 10 to 14 day visit. The visits would terminate with a two or three day visit to Washington. General Westmoreland and I would meet the guests at Andrews AFB, and then helicopter them to Fort Myer, with General Westmoreland at the helm. He liked to fly as pilot, ably assisted by CWO Charlie Astrike, a *real* pilot and a great one. Upon arrival at Fort Meyer, the 3rd Infantry honor guard would render honors to the guests, and Mrs. Westmoreland would take the foreign Chief of Staff's wife to Quarters One for tea, relaxing and visit. I would accompany the ladies, and Kitsey Westmoreland would always invite me inside, but I always knew that the correct response was, "thank you Ma'am, but I'll just wait with the driver outside," Meanwhile, the others would go to General Westmoreland's office in the Pentagon where the foreign Chief of Staff would receive the U.S. Legion of Merit from General Westmoreland, and they would exchange gifts.

As one can imagine, the amount of planning for these visits was incredibly detailed and time consuming. The coordination with every military installation on the guests' itinerary was mind-boggling. We would run about 6 or 7 of these VIP tours per year. It was a full time job for my secretary and me. Occasionally we would run one for the Secretary of the Army. *Everything* had to be *perfect!* I would select the next American Military Attaché to the country, if one had been named, to be the escort officer through the 10-day visit to installations. If the next attaché had not been selected, I would usually select the current American Military Attaché in that country, normally a Colonel. The escort officer would come to Washington before the visit started, for my briefing and resolution of any issues. The Air Force would give me a C-140 Jet Star aircraft for the mission. Another part of the Washington visit, was of course, a reception or formal dinner given by the country's Ambassador to the U.S., at their Embassy, and Katherine and I were usually invited to those. I received some really great mementoes from the VIPs, as well as autographed pictures (they are in the attic somewhere.)

I need to explain our "social calendar" at this point. When we accepted this job in Foreign Liaison, we agreed to attend the social events to which we were invited by the foreign military attaches. We were "connected" to 64 different Embassies. As I mentioned earlier, each Embassy would have an average of 4 or 5 large functions each year. We were attending Embassy functions an average of 4 weeknights a week. This was the only job I had in the Army that my wife had to agree to. There was a small stipend available for babysitting costs. I would race home after work, remember the 1 & ½ hour trip, clean up, put on the appropriate military dress uniform, and then we would race back up to Massachusetts Avenue for the gig. This was not all bad, except for sacrificing my liver for my country-----I started drinking sprite—it only *looked* like Gin! The fun part was getting to know all the attaches, because we would see them virtually every night. We got to know many of them really well, and were invited to their homes on the weekend. The primary reason we could not play hooky from any of the receptions, was that if we missed one, let's say the Pakistani reception, we were going to see the Pakistani attaché the next night at the Indian embassy, and he would very pointedly ask you why we did not attend his reception the night before. We attended two gigs in one evening several times. One thing was common about all these attaches. When a foreign country selects an attaché and assistant attaché to represent their country in the United States, they don't just pick Joe Glotz off the street. All these folks could speak excellent English----the one hardest for me to understand was the Brigadier from Great Britain! And they were outstanding individuals and families. So it was a select group. I could write another book about the great times we shared with foreign attaches, but I will relate just a few experiences that we had.

I guess our favorite military attaché was from Brazil, General Cesar Montagna, and his wife Maria Lucia (Lucy). When they arrived, Lucy could not speak English, but she learned by watching advertisements on TV! General Montagna looked like Santa Claus without the beard. He was just delightful. On one occasion, they invited us to their home. After a reasonable time, we were saying our goodbyes and the General told us not to leave, so we stayed a while longer. After almost everybody had left, we again thanked them for a wonderful evening, but the General told us not to leave. Well, after *everybody else* had left, he sent for his driver and escorted us to his car. We drove across town to an after hour's Brazilian party, where he introduced us to Pele, the famous soccer player! Pele had been designated a "National Treasure" by the Brazilian government, and was visiting. I have his autograph somewhere, in the attic no doubt!

Other favorites were the Indians. Major General Naidu and his wife were great folks and we were invited to their home and to their Embassy on many occasions. His assistant attaché, Major B.N. "Ben" Kumar (and wife Sushila "Sheila") became our good friends and we visited in each other's homes on several occasions. Sheila was a great cook, when it came to the classic India dishes, curry and a dish with a thin, silver (actual silver) film on it? These home visits were almost required to be on weekends, because of the heavy schedule of receptions during the week, but they were very enjoyable. One other very interesting guy I became friends with was the Assistant Air Attaché, one Joginder Singh. He was a Sikh—full beard, full head of hair under his turban, etc, but with a great sense of humor---when I saw him I would ask when he was going to get a hair cut!!.

The Indonesians were nice, folks; General Soesilo and his assistant, Colonel Bambang Sumantri. For all their receptions, the Indonesian ladies prepared all the great food. This was a little unusual, since most of the Embassies hired caterers to do the food---a gigantic business in Washington, D.C.

Some of the attaches went on to bigger, better things. One morning, my boss, Colonel Deaver asked me if I had seen Brigadier General Levingston (Argentina) at the reception a few nights before. I replied yes, that I had talked with him for a while. Colonel Deaver told me that the day after the reception, he had been suddenly recalled to Argentina by the strongman, General L. and was named the new President of Argentina! How is that for a promotion? He later started acting like he was indeed the President, and strongman General L. fired him.

The Russians were very interesting. I played golf with an assistant attaché and when he hit one into the woods, we must have looked for half an hour for his ball. I offered to give him a ball, or more, but I got the feeling that the Russian supply room had given him one golf ball and he had to bring it back! Reckon it was *wired?* Major General Stolnik was the Russian Military Attaché and he was a nice enough fellow. I got to know LTC Demurin, an assistant attaché. He noticed that I smoked an occasional cigar, and one day he told me that he would get me some really great Russian cigars. I thanked him, and for the next 5 times I saw him, he reminded me that he had not forgotten about getting me those great Russian cigars. I said, OK, OK. Then about a month later, he called me and said that he had received the Russian cigars, and would bring them to me. I met him at one of the Pentagon entrances and he made a big deal of presenting me with those great Russian cigars--------from Cuba!

One of the more interesting tours that I arranged was for two Army Officers from the country of Camaroon. I new it would be interesting because our military attaché in Camaroon told me that the senior officer was a Colonel, and the other officer was a Major, but was a Prince in the Royal family. Well, doesn't that bring up a host of questions, and my protocol officers around the country asked me *all* of them. Like, who was the Daddy Rabbit in this gig? Well, here was the guidance I received. When the two officers were in military uniform, the Colonel was in charge. He should receive the honors from any honor guard. He would receive any gift offered by one of our commanders; all deference would be paid to him as long as they were in military uniform. The Major would definitely take a back seat. *However*, when they changed into civilian clothes for any dinner, reception, evening function, etc, the Colonel would stay in the rear and the Prince would be the honoree, etc. My protocol officers at our installations were very nervous about this, but our attaché assured me that these were good guys and that they understood the delicacy of the situation, and would not be thin skinned---not to worry. Well, it all worked out fine with their visits to our military installations, and when they got to Washington, the Cameroon Ambassador threw a gigantic formal reception in one of the largest hotel ballrooms in Washington. Katherine and I were invited. I did not own a complete tuxedo at that time, but I had a "Fort Sill, Oklahoma" tuxedo. It consisted of tux pants, formal ruffled white shirt, back bow tie, a red cummerbund and an Artillery "fire engine red" blazer. Folks, that's as formal as you can get at Fort Sill, Oklahoma. We go to the reception, and when we walked into the ballroom, with over 1,000 guests in attendance, we immediately noticed that about 200 guys were dressed exactly like me--------***the hotel cocktail waiters!*** Katherine was so embarrassed I thought she would faint. She said that we must turn around and beat a hasty retreat and go home. I said no, that we had dressed up for this gig and we were going to stay and have a good time. All evening, people would come up to me and order a scotch and water and 2 beers. I did make some serious tip money that evening (just kidding)!

For two years in a row, I was assigned the mission of arranging for visits to Washington, D.C. by the entire student body of the Canadian National Defence College, in Kingston, Ontario. I would arrange meetings with our Secretary of Defense, Joint Chiefs of Staff, briefings by senior staff officers of all services, and senior flag rank officers to host luncheons, reception, dinners, etc. It was a fun group, the visits were successful, and the Canadians really know how to say "thank you". After the last class visit, the Canadian Military Attaché to Washington, Brigadier General Brodie, called me and asked me to come to his office in the Canadian Embassy. When I arrived, he pulled a bottle of Scotch out of his desk, and I knew it was going to be a long afternoon. We chatted for a while, he thanked me profusely for arranging everything for the NDC visits, and he asked me if I had ever visited in Canada. I told him, no I had not. He then called one of his assistant attaches, Commander Pete Gardner, into his office and said, well, this is your escort officer for a six-day trip to Canada. Your itinerary is completed and I am sure you are going to enjoy this visit. He apologized for the weather, and cautioned me to bring my "long johns", because we were going to start the trip on 15 December. WOW. I knew Pete Gardner well, we had popped a top or two in the past, and I was delighted he was going to escort me. He was also a great French linguist, which would help. I just now found my notes from that trip and they had been classified Tres Secret, but enough time has elapsed that I believe I can declassify them. They are short, cryptic and are as follows:

Departed Andrews AFB, Maryland on 15 December, by Canadian Forces Military Aircraft and landed at Canadian Forces Base, Uplands in Ottawa. Temp 20 degrees, wind 30 mph, freezing rain—welcome to Canada! To VIP quarters, took on antifreeze replenishment. Night drive around the beautiful city of Ottawa, then to Hull, Quebec for dinner at the La Ferme Columbia. Onion soup as only the Canadians can make it, filet mignon, jug of Medoc Cruse Bordeaux. Back to VIP quarters.

Next day, sightseeing in Ottawa (have pictures to prove it), toured House of Parliament and library, beautiful. Signed the guest book in the American Embassy, --- tried to defect, but was told I was in the wrong embassy---never found the Canadian Embassy! Called on the Foreign Liaison Officer at Canadian Forces Headquarters, met staff, had interesting discussion. Attended Military Attaché luncheon, hosted by Russian Attaché, enjoyed caviar, salad, duck, jug of Dumons Bordeaux Superior.

Late afternoon, departed Ottawa by sedan for Montreal. Arrived Canadian Forces Base, Montreal Management School, met with Commander. Driving tour of Montreal, to dinner in old Montreal at the Saint Gabriel, pea soup, escargots, jug of Macon Chauvenet— formidable!

More sightseeing, Expo, etc. Lunch at the Bluenose, clams, Alaskan King Crab, jug of Entre Deaux Mers. PM, departed Montreal for Kingston, Ontario via sedan. Arrived National Defence College, to VIP quarters. Attended delightful cocktail party at one of the student's home. Met many old friends from NDC. Later attended party at Land Forces Staff College---more friends. Weather turned bad, whiskey haze descended, visibility limited. Terrorized band, blew "Saints Go Marchin' In" and other assorted hymns on trumpet. To VIP quarters.

Next day, awakened by LTC Mike Seay, another U.S type who had defected, who saved my life with an adult beverage. To his house, for Bloody Mary's, then breakfast fit for a king. Met his 200-pound Saint Bernard---sobered up fast. Arrived back at NDC just in time for a delightful lunch hosted by BG Mussells. Departed Kingston, reluctantly, for Ottawa via sedan. Arrived Ottawa.

Departed Uplands for Andrews AFB, Maryland. Arrived 1250 hours. 1300, ready to go back!! I have at least one observation about Canada after this trip. The average restaurant in Canada makes the Sans Souci and Jockey Club in Washington look like McDonald hamburger stands. Awesome.

The most amazing thing about this trip was that they treated me, a little ole Lieutenant Colonel, like a VIP! I was as far from a being a VIP, but I got the 4-star General treatment. I had Generals and Admirals hosting parties, luncheons, receptions, and dinners in my honor. It was embarrassing, (but I got over it in about 15 minutes!). The Canadians really know how to say "thank you".

A very interesting experience that I thoroughly enjoyed was escorting a large group of foreign military attaches to Cape Canaveral and observing a moon shot, the launch of Apollo XIV. We flew from Andrews AFB, Maryland to the Kennedy Space Center in a C-135 aircraft. NASA officials met us and gave us a tour of the Center facilities. We were briefed by NASA in the Visitors Information Center, followed by lunch and then visited the Vehicle Assembly Building. We then traveled to the VIP viewing stand and observed the launch. Although we were a safe distance away from the launch pad, the noise was awesome. We could literally see the sound wave traveling across a grassy field, and when it reached us, it almost blew our shirts off our backs. A good day.

One year, I also enjoyed taking a group of foreign military attaches to Philadelphia to see the Army/Navy football game.

Early in this tour, whom would I bump into? One Hardy Nicholas Rose, my buddy from college dance band days and Korea. We both were assigned in the D.C. area. Somehow we met with an Army Colonel, Bernie Pankowski, who played keyboards and accordion. In fact, he was a "one man band", having rhythm instruments of his choosing wired into his accordion. I do not remember the details of how we met and got together, but he had connections with some Hawaiian folks in the D.C. area. One night at his house, Hardy and I were there, and Lelani (a Hawaiian singer) had been invited. A trombonist, Hal Farmer, was also there. In the middle of "Little Grass Shack", the spirit must have moved us, because without any cues, Hardy and I just took off on a Dixieland version of Little Grass Shack. We all sorta looked at each other after we finished, and collectively said, "By jove, I think we may have come up with something here!" Indeed, we had. Bernie and Lelani knew lots of Hawaiians in the area, other dancers and rhythm guys (bongo drummers, et al), even Luau cooks! We all got together and practiced a bit and then played lots of Luaus around the area. We named the group, the Dixie Five-O. We played several times at the Navy CPO club in Washington, and at many country clubs, on the weekends.

Hardy and I even sat in for a while with the "Anacostia River Ramblers", a *pure* Dixieland Band at a club near the Pentagon. More notes and a great time. One weekend, we were asked to play on the sun deck of the Presidential Yacht "Sequoia", when they invited disabled veterans on board from all the hospitals in the area, and we sailed up and down the Potomac River, playing Dixieland Jazz—a real kick!

This tour of duty in the Pentagon was rather unique. It was much more interesting and enjoyable than the run of the mill action officer tour which can be characterized as all work and NO play! It had been a fantastic assignment! At the end of this tour of duty, I had an interesting conversation with my assignment Chief. I will relate it later.

TWO

Fort Benning, Georgia, Battalion Commander

Near the end of my tour of duty as a Foreign Liaison Officer, VIP Tours Officer, and Foreign Protocol Officer, in the Pentagon, I received a great telephone call from the Chief of the Artillery Assignment Branch, in the Office of Personnel Operations, Colonel Jim Wortham. He said that he wanted me to go to Fort Benning and command the only Field Artillery Battalion at Fort Benning, the 2nd Battalion, 10th FA. My dreams were coming true! He explained the assignment this way, as if I *needed* more motivation. He indicated that it was by far, the largest Artillery Battalion in the world, since our mission was to demonstrate *virtually all* Field Artillery weapons to the Infantry, our biggest and most important "customer". The battalion had 105mm howitzers, 155mm howitzers, 8-inch howitzers, towed and self propelled, searchlights, everything. He told me that he would only assign to me the very best Field Artillery Officers, a promise he certainly kept. He indicated that if any of my officers were just a bit behind the curve, not cutting the mustard, but not bad enough to "can", he would transfer them out over night without prejudice, depending on the situation. He clearly wanted the Artillery to "shine" at Fort Benning. I was flattered, but more importantly, I was salivating and chompin' at the bit. I was assuming command from an outstanding Field Artilleryman, LTC Jim Wurman. Jim and his sweet wife, Margaret, would become great friends of ours. Jim retired later as a Major General, and unfortunately died of cancer.

My assignment Chief, Colonel Wortham, said there was only one test that he knew of, that I needed to pass, to get this job. He told me that the Battalion was one of 5 battalions in the 197th Infantry Brigade; one Artillery battalion, two Infantry battalions, an Armor (Tank) battalion and a Support battalion. He said the Brigade Commander was a Colonel Will Latham, and that he was a tough, physical commander, and was a runner! He said that when he nominated me to Col Latham, the Brigade Commander had only one question---------how far can Hoglan run? *Say what??* Now folks, I had been sitting on my butt in the Pentagon for 3 years, working my tail off, but the only exercise I got was cussing the traffic to and from work. I didn't know what to say to the question, but Colonel Wortham was serious and said I *must* tell him the answer so he could relay it to Colonel Latham. I told him to tell the Brigade Commander that I could run just as far as I absolutely had to!! It worked, and I was hired, but I thought for a time that I had signed my death warrant!

We moved out of our house in Annandale, and moved into a *big,* commander's house on Lumpkin Road at Fort Benning---2 stories plus a full basement. We found out that if you have a house with a basement, you don't throw *anything* away. Don't take out the garbage-(maybe a little stretch)-you may need it, so just put it in the basement. Of course it makes the next move completely impossible!

I had about 2 to 3 weeks before I assumed command of the battalion, and remembering my challenge, I had to get into physical shape in a hurry, so every morning I went over to a large quadrangle (parade field) close to our house and would run laps. On most mornings, I would meet a very nice, beautiful lady, who was also running laps. After just a few mornings, when she would "lap me", I stopped and we met. She asked me what I was doing out here every morning early, running. I told her that I was to assume command of the 2/10th Artillery in the 197th Infantry Brigade in about 3 weeks, and that I had been told that the Brigade Commander was a mean little SOB, who was a physical fitness nut, and I was trying to get in shape. (You know where I'm going with this, don't you??) I then asked her what *she* was doing out here so early every morning, running. She smiled sweetly, and said, "I'm married to the mean little SOB!" I immediately covered up my nametag, but it was too late. Luckily, I fell in love with Mikie Latham and I guess she liked me, because I didn't get killed. I have taken a bit of license with our conversation, to make it a little more interesting, but this is in fact where I met Mikie Latham.

Well, I continued to run and by the time our change of command came about, Colonel Latham had been assigned to be the Chief of

Staff of the Infantry Center, and was now my number two boss, but he certainly kept up with what the battalions in the 197th were doing. The Brigade had been assigned the mission of being the very first VOLunteer ARmy unit "VOLAR" in the Army. This mission was started under Col Latham, and a set of previous of battalion commanders, prior to me. Before this, the 197th was full of draftees and Viet Nam returnees, all "short-timers" and there were many discipline problems, drugs, etc. Col Latham was given the mission of straightening out all this, *and* recruiting a Brigade full of new, volunteer soldiers, a very formidable task. He assigned each battalion in the brigade a State in the southeast----the old "mission type order", that I loved. My mission was "to go to the State of Florida and recruit a battalion of soldiers (about 500)! Each of the other 4 battalions was assigned a different State in the southeast. Col Latham , later Major General Latham, was to "save my life" in Germany. Much more about him later.

The change of command ceremony went well, and the Fort Benning band participated in it. Incidentally, our battalion later cooperated with the Fort Benning Band, and performed with them, down on main Post in front of Infantry Hall, the William Tell Overture, by furnishing the cannons. It was great!

My new Brigade Commander of the 197th was Colonel Ed Kennedy. He was an outstanding Brigade Commander, soldier and gentleman! And, of course, I loved his wife, Dolly. They live in Sarasota, Florida and are our dear friends. Ed retired as a Brigadier General, after a very successful military career.

We continued to recruit new soldiers from the State of Florida. We did many things to advertise our presence there. We used "home town" recruiters, and asked new soldiers from Florida if they would like to return to their hometown for a tour, and help enlist young people that they knew. They would use the local recruiters' offices as their base of operations. The locally assigned recruiters loved it; they would gladly use all the help they could get. It helped greatly in meeting their quota of new recruits. To put the Army recruiting requirement in perspective, right now, our Army must recruit the equivalent of the *entire Marine Corps, every year!* We furnished color guards for all kinds of ceremonies, and festivities, including the color guard for Miami Dolphins football games, the Daytona 500 Race, etc. It was a very successful venture for the entire 197ᵗʰ Brigade. It was interesting that the *old Vets* initially did not like the new VOLAR. With VOLAR came some important changes in the new Army. The Army was transitioning from squad bays where soldiers had no privacy to two man rooms in the barracks. One change that seemed to upset some old soldiers, was that now, beer was allowed in the barracks. When I received this complaint (often), my reply was that we *always* had beer in the barracks. The only change was that now the troops could just put the cans in the trash containers and didn't have to throw them out of the window!

I attended a seminar with some senior officers present. We were discussing several leadership techniques, and I commented that one way I could really find out what the troops were thinking, doing, feeling, was to occasionally visit the barracks on the weekends or after duty hours. One full Colonel said that if he were a Captain, one of my Battery Commanders, and I came into his barracks without his knowledge, he would throw me out of his Battery. I looked him in the eye, and said, "Yes Sir, but you would try to do that only once, and I would get another Battery Commander"! You see, those are *my* soldiers also. They do not exclusively belong to the Battery Commander. Now, I'm not entirely stupid. Of course, I would not just walk in and ask how they liked their Battery Commander, or in any way undercut the Battery Commander. My BCs clearly understood that. I would walk in and the first soldier that saw me would call "ATTENTION!" At first they were surprised to see me. I informed them that I was not there for an inspection, I just wanted to visit for a little while. One asked me if I wanted to have a beer with them and I said "don't mind if I do"! It is amazing what you can learn from your soldiers if you just listen sometimes. It was rarely a "bitch" session. Usually the conversation was about how much fun it was to be selected by the Brigade Commander (an Infantryman) as the best Battalion (Artillery) in the parade and given time off, or beating one of the other Battalions in a basketball game. In other words, it was a good way to judge the morale of the troops, and occasionally I would discover a problem that could easily be fixed. One of the greatest morale boosters for my soldiers was my Battalion Chaplain, (Major) Bob Bell. He was the best Chaplain I ever met, and I had some good ones (and only one bad one). Bob Bell was not just an outsider-----although he wore a cross on his collar, it could have been crossed cannons, because he was a true member of the family. Bob *lived* in the field constantly with my soldiers. We would rotate Batteries in the field for one or two weeks at a time, and he would stay in the field with *all of them*. I had to order him to take a break. He was such an asset. Soldiers will talk to the Chaplain when they will not talk to anyone else. Although I jealously guarded his confidentiality with the troops, he alerted me to so many potential problems, most of which he had already solved. He did so much more than just take his turn at preaching at the Brigade Chapel, but when he did preach, the 2/10th Field Artillery would be there in force. The troops loved him and so did the Officers and NCOs. His sweet wife, Anne was a great complement to him. We still correspond but do not get to visit often enough.

I also had the best Battalion Command Sergeant Major on the planet, CSM Gus Myszka. He also kept his hand on the pulse of the Battalion and was an amazing CSM. He was tough, but consistent and fair, and was well respected by everyone. He kept *his chain of command, those battery first sergeants,* on the ball. Every Friday morning, he would gather all the new soldiers who had joined the battalion during that week, in the classroom, and we would talk to them. He gave me their records and I studied them enough to know something about each soldier. It is amazing what happens when you can call every soldier in the battalion by name. Battalion command is about the last unit (going up the line) where a commander still commands *soldiers, directly,* and you can get to know your soldiers. At brigade, Corps Artillery, Division, Corps, etc, you are commanding a staff and subordinate commanders---your contact with the troops is more remote, naturally (and not nearly as much fun)! That is the reason I have said on many occasions, that if the Army had been smart, they would have told me, "Hoglan, you are going to stay a Lieutenant Colonel forever and just spend the rest of your life commanding battalions." I loved it. And I thought I got to be pretty good at it!

A major reason for our success was the quality of the battalion officers assigned to our unit. I was blessed by having a succession of three outstanding battalion executive officers (XO, 2nd in command). First was Major Bob Thomas, and he was a jewel. I tend to be a little, shall we say, excitable----Bob was smart, steady, a quiet motivator, with a great and dry sense of humor. He and Mitzi were a great part of the family. We correspond often today. Next, is Major Bob Veen. Bob had been one of my battery commanders in the 8/4th FA in combat in Viet Nam, so I knew he would be good, and he was. Similar to Bob Thomas, he kept me under control and he and Carol were great family members. Unfortunately, Bob died later, while on active duty at Fort Monroe, VA. One of the best soldiers I ever served with was my 3rd XO, Major Dick Noack. He was an innovator, a masterful chief of staff, had a great sense of humor, and loved to pick on the Infantry. He had a lot of opportunity, since we were stationed on an Infantry Post. I will just relate a couple of examples of his handiwork.

But first, when Dick and Mary arrived at Fort Benning, we surely wanted to welcome them, and we asked them to dinner at our house. I fired up the three-legged grill in our back yard, and Katherine had bought 4 great steaks, and cut them into shish-ka-bobs-----I wanted so much to make a good impression on my new XO. When the grill got just hot enough, I put the meat on it. After a while, of course, it was time to turn over the meat. In my own, unique, clumsy fashion (without a second glass of wine---I swear), I flipped the grill over and the meat, complete with onions, bell peppers, and all the goodies on the skewers, ended up on the ground, in the dirt, upside down, with all the charcoal, ashes, and the grill on top of them! Until this very day, when Noack visits and we have a meal, he asks if we are having upside down shish-ka-bobs again! Smart aleck! Now to his contribution to the Infantry Center!

We had license plates made with our battalion motto, "Rock's Support". The battalion had been given that motto for it's heroic combat with the 3rd Infantry Division in the Marne region of Germany. The Division is still known today as the "Rock of the Marne". Most of the folks in our battalion bought a license plate and placed them on the front of their vehicles. Dick thought that we shouldn't just keep these to ourselves, but that we should share with those not so privileged to be Field Artillerymen. So late one evening, after he had invited me and all the Lieutenants in the battalion to his house for a party, we quietly visited the other battalion commanders in the brigade. First stop was at Infantry Battalion Commander LTC Chuck Arnecke's house where we installed a license plate on the front of Chuck's truck. Next stop was at Tank Battalion Commander LTC Jim Eddins' house to place a plate on the front of his car. He did not have a mounting bracket, so I rang his doorbell and borrowed a drill! Then we went to the other Infantry Battalion Commander's house, for his license plate. Of course, the brigade commander did not escape. After feeling so "kool" at our caper, we decided to put one on Brigadier General Bill Richardson's car. He was the Assistant Commandant of the Infantry School and was second in command at Fort Benning, after the Commanding General. His garage was closed, so we opened it, and wouldn't you know it, he parked it with the front bumper so close to the forward wall of the garage, that we could not reach the bumper. How un-thoughtful of him! So we took off the official Georgia license plate, threw it over to the side of the garage and put our Rock's Support plate on the *back* of the car. When we thought about it later (some would say *sobered up*), we knew we had definitely left our calling card, seeing as how we were the only artillery battalion on Post, let alone the only one with Rock's Support as a motto. I waited for *the* phone call from the General. It never came (until years later when BG Richardson was a four star general and I was a brigadier general). More about that later. (How did I ever survive?).

Of course, from the very beginning, we continued to do battalion and brigade runs. I will never forget my first battalion run. It was about five miles long, and we ran in fatigue pants, combat boots (the absolute worst foot gear to run in—they run in athletic shoes now), and tee shirts. I had *never* run that far in my life! Colonel Latham had set a high, but fair standard: the Commander *led the formation!* How can you argue with that? He would fire a commander that did not lead his troops (and he did). If he caught a commander having a staff meeting in the mess hall over coffee and donuts, and the CSM or somebody else was out leading the troops on the run, the commander was relieved of command---period! On that first run for me, I thought surely that I was going to die. I thought that maybe they would name this hill in my memory, because I didn't think I could finish the run. That is when I discovered that you could run a lot farther than you think when you have 500 of your cowboys behind you. There is *no way* you can drop out of the run in front of your troops. I learned something about setting the example that day. The run got a little easier, but never was really easy for me.

I also had some fine battery commanders and staff officers. Major Jim Pongonis was my S-3, Operations Officer, and he and his wife Sandy were great members of the family. They live in Dothan, Alabama and we correspond regularly and see them occasionally. Larry Aaron, Ed Irick, Bennie Williams, John Routon, Frank Mims, Rosie Adams, Mike Wells, Bob Balog, Bruce Minger, Ron Kilpack, and Chuck Ames, and others were fine officers and distinct assets to the battalion.

In those days, battalion command was anywhere from 6 months to one year. We changed brigade commanders after I had been in command about 1 year. I was so fortunate to have Colonel Bill Steele take command of the 197th Brigade. He was another outstanding commander, soldier and gentleman, and his wife Ginny was a sweetheart. How could I be so lucky as to have two of the finest officers I ever worked for, Colonels Kennedy and Steele, as my brigade commanders? Example number two of Dick Noack's capers: On New Years Day, as was the custom, the commander would invite all the officers and spouses in the unit to call on the commander, usually at his quarters. Colonel Steele did that, and Dick Noack lined up the junior Lieutenant in the battalion, 2nd Lieutenant Bridges, who looked like a cross between Tarzan and Robert Redford, to be the first in line when we rang the brigade commander's doorbell. When Ginny Steele answered and opened the door, Lt. Bridges presented her with a dozen red roses, and said, "Mrs. Steele, please accept this small token of our esteem, admiration and love for you, from the officers and ladies of the 2nd Battalion, 10th Field Artillery." I thought Ginny was going to melt right there. Then Dick Noack gave the signal to two gun crews, with 105-millimeter howitzers that he had set up across the street, and they fired a gun salute in honor of Colonel and Mrs. Steele. Although they were obviously firing blanks, the concussion blew the windows out of the front of the Fort Benning Chief of Staff's house across the street. He was not impressed! Oh, how did I ever survive? My boss requested the Artillery assignment folks in the Pentagon extend me in command, so I had the privilege of commanding the battalion for two full years, a rarity in those days. I guess they wanted me to do it over and over again, until I got it right!

Colonel Steele went on to command the 5th Mechanized Infantry Division and retired as a Major General, after a distinguished military career. On one of my efficiency reports, he wrote a comment that I am most proud of. He stated that of his 5 battalion commanders, I was the firmest disciplinarian, a polite way of saying I was a hard-ass and did not tolerate lawbreakers. I need to explain this. I developed, over the years a philosophy about soldiers. I enjoyed coaching and teaching my young officers and NCOs what I had learned about soldiers. I told them that there were *expectors* and *expectees*! We, the officers and the NCOs were the expectors and the troops were the expectees. If we *expected* the troops to steal from each other, shoot up with drugs, or throw a brick through the local Gasthous window, they would not disappoint us---they would do that. But if we *expected* them *not* to do those things, *and clearly articulated what the correct standard was, and the penalties involved,* 95% or so would live up to our *expectations,* and there were appropriate ways to deal with the other few. It involves setting a high but attainable standard, then rewarding excellent performance and behavior, and penalizing bad behavior. Simple enough. Almost always, if a unit fails, it is the fault of the expectors, not expecting or insisting on excellence or clearly articulating the expected behavior or performance. There are honest mistakes and not-so-honest mistakes. If a young mechanic was trying to repair a truck engine and just made an error that caused major damage, that is an honest mistake. I always remembered what Lieutenant General Reuben Jenkins told me---you don't discipline ignorance---you educate it. But if the soldier willfully broke the law, he must pay a stiff penalty. I told my soldiers if they behaved and were good soldiers, I would be the best friend they ever had, I would take care of them, and train them *hard* so they would survive combat. But if they did the crime, they would do the time, and I would be their worst nightmare! We were especially tough on AWOLs. I thought that the least I should expect from my soldiers was to show up. I was especially proud of my relationship with my young soldiers. They were always very respectful of me, but were not afraid to come up to me in the motor pool, or on the parade field to talk to me. One day several of my young black soldiers that were very new to the battalion, came up to me, and we were talking. They were nervous, and one sorta looked at the ground and said, "Sir, we have heard about you." I was a little surprised at this, and asked what they had heard. He said, "we heard that you are a tough but a straight son-of-a-gun." I smiled and thought, "that wouldn't be a bad epitaph----here lies a tough but straight SOB." There had been a couple of cases in another unit where they thought a white soldier had been given the benefit of the doubt and "covered for" when he didn't come back from leave on time---in other words, he was AWOL. But one of the black soldiers was given no slack when the same thing occurred. I had learned that you can be tough, and especially train your soldiers hard, but what the soldiers want is *consistency and fairness!* To end this lesson in "Leadership 101", Colonel Steele wrote in my ER, "LTC Hoglan is the firmest disciplinarian of my 5 battalion commanders, but his soldiers **love him,** and will do anything he asks of them". WOW! I'll admit that *love* is a rather strange word to find in an ER, but I am very proud of it.

Of course, one of my bosses somewhere along the line, wrote "this officer may not always be right, but he is never in doubt"! I must plead guilty to that. I am rather opinionated on many subjects, and it seems to get worse with age! Another comment, "this officer performs all things to *his* complete satisfaction!" I guess I am guilty of that also! Sorry for the "Leadership soapbox drill", but it is one of my favorite subjects. I don't want any of my contemporaries who read this to be upset. I am sure that *they* think they know more about this subject than I do. Maybe so. I am indebted to my great bosses I have mentioned (more to come), and all the super Officers, NCOs, and soldiers that made me look good, well at least adequate, but I don't want to forget my contemporaries. They are often overlooked. I have learned much from them. In the 197th Brigade, LTCs Chuck Arnecke and Jim Eddins, my fellow battalion commanders, are at the top of my list. LTC Steve Pawlik was also my contemporary and fellow battalion commander, although he finished his command tour before I had been in command very long, and went off to the Navy War College. You remember, we were together with Colin Powell as instructors in the Infantry School on a previous tour. One day, I noticed a framed sign in Steve's office, with just two words: INCONVENIENCE YOURSELF! I asked about that and he explained it this way. It is fine for the officers to visit soldiers in training on nice sun-shinny afternoons, but it is important that you *inconvenience yourself!* It is important that you also visit them on the gun line at the Graf firing range, at midnight, when it is snowing like crazy and is about 20 below! Inconvenience yourself Lieutenant, Captain, Colonel, and show the troops that you share their hardships, and you are not *too good* to get cold or soaking wet. I submit that is not grandstanding, it's showing a sincere concern for your soldiers. A sign went up in my office that read, "INCONVENIENCE YOURSELF", and I would explain it to my young officers. Thanks, Steve.

LTC Ted Voorhees and LTC Bob Brumback were the other Battalion Commanders in the 197th Brigade, and we all went to the Army War College together in 1975-76.

I mentioned my super Battalion CSM Gus Myszka. Somewhere, we had acquired an old towed howitzer with wagon wheels and a limber (used to tow the gun and carry ammo). CSM Myszka and I were talking one day and he told me we needed a horse to tow the limber and cannon and maybe a second horse to be ridden along side. He said we could build a pen down by the motor pool to keep them in. Since we had been doing such great things for communities in Florida in our recruiting efforts, I wrote a letter to U.S. Congressman Bob Sykes, from Northwest Florida. I enumerated several of our contributions to some of his communities, and told him of our need for a couple of horses to carry on the old horse drawn Artillery tradition. I was aware that Rep Sykes was a reasonably wealthy man, and I was hoping he would just donate a couple of horses to the battalion. Next call I got was from the Chief of Legislative Liaison, Office of the Secretary of the Army, in the Pentagon. I had gotten a *"congressional"*! Not a good thing. A *congressional* is when a soldier complains to his or her Senator or Representative about treatment, whatever. The congressman's office routinely forwards these to the OCLL (Legislative Liaison), who forwards them to the command for a full answer and explanation. No commander cherishes these. It usually has negative connotations, takes time to answer and the answer does not always end the episode. The Chief of Legislation Liaison said that this was the first time he had received a *congressional complaint* from a Lieutenant Colonel, a battalion commander at that! Well, the Army explained to the congressman that they did not have any horses, and that answered the inquiry for the time being. Wouldn't you know, my very next assignment was to the Office of the Chief of Legislative Liaison in the Pentagon, thanks to my ex boss, and former 197th Infantry Brigade

Commander, Colonel Ed Kennedy, who was now assigned to OCLL. When I reported in, my boss, Major General Tom Tackaberry said he wanted to meet the battalion commander that had made a *congressional complaint*. How in the world did I survive?

Well, CSM Myszka acquired two horses, "Short Round, and Projo" (short name for Projectile). I don't know where he got them and was told, "don't ask"! We got a lot of mileage from them, pulling the old cannon in parades and other formations, Christmas caroling in December, etc.

We wanted to spread good cheer and pride in our branch (Artillery), so I would wear red socks with all my dress uniforms. The Commanding General of Fort Benning and our Brigade Commander would always come up to me and raise my trousers leg to make sure I was wearing red socks---probably could not have gotten away with that at any other military installation----so we painted the Infantry Center with Artillery red. Fort Benning remains our favorite Army installation (forgive me, Fort Sill). It is a great family post, and the Infantry folks treated us so good! This was our second tour at Benning and third in Georgia (Robins AFB earlier). So our daughter grew up in her formative years in Georgia, and later graduated from Georgia Southwestern University in Americus, Georgia. And now she lives in Americus. So anytime someone would ask Sonja where she was from, she would, without hesitation, say Georgia. On the other hand, when anyone would ask Steve where he was from (he never went to school more that two years in any one place), he would answer with a question, "what is this *from??* Does everybody have to be *from?* He did not understand the question.

I'm sorta like Steve, after moving 37 times, I'm not real sure where I'm from! But I still claim I'm just a country boy from Pitkin!

Not everything was all work and no play. During this tour at Benning, Steve was 12—14 years old, and he wanted a dirt bike in the worst way. We bought him a new Yamaha 125 Motocross racer! I had a pick-up truck and I would haul him and the bike out into the woods on the Fort Benning reservation and sit on the truck tailgate and watch him ride. It really looked like so much fun. I gave in, and told Mama that if *I* had a bike, it would be so much more fun, riding *with Steve.* I bought a Kawasaki 185cc dirt bike and then the fun began. We rode together, not only at Fort Benning, but later at Fort Belvoir, Virginia (when I was assigned back to the Pentagon), at Carlisle Barracks, Pennsylvania (when I attended the War College), and in Hawaii, through the pineapple fields and on top of the mountains with the exquisite view. The bikes allowed us to spend a lot of great times together. More about that later.

During this tour of duty, Sonja attended Spencer High School in Columbus and Steve attended Faith Junior High School at Fort Benning. Senator Beagle Dog and Goldwater Cat enjoyed Fort Benning also. Senator would escape his tether and chase cars---one day he caught one, and came limping home----not hurt bad, thank goodness. Katherine spent a lot of time retrieving him from "jail" at the pet D (detention) Cell on post.

We had 45 officers in the battalion, most of them married, and Katherine did lots of entertaining. We had all the officers and ladies to our house for dinner several times, as well as lots of socializing with "the stockholders" (the brigade and battalion commanders). I mentioned that on our first tour of duty at Fort Benning, we discovered the Benning Recreation Center in Destin, Florida. On this tour, we used it even more. I would give the battalion a "training holiday" on a Friday or Monday, so the troops would have a 3-day weekend, and all the officers would go to the Destin Rec Center for a 3-day R & R. At that time, a unit could reserve up to ½ of the cabins, plus campground area for tents, trailers, RVs, etc. Many great memories were made. We would play all kinds of games, fish, swim, and boat ride during the day, and on Saturday night have a shrimp-a-peel dinner in my large cabin. My favorite Chaplain (Major) Bob Bell would hold Sunday morning church services on the beach. These were some of the greatest of times, and my officers still comment about these occasions and a strong "family" relationship among us. We fell in love with the Destin area, and have enjoyed more than 40 vacations there. Three generations of Hoglans have worn out 3 sets of quarters at the Destin Camp during the last 40 years. It's why we knew for a long time that we would someday live in this area.

After commanding the battalion for two years, I received PCS orders in the spring of 1974, assigning me to the Office of the Chief of Legislative Liaison in the Pentagon. This had been arranged by Colonel

Ed Kennedy, my first brigade commander in the 197th, who was now assigned as Chief of the Senate Division of OCLL. Off to the "puzzle palace" for my second tour on the Army General Staff. I looked forward to the job, but not the Washington traffic!

As I leave my beloved battalion, I will add a copy of a statement I had posted on my wall.

"A dead soldier who has given his life because of the failure of his officer is a dreadful sight and a crime before God. Like all dead soldiers, he was tired before he died, and undoubtedly dirty, and possibly frightened to his soul. And there he is, on top of all that, never to see his homeland again. Don't be the officer who failed to instruct him properly, who failed to lead him well. Burn the midnight oil, Lieutenant, that you may not, in later years, look at your hands and find his blood still red upon them!"

Author unknown

This says it all about officer-ship and leadership!

THREE

Department of the Army General Staff, OCLL, The Pentagon
Carlisle Barracks, Pennsylvania,
The U. S. Army War College
Shippensburg University of Pennsylvania

We arrived in the Washington area and stayed a few days with the Kennedys in Alexandria, Virginia while we looked for housing. They introduced us to Laura Rosenblum, a real estate agent, who was the wife of Don Rosenblum, later Lieutenant General Rosenblum. Laura had a house in mind for us immediately, in the Mount Vernon area of Alexandria. It was a two story brick colonial very close to George Washington's Mount Vernon and also Mount Vernon High School. Laura's description of the house before she took us to see it was stark! She emphasized that we would need to hold our noses while in the house. A young couple had bought it, and now was moving out into the countryside. They loved animals, but didn't want children. The master bedroom was home to two honey bears, complete with dirt, straw, logs etc. One upstairs bedroom was occupied by rabbits----many rabbits! The other bedroom and the yard were living quarters for several huge, Alaskan Malamute dogs. The couple slept in the basement on a mattress on the concrete floor. Laura was right---the stench was almost un-*bear*-able (pardon the pun). But she emphasized that there was no structural damage to the house. It would be necessary to clean and paint it, but it had a very low price, and was in a very nice, upscale neighborhood. We bought it. We hired a professional cleaning team to thoroughly clean the house. They scrubbed the basement with pine oil, stripped all of the rugs from the floors, removed the Venetian blinds (the odor had permeated the cloth strips), and sanded the wooden floor in the "rabbit room" upstairs where rabbit pee had soaked through the carpet. The entire house was stripped and thoroughly cleaned, with new carpets and curtains throughout. Katherine and I painted the entire house on the inside and wallpapered the bathrooms. When we finished, it was beautiful! And it doubled in value. We only lived in it for just over one year and transferred to Carlisle Barracks, PA, but kept it rented for about 10 years, and made a killin' when we sold it.

The reason that we did not keep ownership of our first house over in Annandale on our first tour in Washington is interesting. When, in 1972, we received orders transferring us to Fort Benning, I asked the chief of Artillery assignments, Colonel Jim Wortham, if it were a good chance I would have another tour in Washington. My house payment at the time was about $310 per month and I was worried that if I didn't keep it rented, I would go broke trying to make those *large* payments! He said, "no, the Pentagon assignment was like the mumps----you only had to do it once." So we sold the beautiful two-story, new house in Annandale. Did not make any money on the deal. Wouldn't you know it; immediately after selling it, the real estate market in the area went bonkers. But why should I worry, I had my case of the mumps---somebody else's problem now—not mine.   You can imagine my surprise when, just two years later, I received orders for the Pentagon again. I asked Colonel Wortham about this and reminded him about his mumps story to me. He said, "Curt, you obviously only had 'em on one side, so we are bringing you back to finish the other side!" When we arrived back for our second Pentagon tour, we couldn't even afford the down payment on our first house in Annandale.   And would you believe, I almost had the mumps a third time, but that story comes a little later.

My assignment in OCLL was very interesting.   I worked for some outstanding bosses, namely Colonel Lee McKinney, Colonel Chuck Franklin, Colonel Bob Sullivan and in order, MG Tom Tackaberry, and then MG Jim Lee. Colonel Kennedy, my buddy and mentor was the Chief of the Senate Division over on the "hill" in the Senate Office building, and Colonel "Scooter" Burke (a Medal of Honor winner from Korea) was Chief on the Representative side. My office was in the Pentagon, but as I learned, I spent most of my time pounding the pavement over on the hill in the congressional offices. The OCLL officers over on the hill spent a lot of time with members of congress, escorting them to various military installations, etc. I spent most of my time briefing congressional staff members and responding to their requests for information. My primary job was to get the appropriations bill and procurement bill through the congress. This was done primarily through furnishing fact sheets to the staffers of the "Big 4". These were the House Appropriations and House Armed Services Committees, and the Senate Appropriations and Senate Armed Services Committees. It sounds like a big job, and it was, but I had a lot of help. Virtually, all action officers in the Pentagon were at my disposal to get the information I needed. I didn't have to write any of the fact sheets, but the congressional staffers could be very *demanding* and we always seemed to be in a crisis mode, getting the information to them *"yesterday"!* The Pentagon staff officers knew what we were up against and were almost always very cooperative with us.

A major area of interest that was assigned to me was the Army Tank Program. There were three parts to this program: (1) The new M-1 tank, later named the Abrams tank, was in the Research and Development (R & D) stage, and a lot of money was needed to be approved in the budget for that program. (2) The M-60 main battle tank was in production at the Chrysler Tank Plant in Michigan and required money for its production. (3) The older M-48 Tank was still needed and they were being retrofitted and improved at Redstone Arsenal in Alabama. My primary "customer" was a staffer with the Senate Armed Services Committee. He was extremely demanding and had the well-deserved reputation for being the toughest (I won't say meanest) staffer on the hill. He shall remain nameless, but any senior Army Officer, who ever served in the Pentagon, who reads this, will know whom I am talking about. I would take Army Generals over to brief him and he would sometimes call them a liar and throw us out of his office. Then the General would chew on my butt all the way back to the Pentagon. It got so bad, that my boss, General Lee, called this staffer and told him that the next time he called one of our Generals a liar and tossed him out of his office, General Lee would call his boss, Committee Chairman

Senator John Stennis and have the staffer fired. By the way, he would
have done it too. Things got a little better. He took up most all of my
time, just satisfying his requests. Not only did I have to respond to his
demands for immediate information, I was required to escort him to the
Army tank plant and other facilities at times. I wouldn't say that he was
not on "our side", but he seemed to think that the more he could cause
the budget to be cut, the more points he would score with committee
members. This was no doubt true with some committee members.
Thank God, Senator Stennis *was* on *our* side. One of the things that
have bothered me for some time is that fewer and fewer Members of
Congress (MCs) have ever worn the military uniform. This staffer told
me on several occasions that he was going to make major cuts in our
programs, especially the tank program.

I was getting very frustrated with all of this, and after laying awake
most of one night, I thought of an idea. The next day, I called the Tech
Rep from the Chrysler Tank Plant and we met for lunch. I knew him
well, and he was definitely an asset that I had used quite a bit, furnishing
information, etc. I asked him how many sub-contractors that Chrysler,
the Prime Contractor, used to manufacture our tanks. He responded
that there were first tier subs, second tier subs, third tier subs, and
literally thousands of vendors. It turns that just about everybody in
the manufacturing industry is involved in providing something for the
tank. I asked if he could get me a list of the sub-contractors and quite
a few of the larger venders. He said he could and about two weeks
later called and said he had the list, and brought it to me. I studied it
and sure enough, somebody from almost every State was involved in
the manufacture of our tank and it's associated equipment. We had
been having great difficulty in getting in to see actual MCs. Each
has a "gate keeper" called the Administrative Assistant (the dreaded
AA). Their primary job is to find reasons that their MC can't see you.
Believe it or not, there are MCs, and consequently their AAs, that are
downright hostile to the "military brass." These are just some of the
ones that swear they support "the troops." More about this later. I
made an appointment with Brigadier General Rex Wing, who headed
up a Tank Program Office in the Pentagon. I asked him, if I could get
him appointments with actual Members of Congress, would he go with
me over to the hill. He salivated and jumped at the chance. I told him

about my idea, and asked him to tell his Executive Officer to just turn his schedule over to me. He did.

Here is the way this gig went down. I would call the AA and ask if there was any way I could bring General Wing over to meet with his Senator or Congressman, for a short briefing. Depending on the office, I would often be asked, "What the hell for---we don't even like you guys. My MC usually votes against the military budget." My response, "that is too bad, because we want to award contracts that amount to a lot of money in your MC's home district, and we wanted your member to make the announcement, but thank you anyway." "Whoa Colonel, perhaps I have been a little hasty in my response, but I think we can arrange a visit---when will you and the General be available?" WOW! I had discovered the magic key to Pandora's box. Maybe everybody else in the world knew about "the key", but at that moment I felt like I was the smartest SOG in the whole world. Of course, there were several offices that welcomed us without using "the bait". During this short tour of duty of just over one year, I learned so much about how Congress operates. They scratch each other's backs. I met very often with one of our strongest supporters, Congressman Bill Nichols from Alabama, Redstone Arsenal country. He would ask me whom he should enlist as a supporter for our program. I told him that Congressman Doe was a hard nut to crack and was hostile to us. He said that he would take care of it. Doe owed him one. It's a club that is very difficult to break into, but if you are a member of the club you are over half way home. My secretary would answer the phone and then tell me, Sir, Congressman Nichols is on the phone for you. Not the AA---the Congressman. He taught me a lot about the *real* workings of the Congress. He told me one day, "Curt, I know that the defense of our country is top priority for you, and I appreciate that. But it's not *my* top priority!" That floored me, but he continued, "Getting re-elected is my top priority, because if I'm not re-elected every two years, I won't be up here helping you fight for the defense of our country. And you need to understand and appreciate that. Many of my comrades in the House feel that way. The Senators only have to run every six years, but we House members are running all the time, and must go back to our districts constantly to keep *running.*" Congressman Bill Nichols was a real patriot, and one of my heroes. By the way, he and Congressman

Eddie Herbert (A-bear) used to crack me up telling the funniest stories about a certain Congresswoman. Sorry I can't tell any of them here---the censors would get me. Eddie Herbert was also one of my heroes. My little combo (more about that later) made history by playing for his birthday party *in the House Armed Services Committee meeting room.* (Complete with larger than life size picture of Mendel Rivers on the wall looking down at us)!

Well, General Wing was amazed and thankful that we got into so many offices on the hill, to brief MCs. The order of march was: I would introduce him to the Congressman or Senator, and he would give a good briefing (not usually more than 20 minutes—their time is valuable and they appreciate the brevity). Then I would close it by stating that in order for the MC to make the announcement in his home district that more money and jobs would be coming, there was one *little* requirement------the Authorization Bill and the Appropriations Bill must pass the Congress, at which time the overwhelming numbers of MCs would say, "you've got my vote, and who do you want me to talk to?" I don't want to make this sound too easy. It was hard work, and we did not *convert* every MC to our cause, but many more than enough. My "hostile" staffer would see General Wing and I in the hallways and he would ask me what I was doing over there so often. I would just say that I had other "customers" as well as him. I think he was amazed that all parts of the Army tank program went through both houses of congress *without a single penny being cut* from the budget. I was a local hero, at least in my own mind. I don't think the staffer ever figured out what happened.

Another "war" story: A new Senator joined the Senate Armed Services Committee. He was very liberal and I think it is fair to say, somewhat hostile to the tank program. So Senator Stennis put him in charge of studying the tank program and reporting back to the committee on it-----an absolutely brilliant stroke of genius. It is easy to sit on the sidelines and carp, but if the Chairman gives you some responsibility for it, you at least must look into it and learn. I escorted him to the tank plant and several facilities and units. His hostility was neutralized, not by me, but by Senator Stennis.

Sometimes I would get a lesson in hypocrisy. On one such occasion, Lee Mc Kinney and I were sitting in the Senate Gallery listening to members making floor speeches concerning the two bills of interest to us. A Senator from Massachusetts (No, no, no, neither of the present Senators from that State, as much as I wished it) rose and made a speech, which was a scathing attack on the Improved Hawk Air Defense System. It was not a great surprise, since this Senator voted "against us more than for us". What was startling and amazing that made our jaws gape, was that the prime contractor for The Hawk system was the Raytheon Corporation from guess where? Andover, Massachusetts! When we returned to the Pentagon, I immediately called the Senator's AA, introduced myself and he was very sarcastic to me and wanted to know what I wanted, seeing as how they really didn't like us. I told him we had just heard his Senator attack the Improved Hawk system, and I couldn't believe they would allow him to speak against it, saying that it was just another example of the Army's "gold-plating", and that we have a Hawk Missile system, and do not need an Improved Hawk system, and urged the Senators to vote against it. He said, well that's the way we feel, so get lost. I asked him if he knew whom the Prime Contractor for the Hawk system was and where they were located. There was an awkward silence of about 5 seconds, and I think he was figuring out that they had just been had. And they had. When I told him it was in Andover, Massachusetts, he yelled %^$#%&, get a fact sheet over to me right now! I did. A couple of days later, I was again in the Senate gallery and the Massachusetts Senator rose, and I will paraphrase, "My distinguished colleagues, the other day, I spoke against the Improved Hawk missile system. It turns out that I had received some incorrect information and was badly miss-led. After looking into the matter closely and receiving briefings on it, I would like to amend my remarks. I can report to you that the Improved Hawk system is absolutely vital to our National Defense," blah, blah. Overt hypocrisy, not even thinly veiled. I would guess one of his staffers got fired! But maybe not!

I do not wish to impugn all politicians, because there are patriotic Members of Congress, and elected officials who are honest and have our country's interest at heart. Unfortunately, there are several that do not fit in this category, which will come as no surprise to anybody.

During this tour of duty, our son, Steve, and I continued to ride dirt bikes. We rode out on the reservation of Fort Belvoir, a close by Army installation. There were several places for us to ride where there were woods, etc to bounce off trees and other obstacles of nature, without interfering with other folks. There was one particular hill, more like a cliff, that we liked to challenge. It was about 30 feet high, and it was almost straight up. We would take a fast run to tackle it. Now, Steve's bike was a 125cc moto-cross racer, with high torque and rpms. With its knobby tires, he could (and did) throw dirt in my face. I remember on one occasion, I took a fast run at the cliff, and about ¾ the way to the top, I ran out of torque, rpms, and ideas all at the same time! I came back down the cliff backwards, at least for most of the way before I was totally wiped out. Would you believe Steve not only laughed at me, but continued to tell the story of my prowess on the dirt bike?

During this tour of duty, Sonja attended Mount Vernon High School and graduated in the summer of 1975. Steve attended Walt Whitman Junior High School and then Mount Vernon High School for his 9th grade.

One last *war* story from this interesting assignment: Normally, I did not escort MCs around the U.S. or overseas. But on one occasion, I was asked to escort 35 Senators, wives, and staffers on an overseas trip. LTC Mike Rhode, over on the Senate office of OCLL was the other escort officer, together with a couple of NCOs. Senator Hubert Humphrey, Chairman of the Senate Foreign Relations Committee, was the delegation leader. He had invited most of his committee members as well as several members of the Armed Services Committee to go on this trip. The Russians had invited him and a delegation to attend the USSR/US Inter-parliamentary Conference in Moscow over the Easter Congressional break in 1974. I still do not have a clue as to what the Inter-parliamentary Conference was! But we were about ready to launch, when just before the Easter weekend, the Howard Hughes seagoing recovery vessel, dredged up some of the remains of a Russian submarine that had sunk in the ocean. The Russians notified Senator Humphrey's office through the Russian Embassy that the Inter-parliamentary Conference had been postponed indefinitely. Now, get the picture; all these folks were dressed up in their Easter finest, now with no place to go. Can't let that happen. Our office got a call that the participants would remain the same, but a new trip, called the "Inspection of the NATO Alliance" would take place in this same time frame. We had, like zero time to plan for this new trip. They specified the exact places they wanted to visit, Brussels, Berlin, Bonn, Vienna, and Madrid. It is interesting that at that time Austria and Spain were not even NATO signatories. We frantically called the American Embassies in these places and told them we were coming, ready or not. I guess they were accustomed to these last minutes taskings, because they were very responsive.

Let me say at the outset that Senator Humphrey was a fine delegation leader and a great gentleman along with his sweet wife Muriel. He certainly treated the escort officers well and was a pleasure to work with---wish I could say the same for *all* the senators and *wives* on the trip. We were in a crash mode for the entire trip, since there were awesome changes from the original trip, but most everything went pretty well. I will only relate a couple of interesting stories from this episode. In every location the local American Embassy would set up hospitality suites in our hotel, with a complete bar, manned by our NCOs. In Vienna, late one night I had gone to bed, and my phone rang. A senator's wife was on the phone, and she said she wanted a Dr. Pepper delivered to her room. I told her that we did not have any Dr. Pepper but we had Coca Cola, Pepsi, and just about everything else under the sun. She said, "Colonel I don't think you are listening. I want a Dr, Pepper and I want it right now." I told her that I didn't think there was a Dr. Pepper in the country of Austria---she reiterated that she wanted one immediately. I said "right away", and rolled over and went back to sleep---I can't *make* Dr.Peppers, and I didn't hear any more about it.

Our last stop was at Torrejon AFB in Madrid, Spain. We departed there on Sunday morning, and the base opened the U.S. Base Exchange just for their last minute shopping, before boarding the C-135 US Air Force jet for the trip back to Andrews AFB, Maryland. Senator Humphrey told me that it was very important that we land at Andrews on time, because he had a press conference with major networks, to report on the group's trip. We boarded the aircraft and I counted noses. Senator X's wife was missing. Senator Humphrey called me to the front of the aircraft and asked me why we were not on our taxiway out to the active runway. I told him that Senator X's wife was not on board, but I would go look for her. I went back to the Base Exchange, and she was still shopping. I asked her if I could help her finish and check out, since Senator Humphrey wanted to get airborne immediately. She told me, "Well I don't think you are going to leave me here", turned and continued shopping. I finally got her to the plane. Meanwhile, her husband was sitting on the plane, enjoying his Martini. Nobody spoke to him about this at all. It's a clubby atmosphere---none of them would speak an unkind word *to* or *about* any other member of the club. They just leaned on the *pore* escort officer, to fix the problem. I couldn't help but think about how this would have been handled if it had been a purely military (Army) gig. Senator Humphrey would have been the General. Senator X would have been the Colonel, Senator X's wife would have been the Colonel's wife, and the *pore* ole escort officer would have been LTC Hoglan. When the aircraft was sensed as not taking off on time, the General would have called the escort officer, LTC Hoglan forward and asked what was the problem. Upon being informed what was holding up the flight, the General would have asked the escort officer to tell Colonel X to report to him. Upon reporting, the General would have said something like, "Colonel, do want your wife to go back to the States with us? If you do, you have about 3 minutes to get that dizzy wife of yours on this airplane or we are going to leave her butt in Spain. Are there any questions?" It wouldn't have been the *pore* ole escort officer's problem. I spoke to the pilot, an Air Force Lieutenant Colonel, and he told me not to worry, he was going push the throttle through the firewall and that we *would* get back to Andrews on time. And we did. When we arrived, I reported to the customs officer and told him, "The airplane is yours". He said, "I wouldn't touch that airplane with a ten foot pole". Good thing!

Allow me one observation about our congressional leaders. It is just my opinion, of course, but it seems that a few of the Senators seemed to think that the laws do not apply to them, just to us common folk, and some of the Senators' wives can be more demanding than the Senators. They run for office every 6 years. I found that the Representatives tend to be more representative of, closer to, and attentive to folks in their districts because they are running every 2 years. This may be an argument for limited terms of office (every 6 months?---just kidding, I think!).

This assignment was very interesting and I now had *two* assignments on the Army General Staff, in the Pentagon, that were very different than most of the other Army staff officers, who were buried in the bowels of the Pentagon, cranking out papers, and begging somebody to "chop" (approve) them. My hat is off to those guys, because I was close enough to them to know what they were going through. Maybe, some civilians think that service on the Army staff in the Pentagon was a *peach* of an assignment, with great working hours and a lot of prestige, etc. For the most part, it is *tough* duty---long working hours, little recognition, and the worst traffic to and from work of any place on the planet Earth! I also worked hard, with long hours, but at least I had the diversion of working with Attaches from 64 countries on my first tour, and then the wild and wooly congress during my second tour!

These were not the typical assignments of action officers on the Army staff. And I am grateful.

I was fortunate to be selected to attend the Army War College at Carlisle Barracks, Pennsylvania after completing only a little more than one year in OCLL. My Boss, General Jim Lee, called me in and asked me if I would extend for one more year in OCLL. He told me that I was about the only officer that could get along with my "favorite staffer" over on the hill, and he remembered that we had gotten the tank program through two congressional budget cycles with no cuts. He said that he would *guarantee my attendance at AWC the following year, and he could certainly do that!* I told him that all 5 of the battalion commanders of the 197th Infantry Brigade while I was there, had been selected for the AWC that year, and it meant so much to me to be classmates with them. God bless him, he released me and did not "ping" me for leaving early. He was such a super boss and gentleman. Another one of my heroes! Another officer in OCLL that I got to know was Colonel Bob Poydasheff. We went from this assignment to the War College together. He remains a good friend and is now the Mayor of Columbus, Georgia.

I mentioned "The combo" that played in the House Armed Services meeting room for Chairman Eddie Herbert's birthday party. I had rejoined the "Dixie Five-O", that I had been a member of on our previous tour in Washington. We continued to play for Luaus and other assorted gigs around the area. It was a blast. Did I work for a living, or just play??

143

Carlisle Barracks, Pennsylvania, The U.S Army War College

When I was selected to attend the Army War College, we were delighted. A small percentage of Army officers were ever selected and we felt very fortunate that we made the list. It was even better that all the battalion commanders that were together in the 197th Infantry Brigade were selected to go in that year. We were to be the "Bi-Centennial Class of 1976, and we made the most of it. We were notified that we would be quartered in Young Hall, a two story building with *forty-eight families!* It was a very *long* building. It was a small apartment so we did not ship much stuff to Carlisle. No problem, we were only going to be there about 10 months anyway, so we put everything we could possibly do without for a year in storage in Virginia: all of our furniture, tools, etc. Little did we know that we would not see any of these things for *seven years!!* More about that later.

Our year at Carlisle was fantastic, primarily because we had a superstar as the Commandant, Major General DeWitt C. Smith, and his sweet wife Betty. He set the stage for an outstanding learning experience. I knew he was going to be good, when he told us that we had all worked hard, and excelled to get here, so he wanted us to relax, get acquainted and spend time with our families, socialize with each other, read or do other things that we had never had time to do before. He said that he understood that we had spent about 20 years or so being very competitive, hopefully for the right reasons. General Smith said that if we were ever wondering if we should read the assignment for tomorrow's class or play golf, *by all means, play golf!* Now this was not an invitation to *waste* the government's money for a year. We had outstanding instructors, speakers, and challenges, but General Smith made it an experience that none of my classmates will ever forget. We had our 10th class reunion in 1986 at the Bowling AFB, Maryland Officers Club, the 20th reunion back at Carlisle Barracks in 1996, and our 30th reunion at Carlisle in October 2006. More about the 30th later.

Our class of 212 students was organized into 10 person seminar groups. LTC Don Infanti was our seminar group leader. He and Norma Jean are our great friends, live in Clearwater Beach, and we visit them fairly often. He later commanded Fort Bliss, Texas and retired as a Major General. Several other of my favorite folks were in our seminar group. Pete Dawkins, the former Heisman Trophy winner from the Military Academy at West Point, New York and his wife Judy, and Dick Stevenson and wife Diane were among them. I was elected social chairman, (CINCSOC) for the seminar group. I will never forget when we invited the seminar group over to our abode for dinner and Katherine fixed Louisiana Cajun Chicken File' Gumbo, Dick stuck his head into the pot and just inhaled!! In addition to Pete Dawkins being in our seminar group, I was privileged to sit next to Pete in the big auditorium when we had VIP speakers. I noticed right away, that when I asked a question, the speaker would look at me with the "that is a dumb question" look and slough me off, with a word or two answer. BUT, when Pete asked a question, the speaker would say, "that is an outstanding question Colonel Dawkins, let me pursue that". So I figured that if I were going to get any of *my* questions answered, I would let Pete ask them! So I *pulled* Pete through the Army War College, by slipping my questions to him---that's my story and I'm sticking to it! He knew it, and gave me a model cannon, engraved with a plaque that reads, "Curt, Thanks for all those questions, Pete". I also was a member of the "Current Events Panel", and we gave speeches and presentations throughout the region. I enjoyed that.

I also participated in the annual sports day when we challenged the National War College to a sports day, and I single handedly sunk our golf team by taking a 9 on number ??, over the water and out of bounds (several times), on the golf course. One of the most enjoyable experiences at the War College was at Christmas time when we opened the Officers' Club to all the nursing homes in the entire county, and War College Students went out and transported the occupants to the Officers' Club for a gala Christmas party. I got to play Santa Claus, complete with costume, beard, etc, for which I volunteered. We did this for a couple of days. I *love* little old ladies, and I had a great time giving out presents and having them sit on my lap. One of my favorites was a little, sweet, black lady that was 98 years old. She sat in my lap, and I asked her what she wanted for Christmas, and she said just visits from her family. This was the answer from many of the guests. It broke my heart to hear many of these elderly people tell me that although they had sons, daughters, and close kin living close by, they almost never were visited by them, and this was the *only* time of the year that they got out. They were not resentful of this—on the contrary, they made all kinds of excuses for it--"my folks are very busy, etc, " We had presents for all of them, plus food and music. This was their favorite outing all year long. My classmates seemed surprised that I was enjoying being Santa Claus, since I was sort of a joker in the class, but I assured them that I got much more out of this than I put into it! It was clearly one of my favorite activities at Carlisle all year.

On top of a mountain, not far from Carlisle, was a great restaurant. One evening, several couples, including Tom and Carol Lightner and the Hoglans, drove up there for dinner. We ordered our food, and it seemed like the service was especially slow, so we each ordered another long neck while we waited for our food. The waitress came out several times and apologized, but said our food was "on the way". Well, after more than an hour, she came over to our table, apologized again and said that there would no food that night! The fire sprinkler system had accidentally gone off in the kitchen and there was about 12 inches of foam all over *everything!* They thought they could clean it up and continue cooking and serving, but it was not to be. So, we drove back down the mountain and began looking for a restaurant that was still open. We finally settled for a bucket of KFC chicken, and some more long necks, and dined in the basement of Jess and Toni Wilkins' quarters. Late! Carol Lightner commented that we should not be upset. We were just "making memories"! Since then, if something goes awry, particularly in our travels, I always remember to try not to be upset; we're just *making memories!*

During our War College year we had the privilege of having *the* military service "show" bands visit and perform for us. The Army, Air Force, and Marine show (jazz, dance, big band, whatever) bands all let me sit in on trumpet, but my favorite was the Navy Commodores. They were great and let me over stay my welcome, probably. A highlight of our year was in the final week; the Army's small jazz combo came to the War College and played for a party. The Army Chief of Staff, General Fred Weyand, was there and I joined in with my trumpet at the invitation of the combo leader, SGM Sheppard. Two of the last full page pictures in our yearbook is of General Weyand singing, and one of me playing the trumpet. Later, in Hawaii, General Weyand and I joined forces and terrorized a party at General Herb Wolfe's quarters, but I will relate that story later.

Our War College Commandant, General Dewitt C. Smith was one of the most outstanding men I ever knew, and his wife Betty was (is) a queen. He loved Dixieland music, which is just one of the reasons I loved this man, and he liked to hear me play Dixieland with the service bands that visited Carlisle. He asked me, while I was a student there, to play "Do You Know What it Means to Miss New Orleans" at his funeral and he reminded me of that wish at our 10th and 20th year reunions. More about this when I discuss our 30th year War College reunion in October 2006 at Carlisle.

During this year, Steve and I continued to enjoy riding our dirt bikes up in the Pennsylvania mountains, riding on the snow mobile trails, with lots of rocks to make it interesting. He attended the 10th grade at David Swartz Intermediate High School, in Carlisle.

This was Sonja's first year in college, and she attended Radford College in Virginia. Since quarters at Carlisle were at a premium, she was not "qualified" for a bedroom, so when she visited us on the weekends, she slept on a mattress on the floor, pulled from under Steve's bed. Senator Beagle Dog and Goldwater Cat survived the experience with their normal aplomb!

I still feel closer to my War College classmates than I do to any other group of schoolmates, comrades, contemporaries, or whatever, that I have ever been associated with! I correspond with many of them often. In addition to several I have already mentioned, some of the other classmates that I admire, respect, and consider great friends, are: Jack King, Jess Stewart, Phil Mason, Jack White, Van VanFleet (of Army, heh, heh), Walt Ratcliff, Jeff Davis, Joe Campbell, John Patton, Jim Shelton, Charlie Searock, Buddy Beck, Tom Lightner, and Don Infanti.

When the War College students began to receive assignment instructions, and negotiations with their respective branches, the Artillery branch assignment representative called me. He said that I needed joint staff experience, and they were thinking about bringing me back to the Pentagon for an assignment to the Joint Staff, (JCS) or the Office of the Secretary of Defense (OSD). Once again, I reminded him of the "mumps" story, and assured him that I had 'em on *both* sides. I told them that I had broken the code---I had discovered that I had classmates that had *never* served in the Pentagon----I asked if we could wiggle this around a little so that everybody got some before they gave me a third helping! About 2 weeks later, I got a call from my assignments officer, and he said that he had located an assignment to a joint staff outside the Pentagon---------Commander in Chief, Pacific Command (CINCPAC) Headquarters in ***Honolulu Hawaii!!*** Now we are cookin'!! I had several great assignment officers in the Artillery assignments directorate over the years. One was Major (later General, and Chairman of the Joint Chiefs of Staff) John Shalikashvilli. I will always remember and appreciate Colonel Jim Wortham, the Artillery Assignments Chief for a number of years.

Shippensburg University of Pennsylvania

While at the War College, I choose to participate in a volunteer Graduate Degree Program, in residence at Shippensburg University of Pennsylvania. Several students opted for this program. We would drive down to Shippensburg some days and nights to take classes. After the one residence year of classes, several options were presented; the two most popular were writing a thesis or working for six weeks in an internship in a government organization. Since I had just completed my "education" as to the workings of the U.S. Congress on Capitol Hill, I opted to do my internship at the state government level. During the year, I had visited prisons in Pennsylvania and written papers on recidivism. I also visited city and state governments and wrote papers on unions in government, since Pennsylvania state government was unionized. My first cousin, James David Cain, was a State Senator in Louisiana and I called him and asked if he would help me with contacts, so I could do my 6-week internship in Louisiana at the State level. He spoke with the Administrative Assistant to the Governor and told me I could work for him! Wow! He promised them that I was not a "spy", and was just a country boy from Pitkin, and was trying to get a Master's Degree in Public Administration. I worked for another one of my heroes, one Dan Borne, the Administrative Assistant to the Governor. He had the utmost confidence in Senator Cain, and told me there would be no secrets between him and me. I attended virtually every meeting he had with officials---sometimes they would look at me a little askance, and he would advise them that I was his assistant and there were no forbidden subjects. He treated me like one of the family. In return I verified to him why I was there and assured him that any reports I made, including the final complete report of my activities made to Shippensburg University would be submitted to him first. He gave me some outstanding projects to lead or participate in. I attended, and subsequently reported on a conference on "Futurism", out at LSU. Dan arranged a helicopter and pilot to take me on a low level (about 400 feet) tour of the Louisiana coast from the Mississippi/Louisiana border to the Louisiana/Texas border. I observed the joint usages of the Louisiana coastal area, by oil rigs, gas wells, shrimp and fishing boats, sulphur wells, hunters, fishermen, etc. and wrote a comprehensive report for the state. I attended and reported on Legislative meetings and the general legislature in session. I was invited to several events, receptions, and parties at the Governor's Mansion, and Dan's wife, Lisette had us over to their house for a great Cajun dinner. I cannot imagine a better "education" that anyone could receive, for my internship. During most of these six weeks, my family and I lived in a motel in Baton Rouge, but Katherine and the kids spent some time in Glenmora, Louisiana with her family. Of course, while living in Baton Rouge, I sat in with a little combo at a hotel----have we been here before? At the end of this internship, I received a Master's Degree in Public Administration from Shippensburg University of Pennsylvania. After finishing my internship in the Louisiana Governor's office in Baton Rouge, we floated off to Hawaii, on "cloud nine", in the summer of 1976.

The Colonel & his Lady, The Pentagon

Dixie 5-O, The Capitol, D.C.

2/10th FA Change of Command, Ft. Benning

Hoglan family at Army War College

Curt & Trumpet at AWC

Chapter Five

THE COLONEL YEARS

ONE

Camp Smith, Hawaii, J-5 Plans Officer, HQ Pacific Command
Hickam AFB, Hawaii, Battle Staff Commander, Blue Eagles, CINCPAC Airborne Command Post

After we left Baton Rouge, we drove to the Grand Canyon, and then stopped in Las Vegas for a visit over night, then on to Yosemite National Park, and on to San Francisco where we stayed at the Marine Hotel downtown and at the Presidio of San Francisco. We flew from the west coast to the Big Island of Hawaii for a few days RR at the Kilauea Military Camp. It was *cold* on top of that volcano! We had firewood delivered to us at our little cabin for burning in the fireplace. We walked across the floor of the volcano, where sulfur fumes were shooting up between the many cracks in the surface of the volcano! Then to Honolulu, where we stayed on Waikiki Beach for a couple of weeks awaiting government quarters at Fort Shafter. I had been selected for promotion and was on the Colonel's list, so we received great quarters on top of a mountain, overlooking the Fort Shafter golf course, the international airport and Pearl Harbor. We had the prettiest view of any place we have ever lived. The quarters were nice, all wood, and were "single wall construction". I didn't really know exactly what that was until I drove a nail into the wall to hang a picture, and the nail came through the wall to the outside of the house! It had no insulation, and of course, no air conditioning or heating---you don't need those things in Paradise! We had a nice "lanai" (patio) with this great view down the mountain. In our yard we had many beautiful flowers, bird of paradise, plumeria, and palm trees, etc.

I reported in to CINCPAC Headquarters at Camp Smith, a few miles from Fort Shafter, but still near the top of the mountain ridge. I was assigned to J-5 Plans Directorate, and worked for a great boss, Rear Admiral McClendon, the J-5. Our immediate boss was Navy Captain Barnette, and the other officers in our office were Army Colonel Ray Pollard, Air Force Colonel Len Clark, and Navy Commander Arv Chauncey. Arv had been released after being held for 6 years as a POW in the "Hanoi Hilton". He was a Navy pilot who had been shot down. He was one of the nicest guys I ever met, and it was astounding considering what he had gone through. He had been held in solitary confinement for most of his years in captivity. He could extend his arms and touch the 4 walls in his cell. He slept every night on a wooden bunk with his wrists handcuffed to his ankles. At first we were very nervous about asking him anything about his captivity, and he sensed this and told us, "Look, I don't mind talking about it if you have questions." One of the most interesting subjects we asked about was how the POWs communicated-----they were all in isolated cells and couldn't see each other. Incredibly, they developed letters, words, and phrases by tapping on the walls of their individual cells. To maintain their sanity, they would, in their minds, plan every single detail, measurements, etc, of a house they would like to build, anything to keep their minds busy. Near the end of their captivity, when the North Vietnamese knew they would be eventually released, they allowed the POWs to congregate. Arv said that one of the things they did was to "tell" each other movies. It was odd to hear Arv say, when asked if he had seen a particularly movie, he would say, "I heard that one".

Upon being released and landing on the first American soil in Hawaii, a Navy Officer assigned to him, met him and told him that his Father had died while he had been in captivity. He was then told that his wife had divorced him and married the Navy officer that was assigned to assist her! I doubt that I could have survived these hardships. And yet Arv was a super individual. He remarried a sweet lady and they were a great addition to our office.

Ray and Barbara Pollard live in Texas and Colorado (summers) and remain good friends. We correspond with them often. Len and Katie Clark lived here in Niceville for a while and we played golf together. They now live in Jacksonville, Florida.

One day in the command weekly bulletin there was a notice about a private pilot ground school at Barbers' Point Naval Air Station. I liked school generally, and I had always wanted to know more about weather, navigation, etc., so I enrolled, without any burning desire to fly an airplane. We had good instructors and the subjects were so interesting and informative, I decided I just might try a couple of flying lessons to see if I enjoyed that. I went up to Wheeler airfield and met a retired, senior master Air Force Pilot, Cal Rich. He took me up for my first flight, and just after take-off, he said that in my Army service I had probably been in small aircraft a number of times and understood gravity and such, so he said why don't you just fly this thing around a little while. *I was hooked! Bad!* One day not long after that, we were shooting touch and go landings, and after several, he asked me to make a full stop. I did, and he asked he how I felt about taking it around the traffic pattern by myself. I said, "Get out of my airplane". He did. I took off and was about half way around the pattern, before I looked over at the other front seat, and realized I was all alone. He was watching from the ground and when I landed, I just greased it in. He said he knew that it would be my best ever landing, because he knew I would really be concentrating. I had soloed in less than 7 hours. There was no stopping me now; I loved it. Cal was my first flight instructor and later my flight examiner. I joined the Barbers' Point Navy Flying Club, and was later elected President of the Club, much to the chagrin of some Navy folks. After I received my Private Pilot License, I continued lessons and eventually received my instrument rating, and after that my Commercial Pilot rating. Harry Cook was my flight instructor and the manager of the flying club.

I really enjoyed making cross-country flights to all the other Hawaiian Islands, and even flew the entire family to Kauai one Christmas. I am sure it was a "white knuckle" trip for them. My favorite aircraft was the T-41 Navy trainer belonging to the club. Although I flew several models of Cessna and Beechcraft, the T-41 was my favorite. It had a canopy that slid back, tandem seating, retractable gear, and a "stick". All I needed was a leather cap and a white scarf, and I would be the "Red Baron". The weather was almost always perfect. The islands have trade winds generally coming out of 45 degrees magnetic north, so the runways are built to take advantage of this----you want to take off and land into the wind if possible. We almost never had storms. I remember only once or twice that I couldn't fly because of high wind warnings. Just before I departed Hawaii, China Lake Naval facility in California gave our club a twin engine Cessna. If I had about 2 more weeks in Hawaii I could have gotten my multi-engine rating.

One of my favorite events was to practice precision landings, touch and goes, at the airstrip on Ford Island, surrounded by "Battleship Row". The airstrip was not long enough to accommodate jets, so it had been turned into a general aviation facility. I would get into the pattern, turn downwind and pull all power, hopefully at the precise instant to glide through the turn cross-wind, then turn final, then set it down right on the numbers of the runway, without having to add power. I practiced it for hours each time I flew. I was doing my touch and go so often, the FAA guy in the tower would often ask me to take over the traffic while he went to get a bite of lunch. When another aircraft would call the tower and request permission to land or shoot a touch and go, I would answer, and say "permission granted, one T-41 on final, enter the pattern 45 degrees to downwind". Or whatever the situation was. My instructor pilot, when I was going through instrument and commercial training, would tell me that I was a real ace at landing the aircraft. I had many more take-offs and landings that any other low-hour pilot. In 10 hours of flying, I may have 75 take-offs and landings. I always thought that the most important thing was to have the exact same number of landings as you had take-offs!!!

OK, back to work! Well, not quite. One day the CINCPAC, (4-star) Admiral Wiesner, challenged my boss, Rear Admiral McClendon to a little game of golf. The J-3, a Marine Lt. General (3 star) would be the CINC's partner, and Admiral McClendon chose me, not because of my golf prowess---but because I probably had the highest golf handicap in all of J-5, around 28 I think. I don't think I had ever broken 90, and often shot over 100. He challenged me to play better than my handicap and we could win. I shot a *76. We won!* Well, my boss loved it. The CINC was a different story. He accused Admiral Mac of running in a ringer, a sandbagger, if you will. The 76 was not *the* story. *How* I shot the 76 was the story. I don't think I made a single green in regulation. I was bouncing balls off trees, skipping across water hazards, rolling through sand traps. At any moment I expected to see a squirrel run over and pick up my ball and take it to the hole (maybe it did a couple of times). I hit terrible shots but scored the best I have ever scored. I'm sure the bad shots, with the CINC as a witness, are the only reason he didn't kill me on the spot!

I enjoyed working in J-5 for a year, as much as you can enjoy staff and paperwork, but at the end of one year, I was asked if I would like to move to J-3, specifically down the mountain to Hickam Air Force Base to the CINCPAC Airborne Command Post. I jumped at the chance and it was a great assignment. When I left J-5, little did I know it would be my very last assignment as a staff officer. I was privileged to be in command assignments for the last 8 years I served in the Army! Wow!

"A soldier should be sworn to the patient endurance of hardships, like the ancient knights; and it is not the least of these necessary hardships to have to serve with sailors."

Field Marshal Montgomery

Hickam AFB, Hawaii, Battle Staff Commander, Blue Eagles, CINPAC Airborne Command Post

I became the Battle Staff Commander of Battle Staff Two in the Airborne Command Post. I replaced Army Colonel Joe Clemons, who was retiring. He was a Medal of Honor winner from the Korean War. Clint Eastwood played his part in "Heartbreak Ridge", the movie. He was a super guy. I had officers from the Army, Navy, Air Force and Marines, and a Sergeant from the Army on my Battle Staff as well as an Air Force Communications Crew of 8 or 10 enlisted Air Force personnel, and an Air Force Air Crew of Pilot, Co-pilot. Navigator, Engineer, and Refueling NCO. The entire Air Force communications and aircraft crew were really outstanding. It was obvious that they had been hand picked. So were the commissioned officers on the joint Battle Staffs. Of course, and as usual, the standard of excellence was set by our boss, Air Force Colonel Bob Shaw. The Colonel had been "Mr. Airborne Command Post", for SAC and other commands, was extremely well respected in this field, and I believe was close to being the senior Colonel in the Air Force. He should have been a General! He and his wife, Evie are great folks. We visited them in California, after we all retired.

The official name of the CINCPAC Airborne Command Post was the "Blue Eagles". We had unique, distinctive "uniforms" (double-knit, dress blue coveralls—my old 1st Sergeants would have died) with unit patches, etc. (Our unofficial name for them was "s___ hots"!) One day in an elevator up at Tripler Army Hospital, an old vet looked at me for a while and asked if I was in the Army (I *did* have on an Army nametag). I said "Yes sir". He then asked, "Whose?" There were five battle staffs in the airborne command post. I was the battle staff commander of Team Two. On my battle staff were Army Major Dick Stilwell, Air Force Major Bob Armstrong, Navy Lieutenant Commander Fred Lohden, Marine Major Larry Adams, Air Force First Lieutenant John Mc Pherson, and Army Sergeant First Class Bobby Anderson. They were my Emergency Action Officer, Logistic Officer, Operations Officer, Communications Officer, Intelligence Officer, and Emergency Action NCO. Later Army Major John Gritz joined our team. During our weeks at home base, Hickam Air Force Base in Honolulu, we worked a 48-hour week. As an example, we would report to the alert shack at Hickam on Tuesday morning at 0900 in the morning. We would routinely get off duty around 0900 on Thursday morning---that would be our 48-hour week. Then we would have several days off before our next 48-hour shift. Now, I don't want to make this sound too easy, or the government may be asking me to reimburse them for too much time off. There would often be other meetings, briefings, and functions that we attended, but the working hours were very good. I made up for all those 6 or 7-day weeks, 12 to 18 hours a day, the Army had squeezed out of me. I took Mama to the beach several days a week, did some woodworking at the craft shop, and continued with my private flying club activities. I rationalized it this way; we were getting paid, not only for what we did, but mostly for what we had the knowledge and were capable of doing, should the emergency situation present itself. All of my officers were required to take a written examination and be formally certified to be qualified in their positions. I had to take a written examination on *all of their jobs,* plus mine, to be formally certified to hold my job---unique in my 30 years in the service.

Without getting into classified information, obviously, the entire 48 hours that we were in the alert shack at Hickam, we were on 15 minute alert to launch our airplane. Our airplanes were EC 135 aircraft. The civilian version was (is) the Boeing 707, 4-engine jet aircraft. In the Air Force the C-135 was a cargo aircraft. The KC version was a refueling tanker. Our version, the EC, was an aircraft equipped with tons of electronic gear and very sophisticated communications equipment. We had to be able to communicate with the National Emergency Airborne Command Post, other major commands, and the National Command Authority (President, Vice President, SECDEF, etc). It was also capable of refueling other aircraft. The minimum alert standard was for us to be airborne in less than 15 minutes from when we got *the call*. And our command practiced this often---during the day and in the middle of the night. Each of my staff officers had their necessary information and gear in black bags, and on alert we kept them inside the aircraft. The aircraft was in a parking slot, just off a taxiway, and next to the alert building, and kept in a "cocked" position. All appropriate switches in the airplane were kept in the "on" position and there was a powder charge in one of the inboard engines, that would be set off to start the engine, (believe it or not) and subsequently start the other engines. When we taxied out to the runway, most of the time, the command would come over the radio, "Blue Eagle", and we would taxi back to the alert shack and secure the aircraft. What made the practice drills so realistic was that when we taxied out on to the runway, the command would often be, "cleared for take off", so you could not cheat. The aircraft had better be fully ready for take-off. On these occasions, we would fly in the local area for 4 hours and would practice sending Emergency Action Messages to other commands.

Under some very precise circumstances, we would be able to release strategic weapons against the enemy. We would have had to receive the proper authenticators from the National Command Authority (NCA), and the entire chain of events would always have to be under the "two man control" rule. It would have been impossible for any one individual to override the system. I carried the "red box" with 2 combination locks, and my NCO accompanied me with a sidearm. When we landed at another base, we locked the red box in the base operations Top Secret safe. Even so, if someone else opened the box, the information would have been useless to *him or her*. I could not imagine a system with more safeguards to prevent unauthorized use or disclosure of this information. When we would send practice Emergency Action Messages to strategic weapons commands, the standing order was that they would *not* answer. For operations security (op sec) reasons, they remained silent and later in the month, a report would be submitted verifying that they received the messages by date, hour and minute. During my military career, I worked with nuclear weapons on several occasions, and it is no coincidence that a nuclear accident never has occurred with these weapons that caused even a partial nuclear detonation. The safeguards built into the systems are awesome!

In addition to performing 15-minute alerts at Hickam AFB, we would deploy to other bases in the Pacific for 10 to 12 day deployments. These would occur about every two or three months, sometimes more often. A typical deployment would be from Hickam to Guam; Kimpo, Korea; Kadina, Okinawa; Clark AFB in the Philippines; Yokota, Japan; and sometimes, Australia, Taipei, and Diego Garcia in the Indian Ocean, In route, we would have a schedule of practice emergency action messages to be sent, staff training exercises, and on occasion we would train flag rank officers in the performance of Alternate Command Authority duties. We would usually stay overnight at these installations, sometimes two nights if we were to fly a local 4 or 6-hour mission in the area.

On one occasion, we were accompanied on a deployment by a Marine Lieutenant General from the Joint Chiefs of Staff. I was to give him Alternate Command Authority (ACA) training during the deployment. Initially, I explained to him the importance of keeping on our schedule, being very punctual for take-off times. I anticipated a possible problem, because everywhere we landed, the base commander would want to whisk him away for briefings, etc. I told the General that we had a schedule to keep, with messages to be sent at precise times to other commands, etc. Sure as shootin', on our first stop, a refueling stop on Guam, the base commander, trying to show him a day's worth of stuff in 2 hours, brought him back to our aircraft about 20 minutes late. Of course, we were all aboard, engines running, and I was standing down at the bottom of the steps. When the General approached me he apologized for being late. I saluted him, then squinted at him, and with a stern upper lip, I said, "No Sir, you are not late, but the rest of us screwed up and got here about 30 minutes too early, *and we promise we will not do that again*"! He said, "OK, OK, I got the message." He was never late for take-offs for the remainder of the deployment!

On one of my last deployments with the Blue Eagles, the Battle Staff Officers were reading an issue of the Pacific Stars and Stripes, and were amused about a story that a group of sailors had become lost when they tried to climb Mount Fuji in Japan at night. When we landed at Yokota AFB, Japan, we went over to the Officers' Club and continued discussing this subject. Somebody said, "Shucks, I'll bet we could do that!" Uh oh! We had a one-day layover there, so we proceeded to prepare for this adventure. Preparations consisted of loading some food in backpacks and striking out. We were not very well equipped to do mountain climbing. We were in our flight suits, and took field jackets, because even in August, we knew it would be cold on top. Footgear was athletic sneakers. I did not divulge to the group what I had packed in my backpack.

We literally hitchhiked to the base of Mount Fuji. We rode in everything from busses to taxis and the backs of trucks. We arrived before dark, and began our climb. Mount Fuji is a beautiful volcano. It is not just a peak in a ridge; it is a perfect cone shaped volcano that rises 12, 395 feet out of a reasonably flat area. We had bought "climbing sticks" with little bells (to prevent straying from the group) and Japanese flags attached. The beginning climbing station (gome) is where you get your walking stick, and begin your climb. The climb is very steep and strenuous. About one-half the way up, one of the NCOs could not make it any farther, and asked to be left and we would pick him up on the way down. We quickly agreed not to do that—we had started this as a team, and we were going to finish it as a team. We took turns carrying him up the mountain. It's a good thing we insisted on taking him with us, because we did not come back down the same way we went up---he may have still been up there! I will quote a passage from a brochure we were given:

"When you leave this station, you walk through weathered pine forests that quickly give way to a steep ledge of rough rocks. Look straight up. That's where you are going, where the trail winds up in erratic loops, each major turn dotted with a stone hut, where the chance to take a well-deserved breather and look around is provided (not much to see at night)". For a large part of the climb, we were below the clouds, and then we broke out of the clouds. The FAA mandates that when I'm flying one of my small, one engine (unpressurized) putt putt airplanes above 10,000 feet attitude, the law says I *must* be on 100% oxygen. Here we were over 12,000 feet. At that altitude, you take about 3 steps forward and then you stop for a few seconds and catch your breath. The big event----the highlight of the climb up Mt. Fuji, is seeing the sunrise over Japan, from the top of Fuji. On a bright morning, the sun pops up over the islands to the east and rises into a clear blue sky above the "land of the rising sun." A moment that goes far beyond picture postcard beauty, it is an experience that borders on elation!

There are several stations (gomes) along the way to the top, where you would encounter a little Japanese man, squatting beside a fire, and he would brand your octagonal walking stick with his station message & logo. I still have my walking stick and there are six brands on it, with six more closer to the base. The most cherished two brands read (in English), "TOP MOUNT FUJI, ALT 12,395 FT", and "SUNRISE, TOP MOUNT FUJI, 1978". As the sun rose, I opened my backpack and we all enjoyed a snack. I had packed two bottles of wine and two loaves of French-style bread. Coming down the volcano was much quicker that going up, obviously. We came down a different route, and I will again quote from the brochure: "The descent can be done in just about 3 hours by using the so-called slide---a very steep ledge of loose volcanic gravel on which you can stride, slide and slip almost like on a conveyor belt. But that takes some skill and a few careful tryouts first." Well, come on, we didn't *need* any more *skill* than we had, we were aces now, and didn't have time for any tryouts! We literally tumbled off that mountain. Coming down we would cover maybe 12 feet per (high speed) stride, and sink up past our (unprotected) ankles, each step. My ankles were black and blue for a month. The brochure recommends setting aside at least 24 hours for the climb. We did the whole gig in about 12 hours. I agree that you will be rewarded with a breathtaking (both literally and figuratively) experience. I now know a little bit about the motivation mountain climbers have for climbing. The feeling of elation and accomplishment even surprised me. But I agree with an old Japanese saying, "A wise man climbs Fuji once, only a fool climbs it twice"!

What a terrific assignment I had for a non aviator (official, at least), ground pounding Redleg, flying all over the Pacific area, on flight (hazardous duty) pay (it ain't the same), but yes, they did pay us extra for doing this! We were well aware that we represented the CINCPAC everywhere we went, so we acted accordingly. The Air Force had a neat rule. On a scheduled aircraft, where the occupants were known, (always on our aircraft), an Air Force Officer of equal *or higher* rank than the most senior officer on board must meet the aircraft. So I was always met by an Air Force Colonel or General. Since we were the CINCs aircraft, it was more often a General. I was embarrassed about this, but I got over it! He would hand me the keys to a sedan, and say, "see you tomorrow when you take-off. If you need anything, call me." In my experience in the military, frankly the Air Force seemed to take better care of their people, up and down the line, than the other services in many respects.

Major General Herb Wolfe was the commander at Fort Shafter, where we lived, and invited us to a party at his house on Palm Circle. He asked me to bring my trumpet. General Fred Weyand, former Army Chief of Staff was there and brought his clarinet and we terrorized the party. General Weyand's clarinet was given to him by Pete Fountain!! And he could play it!

Steve attended Moanalua High School for his last two years in high school, where he played first team soccer. When we left for Germany, Steve went to Murray State College in Kentucky, with another Army brat he was with in Hawaii, a Chaplain's son. We continued to ride our dirt bikes during our tour in Hawaii, riding through the pineapple fields up to the mountain ridgeline. It was very interesting, as we would round a corner and run into a herd of wild boar and other critters. Spectacular scenery. Sonja joined us initially in Hawaii, after graduating from Mount Vernon High school in Virginia, and attending her first college year at Radford College in Virginia. She attended Chaminade University in Honolulu for one semester, but her "Georgia roots' beckoned her back to Americus, Georgia, where she attended Georgia Southwestern University. After our three tours of duty in Georgia, Sonja *thought* she was from Georgia. At Southwestern, she met one Kevin Duggar, a classmate. They visited us in Hawaii and he proposed marriage to Sonja on Waikiki Beach. He did it the old fashioned way, asking my permission first, and I appreciated that.

We enjoyed many visits to Hawaii by kinfolks, friends, etc. My Aunt Bertie and Uncle Joe Howard came to visit and we enjoyed taking them all around the Island. Their daughter, Gloria and her husband Nathan Bray, also visited us, and I flew them around the Island of Oahu. We were also delighted that Katherine's Mom and Dad came for a visit. Katherine's brother, Happy also came and visited us.

Funny, we did not get that many visitors when we lived in Georgia! When we moved from Georgia to D.C. we got a lot of visitors, 25 sets of house guests in the first summer, but when we were sent back to D.C. for a second time, I didn't tell anybody---everybody thought we were still in Georgia.

We did not take Senator Beagle Dog or Goldwater Cat to Hawaii. The State of Hawaii had a law requiring the quarantining of pets for several months and we just did not want them to live in a kennel for so long. So at the end of our Pennsylvania assignment they were retired out in the country to Katherine's folks home in Louisiana and lived happily ever after.

On what was to be my last deployment with the Blue Eagles, although I did not know it was to be my last, we had landed at Kadina Air Force Base, Okinawa. At about 3 AM, I was sound asleep in my BOQ and the phone rang. I answered and the voice on the other end of the line said, "can you be in Germany next week?" To which I replied, "say what?" He said they needed an immediate replacement in Germany. I told him he had the wrong phone number, and that I was just a GI on a mission to Okinawa and it was 3 AM. He said, "Hoglan, 433-44-xxxx"? And I said, "Oh s---!" I had been fortunate enough to be selected for Brigade level (Colonel 06) command, and had been slated to serve my third year in Hawaii, then go to Fort Sill, Oklahoma and command the Missile Brigade there, which suited me just fine. I was really elated at being on the 06 command list, as it was very competitive. Since we had just completed our second year in Hawaii, we were looking forward to our third year in paradise. The assignment officer explained that a Field Artillery Commander in Germany, Bob Basha, had just been killed in a helicopter crash, along with several of his staff members. Another Colonel, Bill Sweet, who was on the command list, already in Germany, and scheduled to assume command of the 72nd FA Brigade, was immediately placed in command to replace Colonel Bob Basha. They now needed a back fill for the 72nd Brigade. My assignment officer explained that although the rules dictated if you turned down a command assignment, you were automatically removed from the command list, he stated that they realized they were "knee-jerking" me, and that if I turned down this assignment, I would remain in Hawaii another year and then go to Fort Sill for the missile brigade assignment as planned. But he said, "Curt, don't turn this one down— it is a great assignment!" Turned out to be an understatement!

I spent the next few hours in several phone conversations with Katherine back in Hawaii. She *really* wanted to stay another year (or ten!) in Hawaii, but as several of our friends know, she is still the best soldier in the Hoglan family, and I did not want to turn this assignment down, and we had never been assigned to Germany, so she agreed to take it. I called my assignment officer in Washington and told him I would take the job. We left Hawaii with 3 days leave en route to Germany. Remember now, when we left Pennsylvania for Hawaii, we put all winter clothes and most of our stuff in storage. We had already put most of our belongings in storage in Virginia before we left for the War College. Can you get the picture?---spending 3 years in Germany in Hawaiian short sleeved shirts? I don't think so. We were allowed to go over our storage inventory, and select specific boxes to be shipped to Germany. We picked out several boxes, as an example, one was marked "winter clothes". After we arrived in Germany and the boxes got there several months later, that one box had one sweater and a bunch of children's toys in it!

Normally, I would have attended several pre-command courses, and a six-month language school in Monterrey, California prior to going to Germany for brigade command. We had heard what a great language school it was, for example, if you were heading for Germany, you and your wife must sit in the German section of the Officers Club, and the waiters would only speak to you in German. You were just immersed in the language. Not to be for us. I was really disappointed about that. Although we were disappointed that our tour in paradise was curtailed from a 3-year to a 2-year assignment, it was a great experience and we thoroughly enjoyed our stay in Hawaii.

169

TWO

Wertheim, Germany, Brigade Commander 72nd Field Artillery Brigade

Goodbye (Aloha) Hawaii, hello (Guten Tag) Germany. We flew into the Rhine Main Airport in Frankfurt, and were met by Lieutenant Colonel Paul McKinney, the 72nd Brigade Executive Officer. The 72nd was located in Wertheim, Germany, just off the autobahn, between Aschaffenburg and Wurzburg, where the Main and Tauber Rivers join in northern Bavaria. Wertheim is a beautiful town of about 20,000 folks at the intersection of these rivers. Our Kaserne (military compound) was located on top of a high hill overlooking the town. It was named Peden Barracks after an Artillery soldier who was a Medal of Honor winner in WW II. Paul drove us to our temporary quarters, a small room above the Officers' Club. The current commander, Colonel Sid Davis, had not departed, therefore we could not move into the commanders' quarters for a while.

We had no car, since the quick orders did not allow me to ship it in advance. We did not receive it for quite a few weeks. I spent the next few days visiting the 4 Battalions in the Brigade, one at Peden Barracks, one in Aschaffensburg, and two in Bamberg, as well as our German counterpart unit, the 12th Panzer Division Artillery, located in Tauberbischoffsheim, a little south of Wertheim. I spent evenings studying my German phrase book. After a couple of weeks, I felt bold enough with my newly acquired German language capability, that we walked down the street to Volkenrot, a tiny village close by, and went into the only Gasthaus in town, The Rose. I spoke to the waiter and *proudly* said, "Guten Abend, herr ober, Kommen sie here, bitte, Wir haben hunger und durst. Ich mochta ein bier, ein glas wein, und swei wiener schnitzels, bitteshoen." He looked at me and said in perfect south Alabama English, "You want home fries or pomme frites with them schnitzels, boy?" Come on man, you don't how long I've been practicing these few words! Incidentally, the schnitzels were great---we were at once hooked on German food.

We were introduced to Walter and Gunilda (Guni) Schelauski. Guni was the President of the German American Club in the town. They were terrific. We would never be able to repay them for their hospitality and their introductions to the great people of Wertheim. In the next two years we were to spend many pleasurable hours of socialization with them and the citizens of Wertheim.

One of our first introductions to the citizens of Wertheim, was a "fest" in the town. Germany is noted for it's fests—they will celebrate taking out the garbage, just any excuse, but they really know how to do it right. This fest was held in Wertheim, and the opening ceremony was in Main Tauber Halle, a huge auditorium in Wertheim. Since I was the new commander of the Kaserne, they insisted that I wear my Army dress uniform (normal with the Germans) and be formally introduced to the public. The halle must have held a couple of thousand people, and I was introduced by Walter Schelauski.

The hard-core custom was for Americans to make some remarks in German. My speech in German was literally unforgettable---at least the Germans never let me forget it! For me, I wanted it to be forgettable! I said, "Guten Abend, meine Damen und Herren. Danke Shoen, Auf Wiedershen!" (Good Evening, my ladies and gentlemen. Thank you, and goodbye)! People just cheered, and I began to wonder just what I had said! I was to repeat that speech many times in the future---my German friends teased me about it, no end. Anyway, after my introduction and splendid speech, Walter walked over to the edge of the stage, and walked back to me and handed me a trumpet! Until this day, I have no idea how he knew I had ever played the trumpet. The crowd got really quiet. They were wondering what in the world was going to happen. So was I. I looked over at the German Um-pah band on the edge of the stage, and they looked at me. They didn't speak any English, and I had just uttered every word of German that I knew. I did *not* want to order a schnitzel at this moment! Just as I began to hyper-ventilate, and was considering faking a heart attack, it came to me, thankfully. (Have we been here before?) I said "Saints Go Marchin' In??" They grinned and said "Jawold, Jawold!" We ripped it. The Universal Language. I was saved once again.

This was such a fantastic assignment, and we have so many great memories, I must resist the temptation to write another 100 pages about it. In addition to commanding the four Battalions mentioned above, I was responsible for a Military Community. We were technically a "sub-community" to the larger military community in Wurzburg, but don't let anybody in our community hear you say, "sub"-community. We weren't *sub* to anybody. On my Kaserne, I had family housing (stairwells as well as single-family housing), Post Exchange (PX), Commissary, Chapel, Elementary School, Gymnasium, airfield, troop barracks, community center, medical clinic, rod and gun club, and bowling alley. I had everything that a major military installation had, just on a smaller scale compared to some others. Most of us "killers" (combat arms officers) may not admit to this, but I enjoyed being the Community Commander as much as being the Tactical Commander of the four Field Artillery Battalions, maybe even more. And I really tried to take good care of my community.

One of the reasons that I really enjoyed being the Wertheim Community Commander was that I had the best Deputy Community Commander on the planet Earth. Herv Reviere (and his sweet wife, Nancy) was an outstanding officer and performed all his many duties in an outstanding manner!

Since I wore two "hats", I had two bosses. My tactical boss was Brigadier General Vince Falter, an outstanding officer and commander. He was in Augsburg, down south, not far from the VII Corps headquarters in Stuttgart. My indorsing Officer (Vince's boss) was Major General George Patton, III, and later, MG Will Latham. The Corps Commander was Lieutenant General Julius Becton, a super soldier, and one of the best senior bosses I ever had. My community boss in Wurzburg was Major General R. Dean Tice, and later Major General Sam Wetzel. General Tice was a trip. He was also the Division Commander of the 3rd Infantry Division (the Marne Division, famous for the battle of the Marne in WW I.) Since the 10th Artillery was the "Rock of the Marne" Regiment, we had a special bond. He made every soldier in the division sing the division song, as well as those of us outside the

Division (since they made me a "Marne Assn. soldier for life", I was not "outside"). But I had to stand in front of his desk and sing "Dogface Soldier" the division theme song. Let's see if I remember it:

I wouldn't give a bean, to be a fancy pants Marine,
I'd rather be a dogface soldier like I am.

I wouldn't trade my old ODs for all the Navy dungarees,
For I'm the walking pride of Uncle Sam.

On all the posters that I read, it says the Army builds men.
Well, they're tearing me down to build me over again.

I'm just a dogface soldier, with a rifle on my shoulder,
And I eat raw meat for breakfast every day.

So pass the ammunition, keep me in the 3rd Division,
Your dogface soldier boy's OK.

(Approximately! If I screwed it up, forgive me General Tice, it's been 28 years, you know!)

One perk I enjoyed by being a separate brigade commander, was to be invited to attended the Corps Commander's (LTG Becton) Conferences, as well as those held by the Commander in Chief, U.S. Army Europe (CINCUSAEUR). General Kroesen. At General Becton's first command briefing he told us his command philosophy and also explained his new policy of *not* losing leave time. It was almost a tradition that commanders in particular, would lose many days of leave every year because they were *"just too busy"* to take the 30 days. I had fallen into this trap and lost the full 30 days on several occasions. One of General Becton's good friends had been a workaholic, consistently lost most of his leave days, then retired and intended to get reacquainted with his family, only to die shortly thereafter. General Becton stated that his policy was that **nobody in VII Corps** would lose any leave.

The two heavy hitters (2-star division commanders) sitting down in the front row looked at each other and snickered. General Becton added that he expected commanders to set the example, and that *any* commander that did not take a full 30 days leave every year, would be standing in front of his desk, trying in vain to explain the matter to him! He was dead serious. He explained that it was not a requirement that the 30 days be taken all at once and that taking about one week, every 3 months worked well for him. He further stated that if your unit could not operate for a week or two without your hand at the helm, he would indicate on your report card that you had not adequately trained it. How could anyone argue with that?? In combat, if the commander were killed, would the unit just fold? Not if the commander had trained it properly! Not only did I, of course, abide by this policy in my brigade in VII Corps, when I went to V Corps I immediately made it V Corps Artillery policy. The V Corps Commander saw my policy statement, liked it, and made it the firm policy throughout V Corps. A highlight of this assignment was getting to know my counterpart in the German Army. At this time, every American unit had a German counterpart unit. This was a great idea and it was mutually beneficial to both units. My counterpart was Oberst (Colonel) Fritz Kunze, my "brother". He commanded the 12th Panzer Division Artillery in Tauberbishofsheim, a town south of Wertheim. We exchanged visits many times, spent much time in the field together with our units, and socialized a great deal with his officers and wives and our officers and wives. We challenged them in all kinds of activities, to include, volleyball, softball, track and field, rifle competition---they almost always won. I had a skeet range on my Kaserne and we thought we had finally found a sport we could win at, until I saw the skeet trophies in their trophy case. I think we finally won a skeet match. Their hospitality was unbelievable. Try as we did, we could not match their hospitality and hosting of all kinds of events. It was a great relationship for me personally and for our units. Fritz and his Frau (wife), Margaret remain dear friends today and we correspond with them. His boss was Major General Altenburg, Commander of the 12th Panzer Division. I would meet him again in the future. Colonel Kunze retired from the German Army in Koblenz, as a Brigadier General. They would spend 2 or 3 weeks in their casa (villa) on the Mediterranean coast in Spain (Torredembara) every late summer. Germans put their vacations high on their priority list. They invited us to come spend a week or so with them. We did. We had a great time, and looking through their guest book, and talking with them, we discovered that we were the only Americans they had ever invited to their vacation home on the Spanish Riviera.

My battalions had as their partners the battalions in the 12th Panzer Division Artillery, so the partnership went up and down the line of organizations. There were many advantages to this arrangement, from improving our collective war fighting capability, to facilitating communications, and having fun while we were doing it. Like most Europeans, the Germans place more emphasis on being multilingual than most Americans do. But I rarely could get Fritz to speak German with me----he wanted to practice his English.

Another highlight of this assignment was being a member of our local German/American club. Guni Schelauski, our president, ably assisted by her husband Walter, insured that we had a very *active* club. Quite a few of the local prominent citizens of Wertheim were members, including Prince and Princess von Lowenstein, Dr. Gerhard and Annamarie Prager, and Oberburgermeister (Lord Mayor) Karl Josef Scheuermann. The Lord Mayor recently called Katherine to wish her a happy birthday, and Guni continues to call and send birthday cards to us, including our kids, every year. Unfortunately, Walter has died, and Guni grieves for him tremendously. Annamarie and Gerhard Prager were very good friends of ours. Gerhard was a dentist and sadly, died recently. Some of the activities Guni promoted were wine probes (visiting wineries locally and as far away as Trier in the Mosel Valley), picking grapes in the grape vineyards, visits to unique manufacturing sites (for example, glass blowing). What I admired about Guni was that she was also helpful to our young married enlisted couples, showing them where to go for what ever they needed around town, etc. Karen Walker, a German lady married to an American, Jerry Walker, was my Civilian Personnel Officer. They have visited with us here in Florida on several occasions. Monica Deville was my translator and speechwriter and we remain good friends. We have visited Wertheim twice since leaving our tour of duty. It was sad to visit Peden Barracks. The Kaserne is closed now, like many, if not most American military kasernes in Germany, and has been converted for other uses. Bernie Speilmann was a local wine producer and also taught our youngsters gymnastics. On a subsequent trip back to Wertheim, he took us to his grape vineyards and also had a party for us at his house. Our association with the German military and with the local German population in Wertheim made this an unforgettable experience. We made many pleasant memories with many new friends.

Early in our tour, we discovered Garmisch, a beautiful little town in southern Bavaria. Every winter wonderland postcard ever made must have been made in Garmisch. It was also beautiful in summer, but in the winter, with fresh snow everywhere, it was awesome. During our 4 years in Germany, we visited Garmisch 18 times. Steve came over and visited us and we spent one week skiing in Garmisch every Christmas season for 4 years. Mama didn't take to the slopes too well, and she pretty much stayed on the "bunny slope", but Steve and I took classes every year. By the second year, ole Hans had us coming down the *big* slopes like champion Alpine skiers (well, mostly)! We got past "snowplow" turns in the first 30 minutes of the first lesson. At the end of each day, we were pretty much dead soldiers.

Sonja came over and joined us for our first Christmas in Garmisch. Dick and Mary Noack, previously XO in our battalion at Fort Benning, were stationed at Herzo Base, near Nurnburg. Dick was commanding a Lance Missile Battalion there. They invited us down for a visit during Kriskrindle Mart in Nurenburg. We had a great time, but Sonja, Steve, and Katherine say that is the coldest they had ever been. Only the great bratwurst and hot Gluwein saved us from frostbite! In Garmisch, the U.S. Army had several R & R hotels, including the General Patton, where we usually stayed. This was especially beneficial to the young soldiers and families. Living on the Germany economy was quite expensive, because of the unfavorable monetary exchange rate.

As usual, another reason this was such a great assignment, is that I was surrounded by outstanding officers, LTC Paul McKinney, Brigade XO and Major Hervie Riviera, Assistant Community Commander. My operations officer was Major Arturo Rodriguez.-- more about this outstanding officer and his wife, Argie later. Outstanding Battalion Commanders were LTC Joe Britton (and wife Ruth), LTCs Bob Castleman, Jerry Granrud, John Lefebvre and Jack Garven. Joe Britton's battalion was at Peden Barracks, and the other battalions were in Aschaffenburg, and Bamberg. Ruth Britton was the head of our youth program at Peden Barracks and President of the wives club. We correspond with them often. I had a great Command Sergeant Major, Bruno Schacht. He and his wife, Margaret are retired in Washington State and we keep in touch at Christmas time.

In June of 1979, Katherine went to Americus, Georgia to assist in Sonja's wedding plans. I followed shortly thereafter, and we attended her college graduation and wedding. She was a beautiful bride and Kevin Duggar was the handsome groom. At the reception after the wedding, several of our friends from Fort Benning and Columbus attended, and among them were General and Mrs. Steele, my "old" Brigade Commander in the 197th Infantry Brigade at Benning. It was great seeing them, and someone mentioned to him that we were having a little problem renting a car to go from Americus to Louisiana and then turning in the car in Louisiana and flying back to Germany. He came up to me and asked me to hold out my hand. He handed me car keys and told me that he would ride back to Columbus with another couple from Columbus. I told him that I couldn't do that to which he replied that he was not asking me, he was *telling* me what we were *going to do!* He said I was to take his Cadillac, drive to their house in Columbus when we were ready to leave Americus. Then we would swap vehicles, and we would take his RV down to Destin, Florida for a few days R & R, and then to Louisiana. He said that the RV knew the route very well, since he commanded the 5th Mechanized Division at Fort Polk, Louisiana, and had traveled this route many times. He said just put it on Automatic Pilot and it would find the way. What can I say? I saluted with both hands, I think. After visiting the beach in Destin, where we met Sonja and Kevin on their honeymoon, we visited in Louisiana, and then drove back to the Steele's home in Columbus, Georgia. He took us to the airport, and then asked if there was anything else he could do for us. I told him that I kinda liked the shirt he was wearing---he said I could have anything but Ginny! What a great couple. They have visited us in Florida and we keep in touch. Unfortunately, Ginny passed away and we all grieve for her. She was a great, sweet lady! We saw Bill at a briefing we attended at Fort Benning last year and he is doing OK.

In August of 79, Katherine and I took an American Express bus tour, 10 days through Italy. It was a great trip, and when we got to Rome, we stayed and visited with Hardy and Katie Rose. You remember my buddy from dance band days at Northwestern State. Hardy was the Defense and Naval Attaché in the American Embassy in Rome. He had flown 257 combat strikes in the A4 Skyhawk from the aircraft carriers Ranger and Constellation as a Naval Aviator in Vietnam, and had been the Executive Officer on the USS Forrestal. Hardy got us tickets to see Verdi's opera Aida, in the ancient Roman Coliseum no less. Awesome! We had played the theme song from Aida a zillion times at Northwestern. You remember it, Daaah, Da Da Da Dah Dah Dah, Da Da Da Dah Da Dah!. I'm sure you do! We had enjoyed the trip to Italy and especially the visit with Hardy and Katie.

In December 79 Steve visited us again and we went to Paris. Did some sightseeing, almost had our pockets picked in the subway (which is almost required), and enjoyed street corner crepes, cooked to order. I agree with Louis Grizzard, once you visit a restaurant in Paris, and get insulted by a haughty French waiter, you 'bout done Paris. New Years eve in Paris was a little wild.

January, back to Garmisch for another glorious ski week. In February, Katherine and I teamed up with the Williams' for a trip to London. LTC Gene Williams was a Maintenance Battalion Commander whose battalion headquarters was at Peden Barracks. His subordinate units were spread all over the VII Corps. We had several tenant units at Peden that were not under my tactical command. I had a special relationship with Gene; we were in love with the same woman! His sweet wife, Mary Lou, was my personal secretary, in the Brigade Headquarters. She was a great secretary, and is a super lady. They were close friends with Guni and Walter and were very active members of our German/American club. They live in Solado, Texas, near Fort Hood, remain dear friends, and we visited them last year. (They are to visit us this week!————————They did!)

In May, we were invited by my "brother" and German counterpart, Oberst Fritz Kunze and Margaret to spend a week with them in their casa (villa) on the Spanish Riviera. We had a wonderful vacation, and visited little villages in the surrounding area.

In June we drove to Oberamagau and attended the famous, all day "Passion Play". It is only performed once every 10 years, so we were fortunate to be in Germany when it was presented. The town is also noted for its arts and crafts. Every carved wood product must have been made there.

I have procrastinated long enough. The following is an interesting, but not so pleasant experience I went through while I was the commander of the 72nd Brigade in Wertheim. We had a newspaper, the Valley View, and I was the publisher as the commander of our little community. A new soldier was assigned to the headquarters with a Public Information Military Occupational Specialty (MOS). Obviously, he was assigned to produce our newspaper, under the supervision of my S-1, Captain Jerry Jobe. One day soon, Jerry came running into my office, and showed me a copy of the newspaper our new "editor" had published. It was scathing attack on our community, and our female soldiers in particular. He was very militant, with a chip on his shoulder and a very bad attitude. That is OK, if he kept it to himself, but his biases have no right to be included in our community newspaper. He claimed that the female soldiers were little more than whores and then it went downhill. It would clearly have undermined the morale of my entire community, and it was *not true!* Well, I went ballistic---I think I mentioned earlier, I'm not calm, cool, and collected, when excited, and I got excited. I asked Jerry how many copies had been produced and where were they? He said, 3,000 and they were all in his safe. I asked him to bring me 3 copies and then I told him to take the remaining 2, 997 out to the (S-2) Intelligence Officers' classified document burn barrel and burn all of them!

The word got out, quickly. I sent copies to my chain of command, including my Indorsing Officer, Major General Will Latham, now the Deputy VII Corps Commander (remember him from Fort Benning days?—I told you he would save my life in Germany---now was the time!) The word spread, and even the Sergeant Major in the Office of Information in the Pentagon wrote in their newsletter about "a commander in Germany" who had burned a newspaper and likened me to Hitler burning books. Several senior officers were "what iffing me" and "why didn't you tell us in advance", and "why did you *burn* the copies", etc. I could read between the lines, and here is how I interpreted what they were all saying; "Curt, lightning is going to strike you, and if I am standing too close to you, I am going to get burned bad, so you are on your own!" In short, I was dead meat!!

Then I got a call from MG Latham. In his normal quiet manner, he asked how things were going. I told him not so well and that I felt like I was way out on a limb and everybody was sawing on it. He said, and I will paraphrase, "Curt, you did *exactly* what I would have expected you to do. I would have been disappointed if you had done anything different. According to Army regulations (and he quoted them), *you* are the publisher of that newspaper, and in the Army regulations, there is no such thing as "freedom of the press". If you, as the publisher, think there is anything in it that would be detrimental to your command, you are completely within your right to withhold distribution and burn it if you want to. The USAEUR Information Officer, Lyle Barker will call you and tell you that the regulations back you up. One more thing, *nobody* is going to hang you over this unless they walk over my broken body first! And I just went in and told the Corps Commander, Lieutenant General Julius Becton that, and he agrees with me"!

Now, I have probably stated this a little more dramatically than he did. I told you I'm a wing flapper and he is cool, but the effect is the same. He saved me. This "mean little SOG" that I met at Fort Benning earlier, is about 12 feet tall in my book.

Back to the pleasant, fun times. On one of our many (18) trips to Garmisch, we were in a PX, trying on clothes as I remember, and we looked up and saw, one Hardy Rose! We had another great visit and reunion. Later, Hardy and Katie Rose visited us in Wertheim and went with us on a German/American trip to Trier in the Mosel Valley. So Hardy and Katie knew Guni and Walter. Do you think maybe Hardy and I were joined at the hip? After we both had retired from military service, we had another great visit when we attended a Demonaires Dance Band reunion at Northwestern, and, naturally, got our axes (horns) out and terrorized the jazz band with a little "Saints" and other assorted hymns. I have told Hardy that he appears in my autobiography almost as many times as I do!

One of the activities that we enjoyed in Germany was going on Volksmarches. It is the national pastime. A ten to twenty kilometer track (trail) is designated for the participants to walk. They traditionally go through some of the most picturesque scenery in Germany. Every village sponsors one or more per year. Every four or five kilometers, a rest stop is set up with libations and bratwurst. At the end of the march, everyone gathers in the tent for more snacks, drinks, and usually listens to a live German band. Large medals are given out to all who complete the event, and your logbook gets stamped. We each have twenty-five or thirty of the beautiful medals somewhere.

We attended Oktoberfest in Munich several times. Katherine loved the whole chickens on a rotisserie grill. On one occasion we were riding the "largest ferris wheel in the world" with my Command Sergeant Major Schacht. We were looking down at hundereds of thousands of people and I noticed he had a troubled look and I asked him what was wrong. He said. "Sir, just look down there---a couple hundred thousand civilians, and nobody's in charge!" Just like a CSM!!

I have summarized many of the pleasant experiences and fun times we had in this two-year assignment. As I read over it, one may get the impression that it was all play and no work. I want to assure you that there was plenty of serious work, field maneuvers, artillery firing at Graf where you were either up to your knees in mud or snow (sometimes both), taking care of and training soldiers, etc., but it is much more interesting and fun to relate the fun times. *And it **was** fun, (even the firing at Graf)!!*

And hopefully, it is more interesting and entertaining to the reader if I skip over the hard work, which can be boring to read about, and concentrate on the more interesting and entertaining experiences that we had. Great memories!

Curt & Aero Club Beach Sierra

Battle Staff Two, Blue Eagles & EC 135

BS Two, Ready to Climb Mt. Fuji, Japan

Curt & Trumpet, Festival in Germany

Curt, Katherine, and Sonja Wedding

Chapter Six

THE GENERAL OFFICER YEARS AND FAREWELL TO ARMS

ONE

Frankfurt, Germany, Commanding General, V Corps Artillery

Toward the end of my two-year assignment as 72nd FA Brigade Commander, I was contacted by Lieutenant General Willard Scott, V Corps Commander in Frankfurt and asked to come to see him. I did and he interviewed me about becoming his Corps Artillery Commander. Although the slot had been filled by a Colonel for quite awhile, he was interested in getting it back in the hands of a Brigadier General, which was what the Table of Organization (TO) slot called for.

Brigadier General Vince Falter, CG, VII Corps Artillery Commander had recommended me for the job, as well as Major General Latham, and Lieutenant General Becton (not *puny* guys to have on your side). My assignment guys back in the Office of Personnel, Washington, D.C. also supported me. General Scott was a noted Field Artilleryman, and an outstanding officer, leader, and gentleman. His sweet wife, Dusty, was a jewel. Now, I was a Colonel and had not been selected for promotion to Brigadier General. I told General Scott that I did not have a clue if I would be on a promotion list since that was completely out of my hands, and of course, he knew that. At that level, the odds are pretty fierce, particularly for *a country boy from Pitkin!* But I told him that if he would take a chance on me, I would give the job my best shot, promotion or not. He hired me. Another command. I was elated.

My office and staff were in the Corps Headquarters, the Abrams Building, in Frankfurt. I had two FA Brigades under my command: the 41st at Babenhausen under the command of an outstanding officer, Colonel Gus Cianciolo. Lots of other folks must have also thought he was outstanding. He later retired as a Lieutenant General. His wife, Sheila was an outstanding asset to the Army as well. The other Brigade was in Giessen, commanded by Colonel Bob Clewell, ably assisted by his wife, Sue, another outstanding couple. The 8 battalions in these two brigades were scattered around V Corps area of operations (AO). All 8 battalion commanders were fine officers and superb leaders. Among them were LTCs Jim Chapman, Kelly O'Malley, Jack Reavill, Ed Carlson, Stan Whitmore, Mike Brokovich, Bob Brown, Jim Reynolds, Bob Castleman, and Joe Nickens. Just surround yourself with outstanding leaders and you will be successful. Another truism is that when it comes to bosses, you win with a winner and you lose with a loser. Although you seldom get to pick your bosses, occasionally you can influence that. Not all "*my*" losers were those retired on active duty (ROAD) Captains that I worked for in the early years. I can remember a couple of Generals that I would not want to work for again, but I will not mention them by name. They were more interested in themselves than they were the troops. That was very, very unusual. Almost all senior officers I met in the Army were really outstanding officers, leaders, and men!

My Deputy and Chief of Staff was Colonel Mike Daley. Mike was one of the most outstanding soldiers I ever served with. He was clearly the smartest and had a PHD in Nuclear Physics from Tulane. But he also had more than his share of common sense. My staff thought he was a master magician. I *knew* he was. He had commanded a battalion in Germany, and had extensive experience that made him a superb officer. Mike lives in Carlisle, Pennsylvania and we correspond frequently. We visited with him last year. We also had some outstanding officers on our staff: Lieutenant Colonels Bill Ryan (& Carol) and Bob Brown (& Lenora), Ed Irick (& Carol), from 2/10th days at Benning, Mike Mountain, Ted Coberly, and Jimmy Kilpatrick, to name a few. My outstanding Aide de Camp was Captain Mike Sweet. He and Vicky were outstanding assets to me and the command. My Command Sergeant Major was Frank Venagas, and later, CSM James Edwards.

We lived in a military housing complex in Bad Vilbel, a small town just outside of Frankfurt. General Scott and Dusty were our neighbors, as well as Brigadier General Gene Stillions and wife Gin. We were (and are) good friends with the Stillions. He commanded the V Corps

Support Command, with units scattered much like my units. When he departed, he was replaced by BG Ken Lewi (& Jean). One of the Deputy Corps Commanders while we were there was Major General Phil Feir (and wife, Mary Deane), with 3 great kids. On one trip to Berlin, we hung out with Mary Deane as we toured East Berlin. We hear from them at Christmas, when Phil writes their annual Christmas letter poem. It's usually hilarious. We were also together one Christmas in Garmisch, skiing the slopes. Another close neighbor and one of my all time favorite Field Artillerymen was Brigadier General Joe Owens, V Corps Chief of Staff. Glen Watson replaced him when Joe departed Germany.

When I commanded the 72nd Brigade, one of my four battalions was a Lance Missile Battalion, in Aschaffenburg. Now, in V Corps, I had two Lance Battalions. There were no firing ranges large enough in Germany or anywhere on land in Western Europe to accommodate the live firing of Lance missiles. So the battalions would go to the Greek Island of Crete, and fire from the NATO Missile Firing Installation (NAMFI) into a restricted area in the Mediterranean Sea. I had visited NAMFI several times with my Lance battalion in the brigade, before moving to V Corps, and accompanied my two Corps Artillery battalions for several more firings. In fact, I visited there a total of nine times in four years, for our Lance missile firings. NAMFI was a NATO command and was commanded by a Greek Major General John Mastigakis. John was a wild man, and we got to be very good friends. He would take us to his officers club and also go with us to eat out on the economy. Our favorite restaurant was rather austere, had a dirt floor, but also had the best swordfish steaks on the planet.

In August of 1980, we received a phone call from our daughter, Sonja, and she told us she was pregnant. I let out a rebel yell you could have heard back in Georgia. I was ready to be a Grandpa! But, Katherine protested mildly and said that she was not ready to be a Grandma. Sonja replied that she *was not asking* for permission, she was *telling* us the facts. I told Katherine that I could only think of one thing bad about this new development, and that was that after the birth of our granddaughter (I ordered a girl), I would have to sleep every night with an old Grandma. She replied and I quote verbatim (some things you don't ever forget), "You don't *have* to GI, you *can* sleep in the garage!"

End of that conversation! We made up on a river excursion on the Rhine River Enflamen and a driving trip to Austria. Once a year a special event occurs on the Rhine River. Fires and mirrors are set up outside all the castles along the Rhine River, and from boats, it looks like all the castles are on fire. It ends with a spectacular fireworks display in Koblenz, where the Rhine and Mosel rivers meet.

In October, we visited Berlin, East and West and stayed with our all time favorite Chaplain, Bob Bell and Anne. We crossed the border at Checkpoint Charlie and witnessed first hand what a bankrupt system was in place in East Berlin. In West Berlin, folks were driving Mercedes, and BMWs and the gasthauses were filled with Germans, singing with music and beer flowing. In East Berlin, it was eerily quiet, no music, no laughter, and the few cars were made out of plywood (the termites are going to eat your car), and have one-cylinder engines that sounded like Briggs and Stratton lawn mowers. And we were told that this was the "showcase of Eastern Europe". I just do not understand how such a bankrupt system lasted as long as it did. I attribute its demise to the communications revolution. The Eastern Europeans had been told for so long that they had it made, and then the word got out. Man, did it ever get out!

In January of 1981, surprise, surprise, Curt came out on the Brigadier General promotion list. Whoopee! But more importantly, on 17 March, our first grand daughter, Jennifer, was born in Americus, Georgia. Katherine was present at the scene. Now, we had picked out names for the grand kid(s) to call us. I wanted to be called Opa (German for Grandpa), and Katherine wanted to be called "Mommie Kay". (She steered away from Grandma or Granny). Little did we know that what *we* wanted to be called did not matter in the slightest. More about what we were named, when, and by whom, a little later. We were just so happy that Jennifer was a beautiful and healthy baby, *and I got the girl I had ordered!* I was sure she would be a beauty queen and she was! In fact, President Jimmy Carter gave her the trophy in the Miss Peanut contest in Plains, Georgia about 18 years later.

In February 1981, I attended a General Officer Orientation Course in Washington, D.C. This "Charm School" was to prepare all the new Brigadier Generals for the wonderful things to follow, etc. It worked for some, better than the rest of us! I had several close friends in the class, including my friends and War College classmates, Pete Dawkins, Al Wheeler, Jim Shelton, Hank Skeen, Don Rogers, Don Phil, Fred Hissong, and Gerry Bethke Good year..

In May, Katherine's brother, Harold ("Happy") Elliott visited us in Germany. He had been stationed in Germany years before and spent time in Lebanon during that crisis. We visited in Trier, Luxembourg, Verdun, and Paris. We also took Happy to Garmisch and Berchesgaden. On 16 June, I attended a senior commanders' conference at Fort Sill, Oklahoma and took a few days leave and visited in Louisiana and Georgia. In July, Steve arrived in Germany for another visit, and stayed for several months.

On 1 October, I was promoted to Brigadier General. My two Brigades held a great troop formation in Babenhausen, and the V Corps Commander promoted me. He pinned on one star and Katherine pinned on the other one! We had many German friends attend the ceremony. A large delegation from Wertheim attended, including many of our German/American Club friends, and Prince and Princess Von Lowenstein.

Remember, back at Ft Benning, when I was a major at the Infantry School, I said that a friend of mine on the Infantry School faculty was Marine Lieutenant Colonel P.X. Kelly. Well, we sorta kept track of each other, and when I was promoted to Brigadier General, he was the Commandant of the Marine Corps (4 star General---the man did good, deservedly). He sent me congratulations on my promotion, and enclosed a copy of a story he thought would be appropriate. It read as follows:

At the battle of Waterloo, Colonel Clement, an Infantry commander, fought with the most conspicuous bravery, but unfortunately was shot through the head. Napoleon, hearing of his gallantry and misfortune, gave instructions for him to be carried into a farm where Larrey the surgeon-general was operating. One glance convinced Larrey that his case was desperate, so taking up a saw he removed the top of his skull and placed his brains on the table. Just as he had finished, in rushed an aide-de-camp, shouting: "Is General Clement here?" Clement, hearing him, sat up and exclaimed: "No, but Colonel Clement is." "Oh, mon General," cried the aide, embracing him, "the Emperor was overwhelmed when he heard of your gallantry, and has promoted you on the field of battle to the rank of General." Clement rubbed his eyes, got off the table, clapped the top of his skull on his head and was about to leave the farm, when Larrey shouted after him: "Mon General----your brains!" To which the gallant Frenchman, increasing his speed, shouted back: "Now that I am a General I shall no longer require them!" ("Generalship—its Diseases and Their Cure" by Major General J.F.C. Fuller)

CINCUSAEUR, General Kroesen, had a written policy that new BGs were to call his XO and make an appointment to come visit him. I did. The XO at that time was Colonel Joe House. We were together for a couple of assignments after that and Joe and Sue remain good friends. When I went for my office visit with General Kroesen, he welcomed me, and told me that since I was not new to the command and had already been there about 3 years, he did not need to explain any policies to me. He just wanted to know my thoughts about all aspects of the command. WOW! It's not often a 4-star CINC wants to know what *I think!* But that is the way General Kroesen is. I have so much respect for this man. He enlisted in the Army as a buck private and retired as a four star General. Not many can say that, and he was (is) universally respected. His commanders' briefings were great and sometimes funny. He had a terrific sense of humor, as well as a very strong bladder. During the briefings, only after his senior commanders were red in the face, squirming with their legs crossed, etc, would he finally announce *"a whiz break for you older fellers!"* Norm Schwarzkopf was a Brigadier General and good friend and also attended the briefings. We laughed at the "older fellers"! Then we whizzed!

A perk we received, because of my promotion, was a "VIP" trip to Berlin on the CINC's train. General Gene Stillions and his wife Gin, went with us. I knew it was going to be a first class trip, when the steward called me, said he was going grocery shopping, and wanted to know what we would like to eat on the train. He recommended the chateaubriand for two as one meal, and I told him that would be fine, along with anything else he recommended. When we reached the East German border, we had to stop for a couple of hours while they adjusted the train wheels, because the track gauge (size-width) changes between

East and West Germany. When we arrived in Berlin, Gene and I received classified briefings on the Berlin Brigade and other pertinent subjects. Then we had a helicopter ride at low level, over-flying the Berlin Wall. The ladies then joined us for a driving tour of Berlin and several segments of the Berlin Wall. It was during this driving tour that I experienced the crowning achievement of my military career-------*I urinated on the Berlin Wall!* And I have pictures and 3 witnesses to prove it! (well, at least 2 that admit it). Most satisfying "whiz" I ever had!

In May, Katherine and I took some leave time, and checked into Ramstein AFB for space-available flights. We flew to Torrejon AFB, Spain, and visited several areas in Spain. We had contacted Manuel Gordo, remember the Spanish Captain we had sponsored at the Infantry School at Fort Benning years ago, and let him know we were coming to Spain. He had invited us many times. He was now a Brigadier General and was assigned to the Spanish Army Headquarters in Madrid. He met us and we traveled by car to the northern border of Spain. He had several assignments at the mountain ranger school in northern Spain and they had continued to live in Jaca. It was on the southern slopes of the Pyrenees Mountains. Over the mountain was France. His beautiful wife, Charo welcomed us into their home and we were treated like a King and Queen. We visited in the area, including an old castle, complete with a dried up moat where deer were lounging around. After a few wonderful days, Manuel drove us back to Madrid and we grabbed a flight to Athens, Greece.

This was one of our first experiences in space-A flying. The main thing about it is, you can't have a fixed schedule of where and when you want to go somewhere. You just take a flight wherever it is going. It was a fun trip. After arriving in Athens, we visited the normal tourist attractions, the ancient Greek buildings, Parthenon, etc. Since I had already visited the island of Crete 9 times for my missile firings, I wanted to take Katherine there. So we bought air tickets and flew from Athens to Crete. My buddy, Major General John Mastigakis met us and the fun started. John threw a big party for us at his home and tried to teach Katherine some Greek dances. He also took us to the firing range and Katherine was able to observe missile firings by the Lance, Hawk, and Nike Hercules missiles. She also got to eat a swordfish steak at our favorite "dirt floor" restaurant. We toured the island, and met an old gentleman that loved Americans---he said he was liberated from the Germans by the Americans. It was a wonderful trip.

Once during this assignment, I had to pick up a visitor at the train station in Frankfurt. One of the very first things you learned in the "Gateway" language course that was required if you had not attended language school (and I took Gateway One three times!), was how to ask directions. All my German friends would tease me about it, and greet me with, "Vo ist der bahnhof?" (Where is the train station?). On this occasion, my driver, Sp-4 Danny Lucas, and I left the Abrams building heading for the train station. Each one of us thought the other knew where it was, but we discovered that neither of us knew. I saw an elderly man walking along the sidewalk with his cane, and I told my driver to pull over. I rolled down the window, and said, "Entschuldigen Sie bitte, Vo ist der bahnhof." (Excuse me please, where is the train station?") The old German gentleman looked at me and said, "Vo ist der bahnhof, Vo ist der bahnhof. That's all you Americans can say. As I recall you didn't have any trouble finding it in World War Two!!" He may have had just a hint of a smile. I think. Not sure.

The German counterpart to the U.S. V Corps was the German III Korps, headquarters in Koblenz. My main man, Fritz Kunze had been promoted and was now assigned to III Korps, so we continued our professional and social association. His boss, MajorGeneral Altenburg, Commander, 12th Panzer Division had also been promoted and was now Lieutenant General, Commander of the III Korps, so we kept following each other around, so to speak. They invited us to virtually all functions in the Korps. General Altenburg insisted that I always bring my trumpet and terrorize his musicians. When I departed Germany, they gave me a beautiful German bugle. Later, we were to meet General Altenburg when he and his wife visited Fort Bragg.

One not-so-pleasant experience was our inconvenience caused by a terrorist group called the "Red Brigade". This started when Brigadier General Jim Dozier was captured by a cell in Italy and held captive for a while until he was rescued. Then, General Kroesen, his wife, Rowe, his Aide and driver were in his armored plated Mercedes (first time he had used it), and they were ambushed. A rocket-propelled grenade hit the rear panel just behind the back seat. They only received scratches;

the armor saved their lives. General Kroesen played this down and was rather, I think the word is non-plussed about it, and just said we would continue doing our jobs. Immediately, both Corps put an anti-terrorist plan into action. All General officers turned in their old Ford OD sedans. We were issued new, unmarked Mercedes, and the license plates were changed every week. My driver was issued a .38 special pistol, and had to attend a special drivers escape and evasion course. We were instructed not to take the same route to and from work and to vary the times. "Panic" switches were installed in the senior officers quarters in Bad Vilbel, so that buttons could be pushed in several of our rooms that immediately alerted law enforcement that there was a problem. Armed Military Policemen were stationed around the clock in the housing area for a while. During this time, I went back to the States for a Commanders' Conference, and read about a Military Policeman who was shot at close to our back yard! After all these precautions were taken, the bottom line was, "If a terrorist wants you bad enough, he will get you, but let's just don't do anything stupid and make it easy for him. We will continue to do our job!"

In April 1982, I was invited to Rota, Spain to speak at a Naval Dining In. I had met the commander while visiting Crete, and he asked me to come and speak to his officers. They squired me around, visiting some interesting spots in the area. We visited some very old wine caves, and learned how they made and stored the wine. I really enjoyed the visit.

Near the end of my Germany tour, I received a phone call from General Kroesen. He asked me how I would like to be the Commanding General, First ROTC Region, with headquarters at Fort Bragg, North Carolina. I told him I thought that would be wonderful. Another command, and I was again elated. I was sweating out some boring staff job somewhere. Or worse, back to D.C.

I paid a final courtesy call on General Kroesen and thanked him for creating such a great leadership climate in USAREUR. He showed me a new aquarium with fish in his office. He said that his wife, Rowe, got it for him and told him to watch the fish and it would relieve stress. He laughed and said when he left Germany, the fish and the aquarium were staying in Germany. (I think the fish only spoke German anyway!

The Change of Command of V Corps Artillery was held on 18 August 1982, and we departed for Fort Bragg, North Carolina.

Oh yes, early on, Jennifer could not say Mommie Kay or Opa, so she forever named us, Kay Kay and Paw Paw. And Kay Kay and Paw Paw we remain today!

"War is an ugly thing, but not the ugliest of things; the decayed and degraded state of morale…, which thinks that nothing is worth war, is much worse. A man who has nothing for which he is willing to fight; nothing he cares more about than his own personal safety; is a miserable creature, who has no chance of being free, unless made and kept so, by the exertions of better men than himself."

John Stuart Mill

TWO

Fort Bragg, North Carolina, Commanding General First ROTC Region

Auf Wiedersehen, Deutschland. Howdy Nawth Ca'lina. Farewell Wienerschnitzels. Hello Pig Pickin'. After a few days leave, we reported in to Fort Bragg, North Carolina. Lieutenant General Jack Mackmull commanded Fort Bragg and the 18th Airborne Corps. He was an outstanding commander and gentleman. My Headquarters, First ROTC Region was a tenant unit, located on Post at Fort Bragg, so General Mac was my military community boss. He gave us everything we needed and I could not have asked for better support. He and his leaders welcomed us into the community and we moved into very nice quarters. Major General Bob Sullivan, my good friend from OCLL days, recruited me to this position. He was now Commander of the ROTC cadet command at TRADOC Headquarters at Fort Monroe, Virginia. I was really looking forward to working for Bob, but he soon departed his post and my new ROTC boss was Major General Prillaman at TRADOC, another fine officer. My number 2 boss was General Bill Richardson (4-star), Commanding General of the Training and Doctrine Command (TRADOC). The same General Richardson I knew from Fort Benning days, another super soldier and leader. More about General Richardson later.

My ROTC Region Command consisted of university, college, and high school Army ROTC detachments in the 17 States on the east coast of the U.S., plus Puerto Rico, several islands in the Caribbean, and Panama. There were 111 colleges and universities where we had a full cadre of Officers and NCOs, led by a Colonel or Lieutenant

Colonel. We called these full programs "Hosts". In addition to these Host Detachments, we had 86 Extension Centers at other colleges and universities where there were insufficient numbers of cadets for a full host unit. These extension centers did have permanent cadre stationed at these schools, but fewer in number and normally led by a Major or Captain. Then, we had many Cross Enrolled schools, where there were a few cadets. The cadre instructors would drive over from a host or extension center several days a week to teach these cadets. In addition, we were responsible for several hundred high school Army ROTC programs.

First Region was by far the largest in numbers of Schools, cadets, and new Officers commissioned. In fact, when I departed this command for civilian life, my folks gave me an "Iron Mike" statue with a plaque that read, "To BG Hoglan, in appreciation, from 10, 689 Second Lieutenants." Those were the numbers of cadets that we commissioned as Second Lieutenants during the 3 years I commanded the Region. I was the only Region Commander in the history of the Army, as best my staff could determine, to personally visit *all 111* of my host colleges and universities, in addition to many extension centers, cross-enrolled schools and many high schools. It took over 2 years, visiting an average of 2 schools a day, 3 to 4 days a week, but I thought the Region Commander should visit every host detachment, many of which had never been visited by a Region Commander.

My typical itinerary would look something like this: My Sergeant Major, Aide de Camp and I would fly to the first school early in the morning, or for the schools that were far away, such as in Maine, we would arrive the evening before. I would spend about 4 hours with the school in the morning. First, the Professor of Military Science and Tactics (PMS) and his cadre would brief me on their program, numbers of MS I, MS II, MS III, and MS IV cadets in the program, commissioning numbers, Officer Basic Course (OBC) failures if any (BOO, HISS). They would include activities they participated in to support their school, etc. Many of my officers and senior NCOs would act as assistant coaches for varsity sports, furnish color guards for appropriate ceremonies, etc. I insisted that they support their school in whatever way they could. It paid off in the support (minimum or maximum) that we received from the school, and that support was critical. I will give some examples later. After their briefing to me, I would call upon the college or university President (pre-arranged by the PMS). I would ask him or her if they were satisfied with our program and my cadre. I asked specifically what they needed my cadre to do to support the school even more. I then would ask the President to support *our* needs, specific to what ever the PMS told me he needed. This would vary from "Thanks Mr. President----your support and that of your faculty is truly outstanding---we couldn't be happier", or a thinly veiled threat that if we did not get more support we may have to close the detachment (rare, but it happened). I did not feel that we should have to apologize for our program and presence on their campus. It was a very honorable thing we were doing, even if several professors and deans felt otherwise. After calling on the President, I would then speak to all the cadets the PMS could muster depending on their schedules, etc. Then we would have lunch, often on the plane, in route to the next school. I would repeat the schedule at this school, after which we would normally be invited to somebody's house for a party or dinner. I did not encourage this, and had my Aide tell the PMSs that they should not feel like they had to entertain me every waking moment that I was visiting their area. The ole Region Commander would appreciate a night off. Didn't do any good. They knew that this may be their only shot at me in their AO, so we did not get many nights off. The Army aircraft that we used was a twin engine, at my disposal. Someday I may write an account of our flight experiences. Hours of boredom, interrupted by moments of stark terror. Thank goodness we did not have to do all this traveling in civilian airplanes or I would still be stranded at some airport somewhere.

Back at Bragg, I had an outstanding staff, more than 100, and made up of more civilian professionals than military. The civilians were permanent party and gave us the year-to-year stability and experience we needed. Colonel Don Andrews was my Chief of Staff, and was a superb officer. He was complemented by his sweet wife, Mary. My outstanding civilians are too numerous to mention all by name, but George Bond, Charlie Brokmann, and Mary Lou Carter examples.

My AO, the 17 States, was divided into 5 geographical areas. I had a Colonel as Area Commander in each of the areas. The area 1 commander was Colonel Howard Stiles, and he was stationed in

Maine. The other Area Commanders were stationed at Bragg in my headquarters, but visited their AOs often. So I had a lot of help. My other Area Commanders were, at various times, Colonels Dick Noack, Mike McAdams, Jerry Novak, Mike Cockill, Ed Voke, Wilson Barnes, Harvey Fields, Reinhold Kraft, and Bob Frazier.

I also had a great personal staff. My Sergeant Major was Ellis Roach, and my 2 Aides during parts of the 3 years (no one Aide could put up with me for the entire tour) were Captains Joe Rose and Greg Borden. They were my heroes and without them I could not have performed my job---my schedule was horrendous and they kept it, and kept me out of trouble. (most of the time!) And, of course, I had one of the best secretaries in the world, one Mary Lou Carter. My nominees for Secretary Hall of Fame are, Iva Lee Brown (from Fort Benning Artillery Committee days), Mary Lou Williams (from 72nd Brigade—Wertheim, Germany days), and Mary Lou Carter (from ROTC days at Bragg). These folks literally kept me alive, and I will be forever indebted to all of them! My driver was Sp-4 Bob Spears and he was a super soldier. All my drivers for 30 years were hand picked by my Sergeants Major so they *had* to be great soldiers. Not sure *I* could have passed *that* muster!

Not all combat arms *"killers"* would ask for an ROTC assignment. Some considered it a wimpy assignment, but I thought it was great. I had more than my fair share of commanding combat units, and this was a great job to end my 30 years on active duty. The cadets kept me young, and they were the cream of the crop on all the college campuses. These youngsters had it figured out much better that most of their college professors. They were well-motivated, smart young men and women who were patriotic and wanted to serve their country. Our future military leaders!

I met some outstanding College and University Presidents, Vice Presidents, and Deans who were very supportive of my cadre and our program. Utmost among them was Doctor John Owen, President of the Secretary of the Army's ROTC Advisory Board. He was also President of North Georgia College, one of the only 4 military colleges remaining in the Nation. North Georgia is an outstanding institution and I have heard it said there are more officers on active duty from North Georgia College than West Point. I don't really know about that, but you could ask General Bill Livsey. Dr. John is now President Emeritus, and an outstanding leader and gentleman. We keep in touch. Incidentally, the other 3 military colleges, where ROTC is mandatory at least for the first 2 years, are The Citadel, Virginia Military Institute, and Norwich University, and all 4 were in my First Region. Can you get a big picture of me giving guidance to retired General (4-star) Sam Walker, President of VMI? Not a problem. I always got in the last word------"Yes sir"!

Another outstanding leader and supporter of our program was Doctor Almadovar, President of the University of Puerto Rico. I visited him several times. On one occasion, I decided to take an outstanding officer with me, and show him off to the cadets. Lieutenant Colonel Art Rodriguez, a graduate of UPR and their ROTC program, was currently serving as a Battalion Commander of an Artillery Battalion in the 18th Airborne Corps at Bragg. He is the same officer that was my Operations Officer (S-3) in the 72nd FA Brigade in Wertheim, Germany. His sweet wife, Argie called Katherine and they cooked up a scheme to join us in San Juan. They had discovered a business deal in one of the stores, that for the price of a cheap camera, they could get two round trip tickets to Puerto Rico for the price of one ticket. So they boogied off to San Juan. A couple of days later, Art and I arrived and did our thing at both campuses of UPR and a high school in Ponce. I wanted the cadets to see what a successful, outstanding battalion commander looked like, and the cadets enjoyed listening to him and talking with him. After our official visits we took a few days leave and Art and Argie gave us a VIP tour of the island, including a visit to a rain forest, and a Bacardi factory. . We thoroughly enjoyed our visit and meeting Argie's Mother. Katherine and Argie stayed a few days longer after Art and I had to get back to work at Bragg. They continue to be dear friends and we have traded visits.

On other visits to the UPR, I was accompanied by the Honorable Wallace Schottlcotte, the Civilian Aide to the Secretary of the Army from Florida. In fact, Wallace usually accompanied me when I visited all of the ROTC schools in Florida. He was owner of a few motels and active in the local business community and in support of the Army. Time to chase a little rabbit here: On one of my visits to schools in the Orlando area, he took my Aide and I to Rosie O'Grady's at Church

Street Station. It was a great restaurant and club, and after the meal, we went into a large lounge with a big crowd, where a super Dixieland band was playing. Do you see this one coming? After playing a couple of tunes, the bandleader stepped to the mike and said, "Would General Curt Hoglan join us on the bandstand?" I knew I had been set up! Well, they handed me a trumpet and we cooked. It is great to play my favorite music, Dixieland, with terrific musicians---they even made *me* sound good! The crowd was very kind, and everybody seemed to enjoy it. Now, I hate to be a name-dropper, but sitting in the balcony of this room was Michael Jackson and his entire entourage, while I was playing. Earlier they had dined about 2 tables across from us. And wouldn't you know it---he never even asked for my autograph! The next day, Wallace took us by Sea World, and they called me up to poolside and I thought Shamu, the killer whale, was going to bite my head off.

Back to UPR and President Almadovar. On one visit, he told me one of the funniest stories I ever heard and swears it was a true story. He had been invited to Oxford University in England along with many education dignitaries for some big gig. They seated him at the head table in this large banquet room with several hundred folks attending. He was seated across from a black, African gentleman, with full beard, a large turban, and a brilliantly colored robe. He noticed that no one was speaking to the gentleman and that he was not communicating with anyone either. There was obviously a language barrier. Dr. Almadovar felt a little sorry for the gent, so as they were eating their soup, Dr. Almadovar leaned forward and asked, "Likee soupee?" The gentleman smiled and nodded his head. Our good Dr. A felt better---at least he had communicated with the man. Still, throughout the meal, no one had any communications with this gentleman. During the main course, Dr. Almadovar leaned forward again, and asked, "Likee steakee?" Again the gentleman smiled and nodded his head. This pleased Dr. Almadovar. Well, after the meal, the Master of Ceremonies arose and introduced our friend in the colorful robe as the featured speaker for the evening. The gentleman gave a stunning, spellbinding 45-minute speech that had everyone sitting on the edge of his or her seats. And of course, he gave the speech in the very best King's English, being a graduate of Oxford. He received a standing ovation from the crowd. Dr. Almadovar said he felt so embarrassed that he wanted to crawl under the table. He did not have time for a getaway however, because immediately after the speech, our new friend came back to the table, sat down, leaned across the table, smiled, and asked Dr. Almadovar, "Likee speechee?" I love it!

In addition to meeting all of the 111 host detachment commanders (PMS) at their campuses, I had a lot of interface with them at the Area Commanders' PMS conferences, and at our annual Region PMS conference, as well as their visits to ROTC summer camp at Bragg and on other occasions. I spoke at many Commissioning Ceremonies, Banquets, Dining Inns, Military Balls, Graduation Ceremonies, etc.

I enjoyed meeting and associating with a large group of outstanding Americans, by attending meetings of the State Adjutant Generals, Civilian Aides to the Secretary of Army, Reserve and National Guard Commanders, active duty senior officers and commanders, College and University Presidents, Deans, and High School Principals. We have a lot of great patriots out there. And we need them to combat the apologists and traitors----oops, the soapbox almost came out again!

Another one of my favorite people was Major General Gene Salet, President of Georgia Military College, in Millegeville, Georgia. After he retired from an outstanding military career in service to our nation, he was still wearing the military (Army) uniform. He and I hit it off from the very first time we met. I was in awe of this man. He joined the Army, the month and year I was born, and was still continuously wearing the uniform. He was one of my (our) greatest supporters. He is now deceased, but remains one of my heroes.

In May, 1983, Colonel Dick Noack and Mary arrived. I had requested Dick to be assigned to my staff. He immediately came over to our house and ordered "upside down shish-ke-bob"! Smart ass! Remember? He was my outstanding XO in the 10th Artillery at Fort Benning! I just could not get away from this guy. He was/is one of the most outstanding officers I ever served with, and one my very best friends, and I am so glad I was able to get him assigned to what was to be our last assignment together, and our last assignment in the Army. However, he ain't gettin' away completely clean (as usual)! I assigned Dick as Area Commander for the 12 major Universities, other colleges and high schools in Pennsylvania. He obviously did an outstanding job. At one of our annual PMS Conferences, I believe it was in Atlanta, where all Area Commanders and all 111 host detachment commanders

(PMS-Colonels and Lieutenant Colonels) as well as staff and others were attending, I had asked General Bill Richardson, Commanding General of TRADOC (our BIG boss) to attend and be the main speaker. He accepted, and before I introduced him, I announced to the entire group that I had a confession and an apology to make publicly. I told the audience, and reminded General Richardson of the "Rock's Support", 10th Field Artillery, "license plate" episode, where, at Fort Benning, years ago, when he was the Assistant Commandant (one star), we put our Artillery license plate on the *back* of his car. I told the group that General Richardson was such a gentleman that he never, never called me about the incident. I then looked at General Richardson, and told him. "Sir, from the bottom of my heart, I want to confess to you in front of all these witnesses, that the whole thing was Dick Noack's idea"!! He acknowledged that, and noted that Dick never was selected for promotion to Brigadier General!! He was kidding because he knew that Dick was an outstanding soldier and leader. I wish he had been sitting on Dick's promotion board! Folks, there *is* some luck in this promotion stuff. I know *I* was lucky! But, hopefully good, or at least adequate, well, would you believe semi-adequate?

In April 1983, I was called back to Northwestern State University and inducted (first inductee) into the NSU ROTC Hall of Fame. I have returned several times to speak at their Military Ball, etc.

In addition to all of our other programs and activities, we also administered a summer advanced camp for all MS IIIs. These were all ROTC juniors (advancing to seniors) in the entire Region from 17 States and Puerto Rico. It was a huge endeavor. This is where the 18th Airborne Corps, the 82d Airborne Division and everybody at Bragg and elsewhere supported us to the max. We could not have conducted this intensive training without terrific external support. I thought this was our shining hour. Our staff and the PMS worked all year to provide a real challenging, and learning experience for our cadets. Many pre-camp meetings and seminars were held, within our own command and staff, but with all the support agencies as well.

Most of all the 111 PMS visited the advanced camp to monitor how their cadets were doing.

Fort Bragg provided barracks for the several hundred cadets attending the camp. Toward the end of each camp, we invited Presidents,

VPs, Deans, or Professors to come to visit the camp. We even invited them to participate in some of the physical exercises that their students were doing, and some times got them to participate—they got a real appreciation for what the cadets were going through!

The Leadership Reaction Course is an excellent example. Without exception, these academics stated that they thought that our program was very challenging and worthwhile. I wish we could have gotten every academic into the program.

Still, another great program offered by Fort Bragg, was Airborne School for my cadets. My cadets could attend an outstanding airborne school, conducted by the 82nd Airborne Division, *the* premier Airborne Unit in the Army, and graduate as qualified as parachutists. Now, Fort Benning never liked this, and officially complained that they were the only sanctioned, official, Airborne School. Technically , they were correct, But it would cost me too much money to send all my cadets that wanted airborne training to Benning, when we could do it at Bragg in conjunction with summer camp! Duh! I understand that Fort Benning eventually won the argument. But the 82nd at Bragg did a terrific job in conducting airborne training for several years for us!

Am I permitted to chase another rabbit? It's my gig, so I guess so. After a couple of summers, I got this crazy idea that if my cadets were going to airborne school, and jumping out of airplanes, I should do that too. I was almost 50 years old, but I never wanted to ask my troops to do anything I would not do. So guess what, dear friends, I enrolled in Airborne school!

The first week was hell! All those NCOs in the 82nd knew who I was although I wore no rank on my fatigue uniforms. I would jump out of the 34-foot tower, slide down the cable to the dirt berm, hit it, and double-time back to the sergeant, salute and report. He would say, "Soldier, you had your eyes closed, go back to the rear of the line;" I would respond, "Well hell yes, you don't think I would jump out of this dang thing with my eyes open?" I would then go to the rear of the line. No slack! I think I must have set a record for the number of jumps out of the 34-foot tower! And PLFs, and the suspended agony harness trainer---well, some of you know!

Against all odds, I graduated from Airborne ground week----then, the day before I was to jump with my cadets, I fell, had major knee surgery and never got to jump---this was one of the major disappointments of my military career. I survived the hardest part, but......! I have tried to make sense out of all this---I think that the good Lord was telling me not to abandon a perfectly good airplane in the air---if it is on fire, that's one thing, but if it's still flying, stay with it!!

While this was a great assignment, not all was sugar and spice. I should relate one not-so-pleasant experience. I dreaded visiting the colleges in Philadelphia. For one thing, it seems like every time we visited there, they had a garbage strike. I told the assistant City Manager that they should encourage citizens to put their garbage in bags, and lock them in their cars, and surely somebody would break into the cars and steal the garbage. He was not impressed with my suggestion! I had 5 colleges in Philly and one in particular, an Ivy League School, stuck in my craw! Once, I visited this school unannounced, and was petrified at what I found. The cadre was not present, except for a couple of officers in civilian clothes. I asked the secretary to contact the PMS and the remainder of the cadre and ask them to honor me with their presence, *in military uniform,* in their conference room, ASAP or sooner. I called the PMS into a private conversation in his office and asked what the hell was going on? He stated that "a Dean had told them not to wear the military uniform on campus-----it would aggravate the anti-military sentiment expressed by many of the faculty." To say that I exploded would be an understatement! After I spoke a few strong words of wisdom, (threats), I instructed them all to go get into their military uniforms and report back to me. Then I called on the University President. I told him that our ROTC program was strictly voluntary---we did not try to cram it down anybody's throat. But, we had some outstanding cadets at this University, and we were not going to raise these young men and women to be ashamed of the military uniform. One million, one hundred and seventy six thousand young Americans had died wearing this uniform, defending our country. I informed him that I had given the following advice to the PMS: If anyone in a position of authority in this institution tells my PMS that the cadre or the cadets were not to wear the military uniform on campus, he has orders to pack up and leave this campus before sundown that very day! He was not to call me to ask permission ---I had given him permission (orders) in advance! I guess this was absolutely the maddest I got in this entire 3 year tour. It is ironic, that in the same State of Pennsylvania, one of the very best universities in terms of support of our program was Penn State---they ain't Ivy League, folks---we had 600 fine cadets there, and the administration gave us fantastic support.

On a good note, one of my fellow Region Commanders was BG Tom Lightner (and Carol). They were War College classmates and another of my "brothers and sisters".

During this tour, I was en route to one of my universities on the East coast and I got a call. My wife had traveled from Fort Bragg to Plains, Georgia, to be with our daughter who was pregnant with her second child (I ordered another grand-daughter). She had not given indications that she was going into labor, so Katherine had left and drove back to Fort Bragg, N.C. I was told that there was a problem with the birth. I called my wife and told her to go immediately back to Georgia. We had a flurry of phone calls and Katherine returned to Georgia. Our daughter had almost bled to death before getting to the hospital----thank God her husband, Kevin had been there and got her to the hospital in time. At the time Kevin was a research assistant at the University of Georgia Agricultural Center in Plains and was close by. After several days, all ended well, and I got my second beautiful, precious grand-daughter, Julie. More about my two girls later.

One of my favorite university presidents was Lieutenant General Russ Todd, President of Norwich University, in Vermont. Most people don't know it as one of the 4 remaining military colleges, but in fact, it is the first university in the USA that made ROTC mandatory, so it is the first military college. I knew General Todd from Germany days and he was/is an outstanding leader and gentleman. Near the end of my 30 years of service, General Todd called me and asked me to apply for a job at Norwich. His Vice President for Administration had died and he wanted me to apply for that position. My final Army assignment in the ROTC business, after visiting and working with more than 111 colleges, would, hopefully be good experience, that would make me competitive for the position. And I would have loved working for General Todd. Anyway, I was excited and thought it would be a great job, but I picked a terrible time to tell my wife, Katherine about the opportunity. It was early spring at Fort Bragg, 1985, and I was retiring that summer. This particular Sunday morning we were sitting in bed, drinking coffee, watching early morning television, and it was snowing outside. I told Katherine about the job opportunity, and then showed her where Northfield, Vermont was located on the map. She immediately got out of bed, went over to the window, pulled back the curtains, came back to the bed and tapped me on the shoulder----I knew something serious was about to occur. She said, "GI, you see that funny white stuff falling out there?" I said, "Yes ma'am." She said, " Now, you have dragged (drug) me to Washington State for nearly a year, Washington, D.C. for 4 years, Pennsylvania and Kansas for 2 years, Germany for 4 years, and Alaska for 3 years. The funny white stuff is called snow and I have seen enough of it to last me more than a lifetime. So, pay attention and read my lips, I only want to have to say this once", to which I replied, "Yes ma'am." She continued, "I want to *live* in the South, and *visit* up North. And when I say *visit* up North, I'm talking about **Atlanta.**" I said, "Yes ma'am," and saluted with both hands. Funny, that was not only the first, but the last conversation we ever had about Northfield and Norwich, in Vermont!

THREE

Army Retirement

All great things must sooner or later come to an end! In the summer of 1985 it happened to me. After 30 years and 7 days on active duty in the United States Army, an organization that I loved, full of officers, NCOs, soldiers, and civilians that I loved and still love and respect, I took off my boots. Forgive me for being a little sentimental, but when you do something for that long, you've got to love it, and miss it. It's been 22 years since I retired and I still miss it, but you can't wear the suit forever.

I claim that I am on "temporary" retirement. As a Regular Army Officer, I am legally subject to be recalled to active duty until the day I die. You Army folks know that. (In fact, I called the Department of the Army a while back and told the DCSPER that I would like to come back to active duty and help them in the war in Iraq. They said they would get back to me. Two weeks later they called and said they were putting me in category 4I. I said that I knew what 4F was, but what is this 4I? They said that when the enemy gets to the corner of 4th and I streets in D.C. they would call me. I think they were trying to tell me *something).* Just kidding.

On 28 May, 1985, my retirement ceremony was held at Fort Bragg. N.C. General Jim Lindsay, then commander of 18th Airborne Corps and one of my favorite officers, was the Presiding Officer.

Our family, son, daughter, son-in-law, granddaughters, brother-in-law, mother and father-in-law, and many, many friends honored me with their presence there. The honor guard consisted of redleg (Artillery) soldiers from the 82nd ABN Div/18th Airborne Corps Artillery.

Farewell to arms and to the Army and soldiers. I will always support you, admire and respect you, and thank you for your service. And a hearty "Gunner's Mate" to the spouses and families. You are all my favorite people!

"I was that which others did not want to be. I went where others feared to go, and did what others failed to do. I asked nothing from those who gave nothing, and reluctantly accepted the thought of eternal loneliness… should I fail. I have seen the face of terror; felt the stinging cold of fear; and enjoyed the sweet taste of a moment's love. I have cried, pained, and hoped…..but most of all, I have lived times others would say were best forgotten. At least someday I will be able to say that I was proud of what I was….

….. A Soldier."

George L. Skypeck

Curt & Trumpet, Germany

CINCUSAEUR, Gen Kroesen & Curt

Brigadier General Hoglan in his Office

Curt's Retirement & Col Dick Noack, Commander of Troops

Chapter Seven

CIVILIAN LIFE

ONE

Florence, South Carolina, Executive Director, Florence County Economic Development Commission

    Several months before I retired from the Army, I made a speech at Princeton in New Jersey. Seated next to my Aide-de-camp was Mr. Ray Trainer, the president of a large manufacturing company. My Aide happened to mention to him that I was retiring from the Army in a few months. When I met him after my speech, he asked me if I would be interested in coming to work for him. (I must have made a helluva speech!) He had manufacturing plants in Trenton, New Jersey and in Hartsville, South Carolina, that manufactured steel ball bearings. He was looking for a Plant Manager for the Hartsville plant. I was flattered but told him that I knew absolutely nothing about ball bearings, steel, or manufacturing in general. (I told him that I might qualify as a tail gunner on one of his trucks in New Jersey!) He told me they would teach me everything about the manufacturing process, and that he needed a people manager and was convinced that I was the man for the job. He invited Katherine and I back to New Jersey, and I toured the plant with him. I was thoroughly impressed with this man. As we went through the plant he called all of the employees by their first name-----over 100 of them-----and they all called him by his first name. I thought that was a bit unusual----it was a union shop, but they obviously had a great deal of respect for each other. Later, he took me to the plant in Hartsville, S.C. for a visit. One big advantage I had in S.C.; at least I could speak their language! Still later we arranged to meet at the Atlanta airport, where he really pushed me to take the job. I would have loved to work for him, but I just felt there was too much engineering and technical data for an ole music major to learn! I reluctantly turned it down. During the weeks that we were in conversation and meetings with each other, we never discussed salary, but I know it would have been a very good one.

I was contacted by the Superintendent of Schools for Dade County, Florida (the second largest in the nation), and asked if I would be interested in applying for the job as one of his Assistant Superintendents. I knew the Superintendent because of our ROTC programs in several of his high schools. This sounded interesting (at first) and I submitted a resume`, was interviewed telephonically by his board, made the final three contender list, and we were invited to Miami for further interviews. It was a nice visit but it did not take very long for the board and I to realize that I wouldn't fit the job. They wanted a computer whiz, and I was not it! Again, I would probably qualify as a tail gunner on a Miami Budweiser truck!

After I chased a few other rabbits, Dr. Tom Stanton, President of Francis Marion College, in Florence, South Carolina called and asked me to consider coming to Florence to be the Executive Director of the Florence County Economic Development Commission. I knew Tom from his days as a Dean at James Madison University in Virginia where he supported my ROTC detachment there, and as President of Francis Marion College where we had a ROTC program. He had supported our programs to the maximum and was an outstanding leader and gentleman. I told him I would be interested, and he hooked me up with the Florence County Administrator, Barry Elliott. Barry and the county attorney, Pete Hyman came to visit me at Fort Bragg, and the hiring process began.

I worked for a board of directors headed by an outstanding gentleman, Allen Lewis. And I answered to the County Administrator and to the Florence County Council. I attended many economic development schools to get up to speed on the technical aspects of the job: The ED basic course at the University of South Florida, and a three summer ED program in residence at the University of Oklahoma in Norman, OK, where I received the designation, Economic Development Executive (one of 13 in the Nation), plus many other short courses. My two great assistants were Pat Olsen, and Sherry Music. I had fine support from my board and many other citizens. Too numerous to list all of them, but in particular, Joe Turner (and Betty) and Joe Geddie (from Carolina Power and Light), Phil Goff (now married to my gal, Sherry) and his boss, Johnny Brown, from the Pee Dee Council of Governments, Florence Mayor Rocky Pearce, City Manager Tommy Edwards, and my all-time favorite small town, country mayor of Pamplico, S.C., Dozier Munn. I need to chase a rabbit here. Now, Pamplico had a population of around 4 or something (just kidding, Pamplico-ites). Dozier was so proud of his little town, and worked very hard to improve it in every way. He would claim that Pamplico had the best tasting drinking water in the nation. He served on many state and countywide boards, commissions, and committees. I loved to ride around in his old pick-up truck that was about old enough to vote. His entire filing system and records for the town were thrown up on top of the dash-board in that old truck, along with duct tape, tools, fishing lures, etc. It was piled so high, seeing over it was a challenge. I didn't want to stir around in it, because I knew there were some strange critters living in there somewhere. Dozier was a great friend, supporter of economic development, and one of my favorite *characters!* Dr. Tom Stanton, President of Francis Marion College, continued to be a strong supporter and good friend. Sadly, I recently learned that both of these gentlemen had passed away. Our son, Steve is a proud graduate of FMC.

Early in my "new" civilian career, I decided that there were several things I did not like about civilian life:

(1) Nobody is in charge! I attended many meetings where everybody sat around the table and took turns saying, "Gee, I don't know, what do you think?" You can guess how much patience I had with that! Contrast this to an Army example----if you come upon two Army Privates out digging a ditch, and you ask, "Who is in charge here", I will guarantee that one of them will say without hesitation, "I am Sir". Somebody is *always* in charge. It greatly simplifies the chain of command, and more importantly, the chain of responsibility. In a unit, the *Commander is always responsible* for everything his unit does or fails to do! Also, in these many meetings, it was amazing to me how civilians could *cram* 20 minutes of real business into a 3-hour meeting!

(2) In civilian life, there are no Non-Commissioned Officers (NCOs) to get the job done. Everybody wants to be either a General or a Private!

When I first arrived in Florence, quite a few of the farmers in the county called on me and wanted me to come see their "industrial parks". I could understand why they wanted to market their land as an industrial park----it would be far more valuable than farmland. After visiting their land, most often my response would be something like, "Sir, it pains me to have to be the one to tell you this, but you do not have an industrial park here. You do not have reasonable access to water, sewer, electrical power, good roads, rail, etc. What you have here is a cornfield, and if we don't get some rain very soon, the corn ain't gonna make it."

With the help of the County Administrator and County Council, and a public minded individual landowner, Mr. Dargan, we developed a first class industrial park on Interstate 95. Ordinarily, it would be against the law to spend public money improving private land, so we passed a county ordinance stating that it would be legal if the county would be in control of land sales (for a specific price per acre to the land owner), and would have the right to approve all sales, including the refusal to sell to polluting industries or other companies not considered to be compatible with our community. The county then provided the infrastructure to the park. I will not try to teach a course in ED here, but if you are going to be successful in attracting industry to your community, you must have a suitable place for them to locate. And it must have the basic amenities already in place (not promised). The infrastructure must always include access to water, sewer, good roads, electrical power, and maybe rail access. When the CEO or plant manager asks where is the water and sewer, the only good answer is, "Sir, I believe it is about 4 feet under your right foot." We ultimately developed 3 industrial parks in the county and were very successful in recruiting many industries throughout the county. During my 4 years in Florence, we realized $410 million in new capital investment, created some 4,000 new jobs, and the unemployment rate in the county dropped from 10.5 percent to 3.8 percent. The largest company in Taiwan, Nan Ya Plastics (Formosa Plastics Group) bought 500 acres in the county and employs about 700 folks. Instrumental in helping us land the Taiwan company was Jim White with CSX Railroad, because the company required rail access. Jim was a great help, and he and his wife, Barbara live in Jacksonville, and we are still good friends today---we visit each other when hurricanes threaten either of us. Caloric, a sub of Raytheon, settled in our I-95 industrial park and hired several hundred employees. There were many more.

I learned that you needed to be competitive in terms of what you could offer industry, but you did not have to be the cheapest place in America. The price of land needed to be competitive and some short-term tax breaks would be helpful, but you did not need to give the farm away. Example: Occasionally a company would visit us and "insist" that an industrial site be "given" to them and all taxes be exempted for 30 years, etc. I would answer, " Sir, I'm afraid what we have here is a case of mistaken identity. You are undoubtedly looking for the cheapest place in America, and we are not it. We are a *quality* place. Now, there is a place near Bumscrew, Montana where there are no taxes, and land is almost free, but there are also no services or infrastructure---no utilities, no fire or police protection, and no education facilities. It has been our experience that companies such as yours need infrastructure and expect an educated work force. Most of our property taxes go to educate our folks. We would respectfully ask you to share in the cost of this important necessity." This approach almost always worked with good companies!

I also learned that most economic development professionals did not have a 'dog eat dog' competitive attitude to the extent that they would bad-mouth other competing communities in an effort to attract industry (the fictitious Bumscrew not withstanding). If the best thing you can say about your community is to run down your neighbors and point out their deficiencies, that in itself makes a statement that companies can see through and will have a negative impact on your own community. The economic development officials that I worked with were generally very professional. We had a strong state organization, South Carolina Economic Development Association (SCEDA), and later, a similar state organization, the Louisiana Industrial Development Executives Association (LIDEA). We also had an outstanding regional organization, consisting of 15 southeastern states, Southern Industrial

Development Council (SIDC). The members were very supportive of each other and I was privileged to serve on the Board of Directors of these ED organizations.

Work hard. Be successful. But then, if we are successful, let the citizens of Florence County know about it so they can feel good. For new plant announcements or major expansions, we would host a big reception at the Country Club, inviting lots of people, including the introduction of officials from the new industry to our community. I would ask the Mayor, President of County Council, Chamber of Commerce President, our State Senator and Representative, and other prominent folks to say a few words of welcome (necessary for keeping *my* politics straight). I would always invite the Governor to the reception and he would attend when it was possible. I got to know Governor Carroll Campbell rather well and I would ask him to call the CEO of companies and thank them for considering Florence County for an industrial site and encourage them to settle in our county and the state. I made a deal with the Governor that paid great dividends. I knew that his schedule was pretty wild and many times he could not attend our plant announcement receptions. So, I arranged for a telephone to be hooked up at the podium in the club, and wired into the PA system. And I gave the Governor the exact time he was to call----it would be timed after the other folks concluded their remarks, and while I was entertaining (stalling) at the microphone. No matter where he was physically located at the time, he was always available by phone. The timing was critical, but it always worked. The phone would ring, and I would answer it. Both ends of the conversation could be clearly heard over the PA system. The Governor would say, "Curt, I'm sorry I cannot be present in Florence today. I'm at a meeting in Washington, DC, but I want to congratulate all the folks in Florence County on this great occasion." He would then name the local politicos---to keep *his* politics straight! Then he would ask to speak to the senior new industry top person there, by name, and of course, I would ask Mr. Doe to please come to the podium, and speak with Governor Campbell. It was a win/win situation for everybody. OK, so it was grandstanding a little bit! Am I too kool or what? But I always gave credit to everybody there, whether they deserved it or not. Especially supportive was my citizens group, Florence County Progress. And they paid for the receptions as well as other kinds of support.

I was fortunate to be selected by my peers and named the "Economic Development Professional of the Year" for the State of South Carolina for 1989. I also received the Governor's Job Creator Award. Part of the reason we were so successful was that South Carolina passed some outstanding economic development legislation. The State and local governments were industry friendly. Governor Campbell was a Republican and the State Legislature was heavily Democratic, but they got together and decided that if the State was going to be highly competitive in economic development, they must present a united effort and they did! South Carolina also had a great Vo-Tech school system. Our local President was Fred Fore and he was a great ally in our economic development efforts. They would even set up a manufacturing line in a vacant building to train workers for a specific company. Education and job training is one of the most important aspects of industry recruitment. All in all, it was a very productive and enjoyable four years in South Carolina.

Rabbit chasing time. Over the years, I never had the opportunity to demonstrate any cooking prowess in the kitchen. My Mom and all my Aunts were great cooks, and I married into a family of outstanding cooks, so I never learned anything about cooking. Now, I could make a peanut butter and jelly sandwich and that is about as far as I went. Just before Christmas, in 1987, Katherine's Dad had a stroke and Katherine left me and spent about a week in Louisiana with her folks. Katherine shopped for me before she left and bought lots of groceries. They were mostly "lean cuisine" meals. The directions on the boxes said "heat and eat". Now, I could handle that. If it had said heat, *stir,* and eat, I would have been in deep trouble. But heat and eat, I can do—no problem. Well one evening I took a box out of the freezer with stuffed cabbage or something in it. It was a nasty, gosh-awful looking mess, and as I put it in a plate and started to place it into the microwave, I reasoned that this thing was going to thaw out and a plate wouldn't hold it without spilling. Ah ha, I needed yonder Revere-Ware Pot. I put the stuff in the pot, placed it in the microwave, pushed the start button and walked down the hall. Well, folks, in about 5 seconds there was a lot of excitement in my kitchen. Sparks, lightening, thunder, etc. I ran back in, and pushed the off button. It did not melt the plastic handle of the pot, but the smell of burnt plastic permeated the entire neighborhood!

I put the stuffed whatever in the trash, and just sorta looked at the microwave for a couple of days. I made another mistake. I told my secretary, sweet Sherry about this little episode, and for the next week, something like 100 people came up and told me that you can't put a metal pot in the microwave. I asked why didn't just *one* of them tell me that *before* I did it. How am I supposed to know about things like that—does it come in a vision at 3 o-clock in the morning, or what? Well, I came up with this story; "Honey, I figured out what to get you for Christmas. This microwave is several years old, and.........."! After staring at this thing for about 2 or 3 days, I knew that I had to try it and see if it worked, so I put a frankfurter in it, pushed start and put my fingers in both ears and held my breath. It cooked the wiener-----I even ate it. Well, the pot survived this experience better than any of the rest of us, but I think that microwave is still perking somewhere in South Carolina. Finally, this story does have an uplifting ending. Since that time, I am not allowed to do *anything* in the kitchen. Not all bad!

"You can easily judge the character of others by how they treat those who they think can do nothing for them."

(Author unknown)

TWO

Lafayette, Louisiana, President and CEO, Lafayette Economic Development Authority

On 1 August 1989, I was recruited to be the President and CEO of the Lafayette Economic Development Authority (LEDA) in Lafayette, Louisiana, serving the citizens of Lafayette Parrish. *Laissez Les Bon Temps Rouler!* The organizational structure was similar to the one in South Carolina, and I worked for a Board of Directors in this job for six years. LEDA had two industrial parks with infrastructure in place. The Chairman of the Board when I arrived was Roland Dugas, an outstanding gentleman who was President and half owner of Acadian Ambulance, the largest privately owned ambulance company in the United States. Roland was a great supporter of economic development and of me personally. He was impeccably honest, forthright, and was one of the few individuals I have ever known, that I never heard a word from anyone, ever, that could be construed as being negative---wouldn't it be fantastic if we all could live up to that standard!

The following LEDA Board members were very supportive of our economic development efforts: Lafayette Mayor Dud Lastrapes, Carencro Mayor Tommy Angelle, Dailey Berard, Dr. Duane Blumberg, and David Sweatt. Mayor Lastrapes accompanied me on industry recruiting trips, including one to Gloversville, NY, where we recruited a leather tanning company, only later to be killed by the State, but that's another story. He was always supportive and I always felt that if I needed the shirt off his back, Dud would start unbuttoning it without me having to tell him why I needed it.

Mayor Tommy Angelle was one of my favorite "Cajuns". He speaks perfect French, at least I thought so, until we got lost in Paris, trying to get back to Orly airport, and no Frenchman could understand his asking for directions! They didn't understand my poor German either. Tommy was one of the board members who came to Florence, S.C. to interview me for the Lafayette job. He is an outstanding gentleman and remains one of my friends, with his sweet wife, Dorothy. They have visited us several times in Florida.

Daily Berard was an outstanding businessman in Lafayette Parish. He was President of Universal Fabricators, a large company in New Iberia, LA that manufactured and refurbished the large offshore platforms used in drilling for oil and gas in the Gulf of Mexico.

Among my outstanding staff members were Joe Bourg, Brenda Buras and Don Babin. They were super, and at my farewell party, I told them that they did most all of the hard work, and I got most of the credit, and *all* of the *blame!* Outstanding citizens of Lafayette Parish that greatly assisted our efforts are too numerous to mention by name here, but I wish to single out two gentlemen that were "partners in crime" with me in the pursuit of economic development. Philippe Gustin, Director of Le Centre International de Lafayette, was a native of Belgium, and of course, spoke fluent French. Lafayette is the "Capitol of Acadiana" a region of south Louisiana where the French speaking Acadians that were exiled from Canada settled. Louisiana was owned by Spain at that time and welcomed the Acadians. Lafayette is the most international city that I know, and has many "twin cities" in other places, particularly cities and towns where French is the primary language. With Philippe, I visited several of these twin cities (officially twinned by Mayors of both cities) in France, Belgium, and Quebec, Canada. He orchestrated an International Business Exchange every year in Lafayette that was attended by trade representatives and other officials from dozens of cities. Philippe's priority was trade and mine was the attraction of industry (and trade), so our missions fit perfectly. Our other partner was Al Steward, Director of the University of Louisiana in Lafayette's Apparel Computer Integrated Manufacturing facility (A-CIM). Al and his resources provided us an opportunity to attract industries and joint ventures associated with apparel manufacturing.

On one particular trip through France, we visited many apparel factories including one that manufactured ladies lingerie near LePuy. By prior arrangement, the local lady economic developer (Dominique) had scheduled this visit, and she and the plant manager met us at the entrance for our tour of the factory. Now folks, I'm just an ole country boy from Pitkin, and I have never known much about these "Victoria's Secret" products. I have heard the big boys and girls talk about them, but I think I discovered where this stuff is made. Now, they were making some of the smallest, flimsiest, sexiest, ladies underthings I had ever seen (and mostly *not* seen)! I'm talking flimsy-----Light duty! They had 2-piece bikini underwear---the top looked more like 2 band-aids, and the bottom,...well, we won't go there! Picture the lineup for our factory tour----the plant manager, then Al Steward, then Philippe and I, followed by our escort, Dominique. We were going through this French lingerie factory, looking at all these skimpy, sexy things being made, going from station to station, feeling these things. And of course, Al is an expert in fabrics and garments; he knows what he is doing. On the other hand, here are Philippe and I----we don't have a clue! Heck, we have all our clothes tailor-made down at Goodwill Industries. But we need to *look* like we know what we were doing, so we were following along, feeling of these exotic, flimsy garments, breaking out in a cold sweat! We made it to the end of the tour, and the plant manager wanted to give us a present for our wives (since there wasn't anything in there that would fit *us*)! (Can you see this coming?) He asked us for our wives' bra sizes. Now, stay with me folks, this is not going to be too bad---I *will* get out of this somehow. Well, the three of us looked at each other, completely dumbfounded. Not a one of us knew our wife's bra size. It was very embarrassing. After an awkward silence, I told the manager that U.S. sizes were completely different numbers than French sizes (thinking that would bail us out). To our dismay, he said "No problem, I can easily convert the numbers---I do it all the time". We were again speechless---we did not know the US. sizes of our wives' bras. After looking at each other for what seemed an eternity, Philippe turned to me and said, "Curt, I don't know-----you know my wife Mary", to which I quickly interrupted, "Not that well Philippe, I swear, not that well--that's my story and I'm sticking to it!"

I put the lacy French bra the manager gave me for my wife in my suitcase and brought it home----I assume we all did. But one thing you don't want to do, is let your wife unpack your suitcase and find a lacy, sexy, French bra in it. That is what you call non-habit forming! So, I unpacked that suitcase myself the first thing and gave it to my wife----I may have done it at the airport, not waiting until I got home. Now, I have not conducted any research as to whether any of the three bras fit (well, at least two of them!). I do not intend to, and I have an idea that I may even be sorry I included this in the book!

In May 1994, one of my board members, Dailey Berard and I made a 10 day trip to Beijing, China. We were invited by the Chinese government to attend the Conference on China Market Economy and Trade. We were among 70 U.S. delegates and over 200 Chinese delegates attending pre-arranged meetings and panel discussions. I carried brochures and catalogs for several Lafayette companies and distributed them to interested parties. We also visited a textile factory, and in Tianjin, a Motorola plant which manufactured mobile phones and VCRs. I also met with members of the Tianjin Economic Development Association. In 1994, the gross national product in the United States was about $6 trillion, the total European GNP was about $5 trillion, and the Asian market was bigger than North America and Europe combined. Even then, we could recognize that China was coming fast as a gigantic and aggressive economic force in the world. Dailey made the comment that Americans often talked about our desire not to isolate China. He said that the choice we confront is whether we want to isolate ourselves from China.

China had 1.2 billion people (1.3 now), of which 820 million were in the work force. In 1992, their economy grew by 13 percent, the fastest rate in the world. My impression was that they were going 100 miles per hour toward capitalism although they will probably never call it that. They want a "market economy", although every official was careful to always say "socialist market economy" (I'm still waiting for a definition of that)! Our Chinese hosts were most gracious---the Chinese are still the most polite folks on the planet. Between meetings we were given tours of Tiananmen Square, the Forbidden City, and the Great Wall. We attended a spectacular banquet in the Great Hall of the People.

I made another trip to China as a Louisiana State Delegation member. We visited in south China and Hong Kong. During both of these trips it was obvious that the Chinese were much more interested in opening up markets in the U.S. for their products. With their ultra-cheap labor rates in China, they were not very interested in making capital investments in factories in the U.S. They have obviously been very successful in finding markets in the U.S. for their products. As proof of this just look at the manufacturing labels and "made in—" tags on most products in our stores. The trade imbalance is staggering as we all know. It was very interesting to see how far China has progressed and how much it has changed since 1994 and when Katherine and I visited (as tourists, this time) for 21 days in June 2006. More about that trip later.

One of our biggest "catches" in terms of industry attractions to Lafayette, was a very large, regional distribution center for Auto Zone. One of their executives involved in site selection and location contacted me early on and indicated that he would like to visit our area, under the condition of confidentiality, that is, without anyone knowing the name and characteristics of the company. This was entirely normal. In order to explain why the secrecy, I need to chase a rabbit here, albeit an important rabbit, one that got me in trouble more than once: When companies are looking for an area to establish a new facility, or substantially expand into an area where they already have a presence, they initially insist on confidentially. This is because of several very important and valid reasons. When a little burg like Lafayette, New York City (well, maybe), Baton Rouge, or even Pitkin is a contender for a new industry, *and if it becomes known in the community* who the company actually is, mysteriously all the surrounding land in the area of that municipality doubles or triples in price. And it is a risk that individuals (in the best interest of the community, of course) will begin to contact the company and promise things that cannot be delivered. Everyone wants to be the economic development professional. In almost every case where we were dealing with companies, they would always, always, initially insist on confidentiality. I understood that, and respected it. But some members of my Board would insist that I tell them everything I knew about the company, early on. Of course, I would divulge everything about the company to my board before we voted to accept the deal, but I got a lot of heartburn from several board members for not telling them initially. It went like this: Board member: "Curt, one of my friends the other day said he heard that LEDA was in the process of attracting a new industry. It is embarrassing to me to have to tell him I don't know who it is. I *am* a board member of LEDA, and I don't even know who you are courting". I would continuously tell the Board member(s), "if that situation happens, and I know it does, just tell them, of course with a knowing smile, that you are not at liberty to tell anyone about the company at the very real risk of losing them to some other community". I doggedly held on to this promise of confidentiality to the prospect company, and it paid off in the long run, although I got a lot of grief from some of my board members. I can understand why some of them would like to appear to be ahead of the curve and be "in the know", but if I told *anyone,* it would no longer be a secret, and that has been proven many times over.

Back to Auto Zone. The primary reason that Auto Zone was interested in Lafayette as a site for a regional distribution center was our proximity to the intersection of Interstates 10 and 49. I recognized that our location was an obvious advantage to distribution-oriented companies and we marketed our location as such. I made several trips to their national headquarters in Memphis, and they visited with me several times. We had other competitors, but in the end, we prevailed and welcomed Auto Zone into our North Park industrial park, and they are flourishing today. In the interest of time (and undoubtedly disinterest by most folks), I will not relate the details, hard work, time and effort expended to land this anchor tenant in our Industrial Park, or other companies as well. As a matter of fact, most of our work would probably be boring to most folks reading this book. I thoroughly enjoyed working with prospective companies looking for a location for their facility. I also enjoyed assisting local companies in growing and improving their profitability. I had one staff member, Don Babin, who was especially trained and devoted all his efforts toward assisting existing local companies. There is a good argument that it is more important to help retain and grow existing companies, than it is to recruit new ones. I did *not* generally enjoy the politics I sometimes had to endure. In economic development circles it is common knowledge that you should try to export your most prolific product. Louisiana, in particular, should try to export its *politics!* *Importing* better roads and highways would be a great help.

I worked as an economic development professional for 10 years and I never stopped learning. In wrapping up this chapter in my life, I will relate a few lessons that are worth passing on. These are not restricted to the field of ED.

Observe strict confidentiality in accordance with the desires of the prospective industry.

Do not promise or imply *anything* that you are not absolutely sure you can deliver.

Don't try to trash your competition.

Don't be afraid of competition. Work hard and your competition will make you look good. Too many folks just don't work at it.

Give your bosses (Board members, etc) credit for your successes. Publicly.

Make *Integrity* your middle name. Always tell it like it really is.

Following is from Dr. Tom Peters' book, "In Search of Excellence" (an oldie but goodie): Your customers are the most important *people* in the world. Treat them like kings and Queens. They are always right (well, almost). Your employees are the second most important *people* in the world. Treat them and take care of them exceptionally well. Set a high but attainable standard, clearly articulate that standard to them. If they consistently fail to meet the standard, let them go. If they meet the standard, show your appreciation, reward them. Your *product (even if it is a service)* is the most important *thing* in the world. Be proud of it. Lay awake at night constantly thinking about how you can improve it. Guarantee it.

In the early 1990's, we bought a house lot in Bluewater Bay, in Niceville, Florida. As I mentioned earlier, after over 40 vacations in 35 years at the Fort Benning Recreation Center in Destin, FL, we had fallen in love with the area. We always knew we would like to retire/

retire in the area of Destin, Fort Walton Beach, or Niceville, Florida. We had maintained contact with folks in Bluewater Bay, a golf and tennis resort, north of Choctawhatchee Bay in Niceville. So we knew the *where?* The only thing we did not know for many years was *when?* In June, 1995, the *when* came to me----in the middle of the night, a little voice said-----*NOW!* I announced to my board that after 40 years in the work force, it was time to fish and play golf.

Rusty Cloutier, President of Mid-South Bank, told me that the bank would like to host a farewell reception for me, and asked me to furnish a guest list for them to invite. I was overwhelmed, and at the party I told my hosts that I felt like Sofia Loren's new little baby boy, when he looked up and said, "Gee, Mommie, is all that for me??" When I called my friend, Jim Bradshaw, local reporter for the daily newspaper, and told him I was inviting just my friends to the farewell reception, he said, "Hoglan, this is going to a very small party, but the editor and I will show up just to make sure *someone* comes!" Jim had been a friend from the day we arrived in Lafayette. In fact, he was calling me in South Carolina and telling me what a great place Lafayette was. The day we arrived he came over to our house and helped us unpack boxes (and drank up all my beer). I picked on Jim just a little bit but not as much as some of my other friends at the reception; I learned that you never want to hassle anybody that orders ink by the ton---you will lose! I thanked everyone there for their friendship and support, then introduced the musicians in the combo. And of course, took my trumpet and terrorized the band with "Kansas City" and a few other hymns. I ended my participation in the reception by reading a telegram I had received. I introduced it by saying it was from a great American, an individual for whom I had enormous admiration and respect. I told them that I was truly honored to receive it and wanted to share it with them. It read:

"Dear Curt, Upon the occasion of your retirement, I wish to take this opportunity to express my sincere appreciation for the outstanding service you have given to Lafayette Parish, the State of Louisiana, and to our nation. I know I speak for all Americans when I thank you for your more than 30 years of service on active duty in the U. S. Army. In your second career, you have worked tirelessly to provide jobs and enhance the quality of life for our people. Lafayette is in your debt and will benefit for years to come because of your hard work, often under difficult conditions and sometimes not understood or appreciated by all. On behalf of a grateful nation and state, I congratulate you upon your well-deserved retirement and thank you for your dedicated service. In my opinion, you are the most outstanding economic development professional in the State of Louisiana and perhaps in the nation."

And it is signed-------------------Love, Mother!   I gotcha!

THREE

Niceville, Florida, Coast Guard Auxiliary Years

Au Revoir, Lafayette, Welcome to the Sunshine State. In June 1995 we sold our house in Lafayette, LA and moved to Bluewater Bay in Niceville, Florida. We put most of our furniture in storage and rented a patio home while our new house was being built on the lot we had previously purchased in Bluewater Bay. We moved into our new home on 1 November 1995. We have been here for almost 12 years and it has been the longest I have ever lived in one place. It is also a record for Katherine in the last 50 years. She says our nomadic days are over and if I want to move again, I can do it alone. So I have stopped looking in the mailbox for PCS orders.

When we moved here, I brought my bass boat, thinking with all the water I would enjoy fishing. Well, it's mostly salt water and I discovered that I did not enjoy salt-water fishing that much. I sold the bass boat and bought a bay boat. After noticing all the red and green buoys in the bay and gulf, I decided that I had better take a course in boating before I ran over somebody, or got run over myself. The local Coast Guard Auxiliary Flotilla advertised a safe boating course and I signed up. It was a very interesting course and I enjoyed it. I thought the instruction was excellent and they recruited me to join Flotilla 18 as a member.

For the next 8 years I thoroughly enjoyed my membership in the Coast Guard Auxiliary. I became qualified as a vessel examiner, boat coxswain, master instructor, Aids to Navigation (ATON) verifier, and Qualification Examiner. At the local Flotilla level, I served as Education Officer, Vessel Examination Officer, Operations Officer, Vice Flotilla Commander, and Flotilla Commander. I served on the Division staff as the Vessel Examination Officer and Chaplain, and on the District Staff

234

as District Vessel Examination Officer. We had about 35 members in the Flotilla, 10 plus Flotillas in the Division, and more than 90 Flotillas in the District reaching from Florida to the Arizona/New Mexico state line. I thoroughly enjoyed working with these professionals involved in the promotion of boating safety. We used our own boats for Coast Guard Aux Patrols, and were reimbursed for gas, oil, and ice. We wore official Coast Guard AUX uniforms and carried large placards on each side of our boats that read "Coast Guard AUX Patrol". Although we had no law enforcement authority, most all boaters recognized us as volunteer lifesavers out there to assist them, well trained, and very knowledgeable in all aspects of boating. They would almost always respond favorably to our cautions and corrections when violations occurred. In those rare instances when they ignored our warnings, the Coast Guard, Florida Marine Patrol, and Sheriff's Deputies were just a VHF radio call away.

After being called out several times for search and rescue missions in the pouring rain, I sold the open bay boat and bought a 25 foot Bayliner Cabin Cruiser. It was a great boat and perfect for patrols. I was so involved in the Auxiliary that Katherine thought I was back on active duty. She asked me where was the check, and I told her it was in the mail---but it never showed up! I attended every course of instruction that was offered to Aux members. It's all volunteer work, but it is very needed and worthwhile. I was surprised at the number of 'boaters' that would invest $500,000 in a new boat and when the dealer would offer a class on it, they would say, "Naw, I've been a boater for years---just tell me which is the front end of this thing and I'll be fine"-----an accident looking for a place to happen. I received much personal satisfaction, knowing I was making a difference in saving lives on the water.

I could write another whole book on dumb and dangerous things I saw boaters doing. I will give a couple of examples: Each year, thousands of "snowbirds" would come from up Nawth to our area for vacations and rent personal watercraft (jet skis). Many times they would violate "no wake zones" and speed through waters where kids were swimming. This is obviously very dangerous, since it is very difficult to see little heads bobbing up and down in the waves. Many times, when I would pull the Jet skiers over, the driver would say, "Yes I saw the "no wake" sign but I thought it was just meant for boats," whereupon I would ask if he thought he was driving a horse and wagon?? Jet skis are boats and are subject to all the laws and regulations of any other boat. One violation in particular that I found very distressing and had very little patience with (it was worth a $1,000 fine by law enforcement) was families in a run-about, with kids "bow-riding"---sitting on the bow of the boat with their legs hanging off the front of the boat. Here's Dad, speeding along and when I stopped them, I would usually ask if he cared about his kids (adults did this also). He then got the "Hoglan lecture about bow-riding". A boat does not have brakes! It will not stop within it's own length when power is cut, even at slow speeds. If the boat hits an object or otherwise stops, and the person falls off the front of the boat, the bow-rider *is going to meet the propeller up close and personal!!* Every year, in our area, somebody is going to lose an arm or leg, or another body part, or worse. One type of accident, and statistic that I found interesting was the number of duck hunters that drown each year. I think one reason that this is true, is that most duck hunters do not consider themselves boaters, and almost never wear life preservers. And when they are discovered drowned, most of them have their flies in the front of their trousers un-zipped, so we know what they were doing when they fell overboard!!! Please wait until you get back on shore before you *whiz!*

As a vessel examiner, I used an approved checklist to insure that boats had all the safety equipment mandated by state and federal regulations. If the boat passed the inspection, a decal would be awarded signifying that the boat met all the requirements. The inspection was voluntary on the part of the boat owner, but most boat owners wanted to be sure they met the standards. We did *not* write citations for violations, but the law enforcement agencies *did!* I inspected more than 100 vessels per year for several years. We enjoyed a close relationship with the Florida Marine Patrol, Okaloosa County Sheriff's Marine Officers, and of course, the Coast Guard. We did joint safety patrols, search and rescue missions, and exercises with them. The AUX taught *all* of the boating safety classes to the public for the Coast Guard. We were authorized to do everything the Coast Guard could do, with two major exceptions---no military duties and no law enforcement. There were two AUX Flotillas in this area and we coordinated our activities, for public education courses, inspection and verification of

ATONs, and safety patrols. We always had a number of AUX boats scheduled for patrol on the weekends and on some weekdays. We were out there in Choctawhatchee Bay and the Gulf of Mexico, primarily to promote boating safety, render assistance to boats in need, and perform search and rescue when directed by the local Coast Guard Station. The minimum number of crewmembers while on CG Aux patrol was two, except for jet skis, and all crewmembers were required to *wear* personal floatation devices (life vests) anytime the boat was under way.

I was privileged to serve with some outstanding people in the Coast Guard Auxiliary. Keith Jerome was one of my mentors, and lives nearby. I went on many patrols as a crewmember on his boat and learned a tremendous amount of boating skills from him. Keith was a true master mariner, a real gentleman, and remains a good friend, along with his sweet wife, Sally. Leland Crenshaw joined the CG Flotilla about the same time that I did. We "grew up" together on the water here, although he had been boating for many years. He was also a pilot, so we often swapped lies, uh, stories about our flying days. Barbara told him if he bought another airplane, he would have to *live* in it! We were boat crews on each other's boats for the 8 years we were in the AUX. Leland and Barbara also live in our neighborhood, and are great friends. John Givens continues to amaze me. John served 34 years in the Air Force, and then 34 years in the Coast Guard AUX. He is the most knowledgeable person I ever met about boating and has occupied every position on the Flotilla staff, as well as many jobs on the Division and District staffs. I have learned so much from John. He and Sarah are good friends and live about 5 miles from here. There are many other outstanding folks that I met in the AUX, in several states in the District, including my two "valley girls", Joann Kaufmann and Phillis King from Texas. These two queens have 35 years of service in the CG AUX, and have contributed immensely to boating safety, and what can I say? They love me (and I love them).

Just after we moved here and I joined the CG AUX, a previous Army friend moved here and attended one of my boat safety classes. It had been several years since I had seen Mike Spigelmire. Mike came to the Infantry Officer Advanced Course at Fort Benning, Georgia as a young Captain. I was a Major, teaching Artillery subjects at the Infantry School. He began dating Dianne, the secretary of the Nuclear

Weapons Committee next door to our Artillery Committee office. Later, Mike and Dianne were married. Although Mike and I were never assigned to the same unit at the same time, we saw them occasionally. After I had retired, he commanded the 24th Infantry Division at Fort Stewart, Georgia, and we attended the Division Artillery Ball. He started out as a new 2nd Lieutenant in the same Division. Mike served on active duty for 32 years and retired in 1992 as a Lieutenant General. His last assignment was as Commanding General, Seventh Corps in Germany. He had a distinguished military career, and I take great pride in knowing that *I taught him everything he knows!!!* After retirement, he worked for four years as an Olympic Committee Director, as Atlanta prepared for the '96 Olympic games. Since then, Mike has worked as a consultant to various defense contractors. They built a home in Kelly Plantation, in Destin, FL, just across Choctawhatchee Bay, about a 10-minute drive from here. I recruited Mike into the Coast Guard Auxiliary and we crewed on each other's boats for 8 years. He and Dianne are great friends of ours, and we see each other often. They have an outstanding son, Chris, who is an Air Force Academy graduate, and is now an Air Force Lieutenant Colonel, a fighter pilot, and just assumed command of a squadron in Texas. I am fortunate to have so many great friends, and I count Mike Spigelmire at the top of that list.

"Don't ever look back, somethin' may be gainin' on you!"

Satchel Paige

FOUR

Travel, Travel, Travel

Before we moved to Niceville, Florida, we went on a short eastern Caribbean Sea cruise out of Ft. Lauderdale in February 1989 and visited Labadee, Haiti; San Juan, Puerto Rico; and St. Thomas. The bug bit us......bad! After we moved to Florida, starting in 1997, we have been on 16 more overseas trips and cruises in the last 10 years. On an early one in 1998, we went on an eastern Mediterranean cruise, visiting Greece, Israel, Cyprus, Rhodes, Crete, and Turkey. The ship sent their daily newsletter around and it warned that unless you were in top physical condition, and could negotiate over rocks and uneven ground, do not try to go on some of these excursions. Well, the next morning, here are all the old folks, in their wheelchairs, walkers, crutches, etc. ready to go on the day's excursion to the Parthenon, Delphi, etc. and all the Greek and Roman ruins. Of course, they made it about 50 feet and had to sit down and wait several hours until the remainder of the group came back for them. Katherine took special note of that and remarked to me, "G.I., (I know when she uses that salutation, something important is about to occur) do you see that?" I replied, "Yes ma'am", as I usually do. She clued me in to the plan ----"When we get *that* old and in *that* deteriorated physical condition, we are going to stay home, rock on the back porch, and maybe drive down to the beach, 11 minutes away, and listen to the waves come ashore, *but*, until then, we are going to *TRAVEL!!* I said "Yes ma'am", as I usually do. I got my traveling shoes ready!

NINE CARIBBEAN CRUISES. Of the 16 overseas trips we have made in the last ten years, nine have been to the Caribbean Sea, visiting 31 islands and countries in the region. Mercifully, I will not discuss each trip in detail. I will summarize the Caribbean cruises; we have enjoyed all of them immensely. Three of our favorite Caribbean islands are the ABC islands in the Netherlands Antilles: Aruba, Bonaire, and Curacao. They were noticeably cleaner than other destinations, and the buildings, particularly in the harbor areas, were painted in pastel colors and looked as if they were painted yesterday. The main harbor in Curacao is really beautiful, with a unique swinging bridge that connects both sides of the harbor.

One thing that every destination had in common was great weather. The Caribbean is a great place to visit in the winter. We never had a rainy, overcast, stormy or cold day. Short sleeve shirt attire every day---Chamber of Commerce weather. I know it rains in the tropics—we visited many rain forests, but we never had bad weather that prevented us from following the schedule. We choose cruises, not just to be on a cruise liner, but our selections are based on destinations---we enjoy visiting new places. We do not attempt to revisit islands, but sometimes duplication happens because of itineraries. And life on the boat is pretty good. Where can you stay in a 4 or 5 star hotel, eat gourmet meals, be entertained with Las Vegas style shows, visit beautiful, exotic places with professional guides, and have such a variety of activities for about $100 a day? Can hardly live at home for that!

Another advantage of the Caribbean is that everyone we came in contact with spoke English. In most all the islands, English is the dominant language. Even in the Central and South American countries we visited, any native involved in their tourism industry spoke English fluently---no translators were ever needed.

And for us lucky Floridians, we have many nearby ports to choose cruises from, so travel to and from the boat is not a problem. Within a reasonable driving distance are Tampa, Jacksonville, Cape Canaveral, Fort Lauderdale, Miami, Mobile, and New Orleans. We departed on several cruises from the Port of Tampa. Bonuses on these trips have been overnight stays with great friends in Clearwater Beach, Don and Norma Jean Infanti.

One of the first neighborhood couples we met when we moved here was Tom and Sheila Kerr. They have become great friends of ours, and have traveled with us on several occasions. Tom is a retired Marine (I don't hold that against him) so we can tell war stories, all true of course. Tom is also a travel agent, so the plan goes like this: I find a tour or cruise that we think we would enjoy, mention it to Tom, and he gets the best price----or----Tom sees one that they think we would enjoy and he tells us about it---or---we find one that we all want to go on. We have been on several Caribbean cruises, one super trip to Alaska, and a nice trip to the Napa and Sonoma Valleys in California with them. The best part is that they are great traveling partners. We are very compatible, close friends, and can stay together for a couple of weeks or so, without wanting to kill each other! When we are not traveling, we visit with each other and go out to eat often. Tom has good tastes in food, wine, and wives----Sheila is a sweetheart. They have three married children---I love Jackie and Sue---Charlie, the son, is OK! No, Charlie is a neat guy, but I really do love Jackie and Sue. Sue and her husband, Pete, live in Pensacola and she is a travel agent, like her old man. Jackie and her husband, Karl, live in Slidell, LA. On several occasions we have departed on trips from New Orleans, by boat or airplane, and have spent the night at their house, and sweet Jackie has driven us to the airport. More about the Alaska and California trips with the Kerrs later.

EASTERN MEDITERANEAN CRUISE. We have been on two Mediterranean cruises. On the first one in November 1998, we visited Athens, Greece; Haifa and Ashdod, Israel; Cyprus; Rhodes; Crete; Kusadasi and Istanbul, Turkey. We flew to Athens, and spent several days there. We had been to Athens earlier and had toured some of the ancient Greek ruins on our own, but on this trip, the tours were more extensive and included many more historical sites and guides to explain their history. Highlights of the visit to Athens were the archaeological sites, including the Parthenon, Acropolis, Olympic stadium, and a full day touring the ancient and mystic city of Delphi. We enjoyed a sumptuous meal and exciting Greek entertainment one evening in the vineyards at an old farmhouse. At the end of our visit to Athens, we were bussed to the Port of Piraeus and boarded our ship.

We sailed on the R-1, a Renaissance Cruise Line Ship. This was our favorite cruise line, because of the outstanding value to price figures (the price included international air fare to the beginning of the cruise in Athens and return air fare from Turkey to the US.) We had a balcony cabin. It was a mid-size ship as were all the Renaissance ships—684 passengers. We liked their rules---no kids below the age of 18 on board (think about it---not all bad), no formal nights requiring tux and formal dress, no assigned seating for meals---eat anytime in 4 great restaurants (included), and no smoking, anytime, anywhere on the ship. In fact, the deal must have been too good, because after our second cruise on Renaissance, the company went bankrupt and folded. They built too many ships too fast (8, I think), and I believe incurred too much debt too soon and could not pay off their debtors.

We spent the next three *long* days visiting in Israel. The ship docked at two ports, Haifa and Ashdod, which enabled us to see as much of Israel as possible. These three days were worth the entire cruise/tour---what incredible history! We visited Nazareth, explored the Basilica of the Annunciation, the Church of Joseph (built over the carpentry shop), and Mary's Well. We drove through Cana where Jesus turned water into wine, past Tabgha where Jesus multiplied the loaves and fishes, and the Mount of Beatitudes, where He preached the Sermon on the Mount. We spent some time in Capernaum on the shores of the Sea of Galilee, and the Yardenit baptismal site where the River Jordan separates from the Sea of Galilee, and where Jesus was baptized.

The next day we drove through the Judean hills and desert on the way to Massada. When Katherine saw the desert, she asked if this barren land was what the Israelites and Palestinians were fighting over. I told her yes, and that the *loser* got possession of the land—that's why they were fighting so hard! In a way, it was a pretty *moonscape* with the only signs of life being a few Bedouins and some goats. There was not a blade of grass, so undoubtedly the goats ate rocks! We arrived at Massada, and ascended by cable car to this mountain top fortress, built by Herod the Great, where 950 Jewish Zealots, men, women, and children, held off more than 10,000 Roman soldiers for over a year in 73 AD. We passed by the Qumran Caves and saw where, in 1947, a Bedouin boy discovered the famous Dead Sea Scrolls, the oldest known biblical manuscripts in the world. On to the Dead Sea, the lowest point on Earth, where I got to float in the Dead Sea, or *on top* of the Dead Sea! The salinity of the water (@30%) makes it super buoyant. You don't have much *draft*, but a lot of *freeboard!* Note that I said *I* got to get in the water. Time to chase a rabbit. About two or three days before we departed for this trip, Katherine fell off a short ladder in the utility room. She wasn't hurt but she bruises very easy, and in about three days she turned black, blue, and purple. So, on this trip, I would not allow her to get into a swimsuit, for fear I would immediately be arrested for spouse abuse!

The third day in Israel, we traveled to Jerusalem and Bethlehem. In Jerusalem we visited the Wailing Wall, and walked along the famous Via Dolorosa, believed to be the route Jesus followed as he carried his cross to Calvary. We visited the Church of the Holy Sepulcher, on the hill known as Golgotha, marking the site of Jesus' crucifixion, burial, and resurrection. We had lunch at a Palestinian hotel restaurant on the Mount of Olives, overlooking the city of Jerusalem.

I requested the Matre' D to write my name in Arabic in a beautiful bible I had bought, with covers of olive wood, laser engraved with the Jerusalem cross. I previously had natives write my name in it also in Hebrew and Greek. We walked through the Gardens of Gethsemane, where Judas betrayed Jesus. In Bethlehem we visited Manger Square and entered the renowned Church of the Nativity, built over a grotto where it is believed Jesus was born.

These three days in Israel were an awesome adventure. We saw as much as is possible to see in three days in Israel. I am glad we went when we did. Even then, many of the itineraries skipped Israel because of the security situation, and now, the government of Israel has curtailed and reduced foreign visits.

Next on the itinerary for this tour, we sailed to Cyprus, an island split and owned/controlled by Greece and Turkey. It has been the subject of wars and squabbles between the two nations for years. It is a beautiful island, hilly, with terraced farmland growing olive trees, figs, lemons, pomegranates, and almonds. The port city is Limassol and we visited the little of town of Lania, a picturesque haven for residential artists. Then on to the village of Omodos, up in the Troodos mountains, where the famous local dry red wine is produced.. It was so quiet and peaceful with narrow, cobblestone streets, and on a hill, that overlooked beautiful valleys. Omodos is also known for its embroidered quilts, tablecloths, and intricate lace handiworks, produced by elderly women residents, whom we met. There is no fighting going on now in Cyprus, I don't think---Unique in today's world.

Our next stop was the island of Rhodes (Greece). We enjoyed climbing over many Greek and Roman ruins of fortresses and temples from the old world. We visited the quaint Greek village of Lindos high on a cliff above the Aegean Sea, inhabited since 2000 BC. It overlooks a harbor where St. Paul landed in 58 AD.

Ready for a rabbit chase? On this trip, our cruise director read a list of questions by previous passengers, most of which bear repeating. One was: "Why did the Greeks and Romans build all these ruins??" (Yes, she was blonde). More later.

After Rhodes, we sailed on to the island of Crete (Greece). We docked at the port of Iraklion. Since I had been to Crete 9 times and Katherine once, we did not take any shore excursions here. We just got off the ship and walked around Iraklion for a while, enjoyed some Souflaki (goat meat), which is a delicacy, and returned to the ship. Crete is the home of the great Minoan civilization. It is the largest of the Greek islands, and the most mountainous.

From Crete, we sailed to Turkey. We landed at the port of Kusadasi and were bussed to the ancient city of Ephesus, stopping on the way to visit the Basilica of St. John, the burial site of John the Apostle. Of all the ruins I have visited, Ephesus takes the blue ribbon---it is tops. It once had a population of 300,000, second in size only to Rome in the entire Roman Empire. The whole city was made out of marble, including the streets. Katherine and I walked hand in hand down the same marble streets that Anthony and Cleopatra walked hand in hand. We visited the old marble amphitheatre holding 25,000 people (big in those days) and many buildings. The two most interesting buildings to me were the community bathroom and the library. Of course, each residence had a bathroom and toilet, but the downtown community one had rows of marble seats with holes in them. Now, marble is somewhat cool to the touch, so the aristocracy would have their servants go sit on the "seats" and warm them up for their masters. That's pretty "kool", pardon the pun! The library was a beautiful building at the end of the main street. There was a "secret" underground passage that led to a house of ill repute on the other side of the street, so the gentlemen could tell their wives they were just going to the "library"!

After a great visit to Kusadasi and Ephesus, we sailed into the Marmara Sea to Istanbul, Turkey, where we stayed for the last three days of our trip. This was a fantastic stop, and I am glad we took advantage of the optional three-day post trip extension in Istanbul. This imperial capital was host to three of the greatest empires of the world—Roman, Byzantine, and Ottoman. It sits majestically astride the Bosphorus River that divides the continents of Europe and Asia. We visited the famous Blue Mosque, built in 1609, and the Christian Hagia Sophia, built in the 6th century AD---absolutely beautiful architecture.

We took a boat ride on the Bosphorus, visited museums, and historical sites and enjoyed delicious meals, complete with belly dancers!

Ready for another insightful question from a passenger? OK. "Does the crew sleep on board the ship?" Nah, we helicopter them in every morning from Miami!!

This first overseas cruise set the stage for many more. We had found a new hobby. We traveled in the Army, but it was usually between assignments, and time and destinations were pretty limited. Now that *every* day was Saturday (except Sundays), we could literally expand our horizons any time we wanted to. I will briefly summarize only a few of our remaining cruises and overseas trips.

RUSSIAN RIVER CRUISE. In July 1999, we embarked on a trip to Russia. (When I retired from the Army, I was not permitted to visit the USSR or any Eastern Bloc country for at least 7 years, because of my security clearances, etc. By 1999, I assured the Department of Defense that I couldn't even *remember* any secrets that long!) We signed up for this tour with GT Cruises, a Russian tour company with offices in New York. We flew from New York to Russia on Aeroflot, the Russian airline, and the flight over there was an adventure in itself. We flew nonstop from New York to Moscow. We were to change planes and fly to St. Petersburg where our cruise-tour began. Although they told us in New York we would change planes in Moscow, they did not happen to mention we would also be changing *airports* in Moscow! You see, they have the international airport in Moscow, but a different airport for domestic flights. I discovered this when we landed in Moscow very early in the morning and I could not find our next flight to St Petersburg listed. I finally found a young girl that could speak very little English and she looked at our tickets and said we had to go to another airport. We had a four-hour lay over in Moscow. I found a taxi driver who pointed to a bus stop across the street and said, "de bus 137." Hokay. We pushed the hand baggage cart through potholes over to the bus stop. At this time, Katherine was wondering if this had been such a good idea after all. After several busses came and went, old muddy number 137 rolled in. *Nobody spoke any English.* We just got on the bus---talk about *faith!* I just held out my hand full of Rubles and the old lady ticket taker took a couple. We departed and immediately found ourselves bouncing along on a gravel/dirt road. At the first stop, an old woman got on the bus with a sack of potatoes, bucket of cucumbers, and a goat! I was then pretty sure we were going for a ride in the country. We finally arrived at what looked like it may be an airport. We did not know *which* airport---we just got off. When we drug our luggage into the building, I looked up and saw our flight number posted immediately in front of me. We were the last two people to get on the plane, and they immediately closed the door. We had used up about 3 hours, 59 & 1/2 minutes of our 4-hour layover time. Five minutes later, and we may still be over there in the Russian countryside looking for a way out!

We landed in St. Petersburg and in the terminal saw a guy standing there holding up a sign that read, "GT Cruises". I ran over and hugged him! He helped us get our checked and hand luggage into his little Volkswagen outside in the parking lot. There were bags in the back seat next to Katherine and I was holding a large one in my lap. He fired it up, and the car would not go into reverse! We unloaded and pushed it out of the parking slot. It *did* go into forward gear and we bounced over paved but full-of-pothole streets down to the docks, where our cruise director, Zina met us dockside the MS Russ, our home for the next 16 days. (I also hugged Zina). Then *everything* turned wonderful. It was one of the most enjoyable and educational trips we ever made. The MS Russ is a long, narrow boat, passenger capacity of @ 280. All the river passenger boats look about the same. There are 18 locks on the rivers and canals between St. Petersburg and Moscow, so all the boat widths are the same. There were about 140 passengers on our cruise and everyone had an outside (river-view) cabin. Except for the male boat crew, which we seldom even saw, all employees on the boat, except one, were women. Zina and all her guides, waitresses, chef, cooks, doctor, language and history teachers, were women. The lone man was Oleg, the "voice of the MS Russ". He would wake us up with the PA system every morning with a corny joke and inform everybody what our activities would involve that day. They were all super friendly and very professional.

We toured and visited many things for three days in St. Petersburg before we sailed, but they would bring us back every night to the boat. We never had to stay in a Russian hotel or eat in Russian restaurants the entire trip. Even when we had all day shore excursions, a box lunch would be prepared and hung on the back of your chair at breakfast. So all other meals would be served on the boat. St. Petersburg has more than 100 picturesque islands, more than 60 canals, and hundreds of bridges. It is considered to be one of the most beautiful cities in the world. Highlights of our stay in St. Petersburg were visits to the Palaces of St. Petersburg. The Hermitage, formerly known as the Winter Palace and home of the Czars, was built by Peter the Great for his daughter. In 1764 it became a museum when Katherine the Great began her private art collection. Today it has more than 1,000 rooms and it would take you nearly three years to spend just 30 seconds in front of each work of art!! Need I say more? Other palaces visited were Peter & Paul Fortress, and Catherine's Palace.

I thought the most beautiful palace was Peterhof, built by Peter the Great, on the Gulf of Finland. It is awesome, very ornate, and has an extraordinary waterfall, the Grand Cascade, with 150 fountains shooting 2,000 jets of water. The waterworks have worked for over 250 years, for 13 miles without pumps, relying on a system of gravity. On one of the three days in St. Petersburg, we carried a box lunch from the ship, and at lunchtime we traveled to a park. The bus stopped and we saw police cars in the park. Our tour guide found out that there had been an assassination ahead of us. A wealthy CEO apparently had not paid his protection money to the mafia. They gave him a *second billing,* with two RPG rockets and a machine gun---he won't get a *third!* Later, our guest lecturer said that the governments of Russia had always been corrupt, even in the days of the czars, but now there was a new dimension ----the mafia (thanks to the U.S.). Our tour guide said they would never find out who killed the man, furthermore, they would not look too hard.

After our three-day visit to St. Petersburg, we cruised out of the city on the Neva River. During the next 16 days we would traverse 1,500 miles through, Lake Ladoga, the largest lake in Europe, Lake Onega, the second largest, connected by the Svir River. Most of our voyage was on the Volga River, connecting with the Moscow canal into Moscow.

One of our first stops was at the tiny island of Kizhi, in Lake Onega, where we had a ½ day shore excursion. Highlight of the stop was a visit to the Transfiguration Church. All the churches in Russia have onion top domes---this one had 22. I think that is a record. The church was made entirely of wood---not even a nail in it.

We visited many of the villages, towns and cities along the Volga River. One of the more interesting stops and shore excursions was a visit to Irma, a tiny village on the Volga. We docked at the riverbank and walked up a trail to the top of a hill. There was Irma, a one street village, dirt road and all. The local citizens had their kiosk tables out in the street, covered mostly with locally produced items and souvenirs. This was common in every town we visited. There were six of us walking along together---the other two couples were new friends from California. As we were shopping, a lady came out of her house and grabbed us and ushered us through her garden and into her house. She had set a table, covered with food and deserts, and of course, plenty of Vodka. Her name was Bakka. She and her daughter served us royally. This was NOT part of the cruise/tour. It was very obvious that she was doing this on her own. Although she had some homemade jewelry for sale in a separate room, she hardly mentioned this. She just seemed to really like Americans, and we had a great visit of more than an hour. We did tip her generously, but you cannot buy the kind of hospitality that she showed. As a matter of fact, we received this kind of hospitality everywhere we went. The Russian people seemed to genuinely like us---not just our money, because we were spending Rubles, and they were not worth anything! And we liked the Russian people---its too bad that the Russian government is so corrupt and so anti-American. If they would just let the people alone, our two countries would get along just fine-----we found that to be true in most countries we have visited. Later, back out on the street, we bought some trinkets, and Katherine bought a sweater hanging in a tree! We came sliding back down the trail to the riverbank where the ship's crew had prepared a barbeque for us. A great visit.

During sailing days, the tour crew (not boat crew) would teach language classes, and I attended all of these and enjoyed them. Spaseeba. They also taught us geography and history classes and they were very interesting. Highlights included several lectures by Dr. Zoya Zarubina.

I fell in love with Zoya. I guess I fall in love easily, but this fantastic lady was a former Soviet Intelligence Officer, drafted into the Soviet Army at age 23, and was the interpreter for Stalin, Roosevelt, and Churchill at the Tehran and Yalta conferences. She also translated at the Potsdam conference and Nuremberg trials. She is a walking, talking, historical encyclopedia, and staunchly anti-communist (she has a choice now). I bought her biography: "Inside Russia: The Life and Times of Zoya Zarubina". I got to know a little bit about her—we had several personal conversations, and she gave me a ceramic Russian doll. Her main hobby currently is sponsorship of three Russian Orphanages. There are many orphanages in Russia---more about that later.

On the boat, as we were sailing, they kept us busy with all kinds of entertainment, including "self-entertainment". The passengers produced skits, under the supervision and direction of the tour crew. They had it all worked out, with script (roughly), complete with costumes. Can you visualize the "kid" dancing to Swan Lake in a Tutu??!! We also had first class entertainers, singers, and dancers, perform for us on the ship. Often we would pick up a troupe of entertainers at one stop and they would entertain us until we reached the next stop. Several times, a combo of musicians would be playing for us at the dock when we were arriving and departing. I had packed my German Pocket Trumpet, of course, heh, heh, and I joined them. I was amazed that most of them were playing American Dixieland music, so "The Saints" and other assorted hymns saved me once more. When our cruise director noticed this, she asked me to be the Master of Ceremonies for the ship's passenger talent show. I did it, under duress, of course, and the ship's band, and the audience had as much fun as I did. At the talent show, I remembered Dr. Zoya's sponsorship of three orphanages, and I told the audience that I thought we should take up a collection for them---we passed the hat and raised @ $400 on the spot. Dr. Zoya now loves me too!

We had an all day shore excursion in Yaroslavl, population of 600,000. It was founded in the 11th century and retains many of the noteworthy monuments of its colorful past. Loveliest of all is the Church of Elijah the Prophet situated in the city's central square. We were there on Elijah the Prophet Day, so it was very special.

We also visited Kostroma, museums and churches, and Uglich, founded in 1148, where the Church of St. Deinitrius on the Blood was built and stands today. An important note is in order about Russian churches. Undoubtedly, Russia has many more churches per capita (or per anything) than any country we have ever visited. This was a surprise to us. We all know that the communists in charge of the Soviet Union outlawed churches. They would not let them be used as churches—they were warehouses, orphanages, etc. during the communist reign. Thank God, they did not destroy them. There are accounts where Russian women took lots of Icons and other religious symbols, artifacts and treasures to Siberia and hid them beginning with WW II. Now the churches have been restored and are used (really used) as churches. I thought the cathedrals in France were ornate---no, they are pretty plain compared to the beautiful and ornate churches in Russia.

After several more stops, we arrived in Moscow. In the capitol city, affluence was noticeable. The people were well dressed, and were driving Mercedes, BMWs, and Porches. The streets were well maintained---we didn't find many potholes. It seemed to be a classic example where all the resources were invested in the capitol city while the rest of the country lived on the breadcrumbs that fell off the Moscow dinner table! We visited in Moscow for 3 days, returning to the ship every night. We had 5 organized visits to Red Square and the Kremlin in 3 days! I guess they really wanted us to see it, and it was certainly worthwhile. We toured the Armory, now the location of a fantastic museum where all the treasures presented to the Czars by foreign heads of state are on display—fantastic treasures that could not be reproduced today. There are three beautiful churches inside the Kremlin that we visited. The office of the Russian President is in the Kremlin and we saw Yeltsin drive by with his motorcade. We shopped in the Gom in Red Square---the largest department store in the world---I say shopped, not bought. Things in Moscow were very expensive compared to the rest of the country. Lenin's Mausoleum is in Red Square---his body is on display---we skipped standing in line to see him! One of the most beautiful churches we saw was the St. Basil's Cathedral with its many colored onion top domes. We spent one enjoyable evening at the Moscow Circus. We were kept very busy and it is impossible to adequately explain and do justice to the sights and insights that we enjoyed, and that includes the entire visit to Russia.

Final comments on Russia (Hoglan's view, with input from Dr. Zoya): The Prussian, Russian, Soviet, then Russian (again) government has always been corrupt. One big difference is that now the Russians are *relatively free* to criticize it openly---our tour guides did! The young Russians really like their newfound freedom (along with mini-skirts, *evil* rock and roll music, and other western *bad* influences.) They would never vote to go back to the communist reign. But the old folks would vote to go back, because at least under the old system, they had bread on their table, *guaranteed*. As we (should) have learned over and over, it is very difficult for a country and society to transition into *our* brand of democracy over night, particularly if they have been under evil dictatorships for centuries! We don't seem to understand that! More soap box later on this subject.

I mentioned that are many orphanages in Russia. On our flight back to the U.S.A. there were three couples seated near us that had adopted children. The process takes about one year. They initiate the application, and tons of paperwork from both countries follows. We were told that it is a very bureaucratic and time-consuming process. Finally, about 1 month before the prospective parents visit the orphanage, they receive a picture of the child. Upon arrival at the orphanage, they stay with a local family while finalizing the process. Most of the orphanages are in Siberia. They are only told the given name of the biological mother. No medical records are shown to the adopting couple. The fee is $30,000 U.S. per child adopted. They are cute kids. Two of the couples had one baby each and they played and slept and never cried or fussed a single time. The other couple had adopted two slightly older children. They told us that unfortunately the orphanage got very little of the money. The government got the most of it.

We would heartily recommend a visit to Russia by Americans. It was very educational as well as completely enjoyable. But in the end, you will be so proud and feel so lucky to be Americans. I guess that is the one common feeling that we had after every trip we ever took. God, help us to keep our great country and our way of life.

WESTERN MEDITERRANEAN CRUISE. Our next overseas cruise/tour was back to the Mediterranean, visiting Spain, Mallorca, Gibraltar, Morocco (Casablanca and Tangier), and Portugal, in Nov 1999. Time for another question from a passenger? Hokay. "Does the ship generate its own power?" Why no, we have this v-e-r-y l-o-n-g extension cord plugged into a wall socket somewhere in Miami! Highlights of this trip were the stops along the Spanish Coast and a visit to the 13th century palace, the Legendary Alhambra. Also noteworthy was the visit to the largest city in Morocco, Casablanca. We didn't see Humphrey Bogart, but we did see the Grande Mosque Hassan II, one of the largest in the world. We fed the Barbary Apes on top of the Rock of Gibraltar, and toured the Casbah in Tangier. We decided that was about all of Africa we wanted to see.

AUSTRALIA/NEW ZEALAND CRUISE TOUR. After another Caribbean cruise, we launched to Australia and New Zealand in Jan-Feb, 2001. First of all, it's a long way from Niceville to Sydney! I paid extra $ and got us Business Class seats. On Quantas Airlines, Business Class is at least as good as First Class on most American airlines. We stayed in the Four Points Hotel overlooking the beautiful, Darling Harbour, and toured the sights in Sydney for five days on our own. The two most famous landmarks in Sydney are the Harbor Bridge and Sydney Opera House. They are more awesome "in person" than in pictures. We went to Chinatown twice and shopped in Paddy's market, where every souvenir in the world is sold. We had to buy another suitcase to hold all the loot.

We traveled by bus about one hour out of Sydney to Featherdale Wildlife Park. This was a highlight, where we fed and petted Kangaroos, Wallabies, Koalas, and other critters. We saw Tasmanian Devils (didn't pet those fellers) and observed feeding time for the huge Saltwater Crocodiles. We visited beautiful Chinese Gardens near Darling Harbour, and went up to the observation deck of the AMP Tower, the highest structure in the southern hemisphere, for spectacular views of Sydney and the surrounding area. We spent a lot of time in the Royal Botanic Gardens of Sydney. I didn't think I was into flowers that much, but thank goodness I really enjoyed them. I did not realize it until later, but we spent more time walking through flower gardens on this trip than any other single thing we did. Every city, and even small town we visited in New Zealand and the two cities we visited in Australia (Sydney and Melbourne) have Botanical Gardens, and they are all huge and spectacularly beautiful. The cities and towns are full of parks, resplendent with trees, shrubs, and zillions of flowers, and spotlessly clean! Where we raise asphalt and concrete, they raise trees, green grass, and flowers. We were in Sydney on 26 January 2001, "Australia Day", a special holiday, when two million other folks participating in or observing 5,000 events joined us! In some regards, it probably beats the crawfish fest in Breaux Bridge, or the frog fest in Rayne, LA!

We sailed out of Sydney on 29 January 2001 (our wedding anniversary) on the Legend of the Seas, Caribbean Cruise Line (I don't know how they ended up in Australia---its a long way from the Caribbean---must have gotten lost). This lil boat weighs 70,000 tons, carries 1,804 passengers, and crew of 735. It is not the biggest ship we have sailed on, but its pretty good size!

We spent the next day relaxing at sea, and docked in Melbourne the following morning. Melbourne is the second largest city in Australia, and of course, is beautiful with lots of parks and greenery. We enjoyed visiting their Botanical Gardens.

Our next stop was in Hobart, in the island state of Tasmania. We took a tour of (can you guess) the Royal Botanical Gardens, including the Conservatory, a large indoor plant and flower area with a fern forest. We continued the tour up to the top of Mount Wellington for great views of Hobart and the surrounding area. After lunch back on the ship, we walked down to the city center and soaked up some more of the local culture at a sidewalk café. Said Hi to all the Tasmanian Devils we saw.

We spent the next two days sailing into and out of, three "sounds" (like Scandinavian fjords), Milford Sound, Doubtful Sound, and Dusky Sound—Incredible, awesome scenery in the mountains, usually on both sides of the ship---snow on some mountain tops, and dozens of waterfalls.

Our first landfall in New Zealand, where we took a shore excursion was in Dunedin, and we thoroughly enjoyed a visit to the (surprise, surprise) botanical gardens. In the interest of time (and possibly boredom), our next stop on the cruise was in Christ's Church, one of my very favorite visits. It is a very beautiful port city and we had our favorite shore excursion here---a 45-minute bus ride out into the country to visit a sheep farm. The Daddy of the farm explained sheep farming to us, and then demonstrated a very interesting and fast sheep shearing in the barn. He then unchained Patty---she had been chomping at the bit to go get the sheep up on the mountain, which started in the back yard of the farmhouse. Patty raced up the mountain, varying directions according to her owner's directions and signals. She went so far up the mountain; I could only see her through my camera's telephoto lens. She circled around in back of the sheep and started them down the mountain. If she crowded them too much and they began to run, she would hit the ground, belly first, and not move a muscle until they settled down. She would rove right and left as necessary to clearly show them the way she wanted them to take to get down the mountain. She circled behind them, right and left, collecting all strays and keeping them on course, but gently, not causing a stampede. She herded those sheep right down the rugged mountain to an open gate into the back yard, where we could reach out and touch them. Then she went over to the side of the yard, lay down, and said. "OK, folks, how 'bout dat?"! She was amazing! I understand that one of the favorite sports is competitive "sheep dogging"!! I see why! The lady of the house had laid out an outstanding buffet around her swimming pool and also invited us to tour her house. We bought a cuddly sheep doll and did not realize it until we got home---if you squeeze it, it goes Baaa! A great day!

We continued up the West Coast of New Zealand to our next stop, Wellington, the capitol of New Zealand. Beautiful churches and cathedrals, a beautiful harbor, and cable cars have often caused this city to be compared to San Francisco. We took a bus tour where we viewed the city from atop Mount Victoria, then to the Botanical Gardens where we again saw beautiful flowers. Enjoyed a museum and watched a parade led by bagpipes and rugby teams in town for an international tournament.

Next stop, Napier that had been destroyed by an earthquake in 1931, and rebuilt in the Art Deco style. We walked around town and listened to a street entertainer that did a great rendition of Johnny Cash's Folsom Prison. The people at every stop in New Zealand were very friendly and seemed to enjoy talking to us and offering to help with directions and suggestions.

Our next port was Tauranga. The ship's Captain announced that our arrival was special in that no cruise ship as large as ours had ever docked there. It must have been announced on shore as well---hundreds of people lined the shoreline and dock area. There was a little ceremony, with the town crier welcoming us, complete with native drummers.

After a day at sea, we docked and disembarked in Auckland, the largest city in New Zealand, with about one million people. It is a beautiful city and we stayed 4 days on our own to take in the sights. We visited the huge Auckland Museum, with a very interesting Maori native gallery, and saw a terrific demonstration of native dances by costumed Maori warriors and ladies. We went up 1,000 feet to the top of the Sky Tower for an excellent view of the city. We then visited Underwater World where we walked *under* sharks and zillions of fish, and then took a ride on a specially built snow cat through an Antarctica experience to see penguins in their frozen landscape. Auckland has a huge zoo with over 600 animals, where we walked through a tropical rainforest, a native New Zealand forest, and an African savannah. They have critters that I had never heard of before (or since). No visit to any town in New Zealand would be complete unless one visits the gardens. Auckland's Winter Gardens include two large enclosed conservatories with every kind of flowers, plants and ferns imaginable. There was even a string quartet playing soothing music and a cat to pet! If anyone asked me to describe New Zealand in three words, I would say, "beautiful botanical gardens." Or maybe, "very friendly people". "Smart sheep dogs", could also apply. In summary, it was one of the best trips we ever made. But it was a long one and we were anxious to get home and see our kitty, Missy.

ALASKA CRUISE TOUR. After another Caribbean Sea cruise, the next cruise/tour I want to summarize is one to Alaska we made with the Kerr's. When we were stationed in Anchorage, Alaska for three years in 1956-59, I was a Lieutenant and we did not have enough money to travel---we never even made it to Fairbanks. On this trip we flew to Seattle on 29 May 2002, and spent a couple of days sightseeing, including an all day trip by ferry out to Vancouver Island. We toured Victoria, capital of British Columbia, one of only two capitals inaccessible by road (do you know the other one? We visited it later). The Buchart Gardens were fantastic, since we now were experts on flowers and plants! We boarded the Ocean Princess in Vancouver and sailed the Inland Passage to Seward. We had a private balcony cabin, with great views. We had great stops and shore excursions along the way in Ketchikan and in

Juneau, Alaska (the other capital not accessible by road). Our favorite stop was in Skagway, the old gold-rush town. We were bussed to the old miners town of Liarsville, and were met by the madam who welcomed us to town. A hilarious skit was presented, and we panned for gold (got some too).

We sailed into Glacier Bay and College Fjord and saw many glaciers, including the Mendenhall Glacier.

At one of our stops, Libby Riddles came aboard our ship and gave an outstanding talk and picture slide show. She was the first woman to win the Iditerod Dog sled race! She brought her lead sled dog on board with her. This is an amazing dog sled race; it goes from Anchorage to Nome and it is literally death defying. It is the absolute definition of endurance.

On to Seward, where we disembarked and were bussed to Anchorage. After spending the night and visiting our old stomping grounds at Fort Richardson, we boarded the private Princess car on the Midnight Sun Express Train for our overland trip to Fairbanks. We stopped for a couple of days at Denali State and National Parks and stayed in the Princess wilderness lodge. It was a beautiful place and one day we actually got to see the top of Mt. McKinley, normally covered by clouds. We took several side trips by bus, viewing wildlife such as moose, elk, caribou, reindeer, eagles, Dahl sheep, etc., and enjoyed a jet boat safari in Talkeetna. Most all the bus drivers were Mormon college kids from Utah. They were delightful, and also worked in the lodges. Most of the bus drivers had memorized long story/poems, like "The Cremation of Sam McGee", and "The Shooting of Dan McGrew." They would entertain us on the bus trips. On several of the wildlife viewing trips, the cruise line would normally guarantee that guests *would in fact, see* the wildlife advertised, or they would return the fees paid for the excursion.

One of our bus drivers related that in one particular summer, the wildlife was so skittish that they stayed under cover. It was so bad that the cruise line paid some of the college students to dress up in animal costumes. It went like this: In this instance, they hired Bruce to wear a moose suit. They would drop him off close to a bus dismount point where the guests were supposed to view the animals. He had a two way radio and when the tourist bus was nearing the stopping/viewing point, they would call "Bruce, the Moose" on the radio and tell him that they were a couple of miles from the animal viewing point and Bruce would don his moose suit. Well, the bus arrived and the guests dismounted and one of them yelled, "Look, a moose." Everybody got excited and began taking pictures of the "moose". Bruce was really doing his thing, and he happened to look in the opposite direction of the bus. There stood the largest carnivore on the North American continent: the Alaskan Brown Bear, looking at Bruce. His heart stood still, then the bear started moving slowly toward Bruce. Bruce started moving slowly toward the bus. Bruce speeded up; so did the bear. Bruce panicked and started yelling, "Help me, help me, I am not a moose." At that point the bear yelled at Bruce, "Shut up fool, you're going to get us both fired!" True story---as all of mine are!

We spent 2 enjoyable days in Fairbanks at another Princess wilderness lodge. We visited the EL Dorado gold mine and panned for gold again---got some more gold---they plant the gold so they can sell you the fancy containers to put it in. We saw a great show at the Palace Saloon in Alaskaland , pigged out on Alaskan King Crab, Lobster, and Halibut (their answer to our Grouper).

A highlight of the stay in Fairbanks, was a paddle wheel boat ride on the Shena River, where we met Susan Butcher, and her dogs, who won the Iditerod 4 times (did I say 4 times?!). This woman is super-human! We docked and visited an Indian/Eskimo village (re-built just for us tourists) and were given a demonstration of a dog sled race (on dry land) by Jesse ?, ---she was the rookie of the year in this year's race (finished 14 out of 65). Those dogs live to run!

We flew from Fairbanks back to home in Florida. The scenery we witnessed on this trip was indescribable. We knew *that* from our 3 years in Alaska, 1956—59, but we were even surprised at how awesome and huge this state is. As with all of our other trips, we have hundreds of pictures, scrapbook items, and movies that describe our travels much better than words. I hope I have peaked your interest in these places. Come visit us to get completely hooked on our wanderings! One more brilliant question from a cruise passenger?? (Aw, stop it!). Overheard in the room where all the ship photographer's photos are displayed, "With all these pictures, how do I know which are mine?" Duh!

EASTERN EUROPE. Two more cruises to the Caribbean, and then, on 28 June 2004, we flew to Warsaw, Poland for the start of our

19-day trip to Eastern Europe. This was a great trip, organized by Grand Circle Travel (GCT), our favorite international travel company. It was special because Dick and Ann Noack went with us.

I need to chase another rabbit here: you remember my great friend Dick Noack, who was my Battalion XO at Fort Benning, then my Area Commander for the State of Pennsylvania in the ROTC assignment in 1982 at Fort Bragg, where we both retired in 1985. His sweet wife, Mary was Katherine's close friend! Mary died after a valiant struggle with cancer. After a few years, an acquaintance called Dick's children, Kathy, Lori, and Mike, and asked them if they would mind if she introduced Dick to a good friend of hers. They all said no problem at all. I thought this was very classy, on the part of the acquaintance and these wonderful kids. To make a long story short, after a while, Dick and Ann were married. She is an absolute doll. All of Dick's kids love her, and so does the Hoglan family. We have visited them in San Antonio and they have visited us here in Florida. We have now been on two overseas trips with them, and we thoroughly enjoy their company and our visits together.

After arrival in Warsaw, we were escorted to our hotel where we met Ann and Dick, our tour director, Paul, and our other traveling companions, and enjoyed a welcome dinner. The next day we set off on a half-day Warsaw city tour. Warsaw suffered heavy damage during WW II, about 85%, so now, unfortunately, there are many new steel and glass, (read ugly) modern buildings that somehow just don't quite fit with the beautiful old architecture. The historic Old Town (closed to all vehicular traffic) has been reconstructed, with narrow, winding streets, churches, and cobblestone streets in the old town square. This was our favorite place to visit in Warsaw. We visited a beautiful park, with 112,000 rose bushes (I counted them) and a statue of Chopin, the most popular citizen of Poland.

This evening, we had dinner in a local home (a trademark of GCT tours). We did not know in advance, but the dinner was at the home of our tour director, Paul, where we met his brothers, sisters, cousins, and grandmothers—it takes a lot of folks to feed a lot of folks! (His Mom was tour directing for another bunch of gringo tourists---we would meet her later, in Budapest). It was delicious meal, pleasant company, and an enjoyable evening.

On day four, we continued soaking up the Warsaw experience, doing many things, but the highlight of our stay in Warsaw was an evening bus trip, about an hour and a half outside the city, in the *country,* at the end of a dirt country lane, to a house, with a separate building having a kitchen and dining area. Several ladies met us in the courtyard with beverages, and then fed us a feast in the dining area (of course I had to have my picture made with them). We then walked about 30 yards to the house, where we entered the small living room. It had a grand piano and about 40 chairs, enough to seat our busload of folks (with no room to spare). They introduced Eugeniusz Chudak-Morzuchowski, one of the most famous Polish pianists, who played many of Chopin's most famous compositions. Our own, personal concert! And he was not sitting up on a stage---we were sitting close enough to touch the piano. He was the best pianist I have ever heard. Afterward he posed for pictures and signed autographs. A great evening.

The next day, we drove a scenic 200 mile route to Krakow, stopping in Czestochowa to visit a 14th century monastery where we saw the Black Madonna shrine. Our local tour director for this visit was a priest who was a comedian. Funny! We thoroughly enjoyed our stay in Krakow. It is the only city in Poland that escaped destruction in World War II. With seven centuries of architecture, it is a beautiful old city, and has been designated a UNESCO World Heritage Site. As in most European cities, it has an old town square, and this one was our very favorite. It is very large, the largest in medieval Europe, with lots of people, pigeons, and horse drawn carriages. There is a covered market place in the center of the square, with every imaginable gift, souvenir, and trinket for sale. On one side of the square is the Church of the Virgin Mary, a spectacularly beautiful and ornate cathedral. Our hotel was two blocks from the square, separated by the "green belt", with lots of trees and flowers, so we spent a lot of hours in our free time, in the square during our stay in Krakow. Also in the square is the 900 year old Church of Saint Adalbert. In most of the old city market squares, they have added "sidewalk" cafes with umbrellas, chairs and tables directly outside the restaurants around the edges of the square, so you have a choice of going inside to eat and have a glass of your favorite drink, or sitting outside when the weather is nice---and it was perfect while we were there---. It was so pleasant to sit outside and watch all the people in the square.

The following day we toured Auschwitz, the largest of the WW II concentration camps, and the site where the Nazis killed about one and one half million people, mostly Jews. Folks, that is a very sobering and sad experience. We walked through the concentration camp's gas chambers and crematorium and saw rooms full of human hair, shoes, and luggage. It is still difficult to believe that humans would slaughter hundreds of thousands of other humans like the Nazis did here. We attended a lecture by Mr. Smolen, an Auschwitz survivor. He loved Americans, especially the U.S. Army---they liberated him and saved his life!

After another day of leisure, spent mostly in the market square of Krakow, we drove through beautiful farm land, 370 miles to Prague in the Czech Republic, After breakfast the next morning we attended a very interesting lecture, "From Communism to Capitalism" by a professor of economics. A quick summary of what he said, verified by other Eastern European natives that we met is in order. They like Americans. The United States is one of the few countries that never attacked any of them. They hate the Nazis, for good and obvious reasons. They hate the former Soviet Union even more----the Soviets treated them horribly. They took away everything---their homes, businesses, their farms, their land---everything. The State owned everything. Since the fall of the Soviet Union, the Eastern European governments are trying to repatriate everything back to the rightful owners, or their heirs, but it is nearly an impossible problem, given the passage of time, deaths and scattering of native populations, etc.

After the lecture, the professor took us on a walking tour of the old town square----more beautiful churches, shops, restaurants, and outdoor cafes. We walked across the famous Charles Bridge over the Vltava River, where a "Dixieland" jazz combo was playing. One afternoon we went to the countryside by bus and toured Sychrov Castle. We enjoyed a private concert, in the castle chapel, and dinner in the Baroque Salon. On a morning tour, we visited Hradcany, the castle district in the city of Prague. It is a massive complex including palaces, churches, and museums. We toured the Prague Castle and the flag on the roof indicated that the President was in his office complex. The city did not sustain major damage in WW II, so the architecture spanning six centuries has been preserved. Prague has the most beautiful buildings of any city we have visited in Europe.

On our own, with Dick and Ann, we had a bratwurst lunch at Prague's famous U Fleku Brewery and Pub, operating continuously since 1499! We sampled honey vodka and famous bohemian beer. After brewing beer for 500 years, they got it right! One of the most interesting tours was out in the country to the small village of Nosalov. After a walking tour of the village, we enjoyed a delicious dinner and a lively program of polka music and dance.

After an early breakfast, we began our 300-mile drive to Budapest. We drove through some of the most beautiful farmland imaginable with fields of grain, wheat, corn, sunflowers, and other crops. We stopped for lunch in Bratislava, capital of Slovakia, with a view of Bratislava Castle perched high above the Danube. We arrived in Budapest in the early evening, checked into our hotel, and had dinner on our own. Until it was unified in 1872, Budapest was two cities, Buda and Pest separated by the Danube River. The first morning we had a city tour, including Hero's Square, with the Tomb of the Unknown Soldier and other monuments. We visited Castle Hill, 180 meters above sea level on the Buda side of the river, home of spectacular Matthias Church (where all the Hungarian kings were crowned), and many historic buildings, hotels, gift shops, and cafes, and a great view of the Danube River and Pest across the river. Budapest also has beautiful buildings and architecture.

The next day we had a full day tour to the Danube Bend, traveling by boat to Szentendre, one of the most charming small towns in Hungary---an artists' town full of museums, folkloric architecture, and culture, not to mention zillions of gift shops where Katherine and Ann put big dents in credit cards.

The next day was one of my very favorites on this trip. We had a long, 60-mile ride on winding roads, out into the Hungarian countryside to a small medieval village of Holloko, population of 400. Maybe one of the reasons I liked it so much is that it is not *that* much bigger than Pitkin! Founded in the 13th century, it has changed very little in over 700 years, and is now preserved as a UNESCO World Heritage Site. We were met by a group of ladies in beautifully embroidered skirts of puffed silk, costumed as in the old days. They treated us to popcorn, popped on an open fire in front of us, and danced and sang for us. We strolled the cobblestone streets (2)!, visited their church and several shops, and then our tour guide separated our busload into several smaller groups for a local family lunch, which was spectacular! Our group's family hostess was Margaret. She escorted us down a dirt road to her white, spectacularly clean, house. She introduced us to her grandson, about age 9, and her Mama (and my sweetie), about age 80. (You know how I feel about little old ladies!) We had a lunch to remember—including hand made noodles, all kinds of other goodies, and gallons of homemade wine. I know that the tour operators pay these families to entertain and feed home hosted lunches and dinners to us gringos on these trips (one of the very best things we like about GCT). But I assure you that money cannot buy the hospitality that the families demonstrated. Interestingly, we did not see an adult man in the village of Holloko---I suppose they were in the fields, working.

The next day was our last full day in Budapest, and last day on our 19-day trip, visiting Eastern Europe. We rode the subway back down to our favorite fussgangstrasse (walking—no cars) street. We browsed, shopped and had lunch (our last shot at Hungarian Goulash), and took the subway back to the hotel. That night we had our farewell dinner and party at a restaurant on the Budda side of the river, with gypsy music and dancing. On the way back to the hotel, the bus driver took us back to the top of the hill where we enjoyed fantastic nighttime views of the city and river. The next day we returned home to Niceville. It was a great trip, made more special because super friends, Dick and Ann Noack, joined us.

In November 2004, the Fab 5 (actually 4 out of 5) Alaska reunion group met in Mobile and took a short 5 day Caribbean cruise with stops in Playa Del Carmen and Cozumel, Mexico. That was our reunion for 2004 and all had a great time.

ITALY. After two more Caribbean cruises, we launched on another Grand Circle Travel trip for 21 days in Italy in May/June 2005. Dick and Ann Noack accompanied us again. We spent one week in each of three places: Rome, Sorrento, and Montecatini, and took side trips out of the three hotels. We like that, seeing a lot of places but only packing and unpacking three times.

Everybody has been to Rome so I won't dwell on that portion of the trip. We had been to Rome before, so we again did the standard bill of fare, Vatican City including St Peters Square, the Basilica, Sistine Chapel, and the ancient Coliseum, Roman Forum, etc. The history and sights are never boring, but Rome is still noisy and full of 'liddle biddy' cars and motorbikes, all blowing their horns, all the time. Did I mention *noisy?*

Our next stay was in Sorrento, a beautiful seacoast town, and our favorite. Our hotel, the Michelangelo, was conveniently located a short walk into downtown with lots of shops, and small parks—lots of plants, flowers and greenery. The town is located on high ground, overlooking a harbor on the southwestern coast of Italy. On the day we arrived we had an Italian language lesson (as it turns out, Italian is spoken more with your hands than with your mouth!). Our teacher was our tour director, Ann. She was an American, married to an Italian, and had lived in Sorrento for many years.

The next day, we had a home-hosted lunch at Luigi and Theresa's home. She had a separate building in her garden with a kitchen and large dining room. We had a delicious lunch with lots of wine and limoncello (a potent beverage made from lemons and other exotic herbs). We enjoyed a full day excursion to the Isle of Capri, taking a hydrofoil carrying 100 folks from the port at Sorrento. Capri is a beautiful island, very mountainous and scenic. The main town is the port, of course at sea level, but we also traveled to the top of a mountain where the picturesque village of Anacapri is located.

On one day we toured the ancient city of Pompeii, which was totally buried and destroyed when Mount Vesuvius erupted in AD 79, and was not re-discovered until the 17th century. This was one of the more interesting tours on the trip. They have literally unearthed the ruins of the old city and the excavations continue today. We visited a farm, and observed cows, pigs, chickens, rabbits, and the making of olive oil and cheese (I'm sure this was interesting to the city folks!) We then made our own pizza and limoncello for lunch. We took a full day bus trip from Sorrento to Amalfi, and the coast drive was awesome. It follows a road literally carved out of the side of a cliff, with the sea @ 500 feet straight down below. It makes the highway 1 drive along the California coast look like a boring ride on flat countryside! Towns along the way were built into cliffs as well. I have many pictures---come see us for the virtual tour.

After a great stay in Sorrento, we headed north to Montecatini, in Tuscany. The next morning, we had a walking tour of the town; famous for its spas, believed to cure many ailments. We were entertained by a string quartet while we visited a huge spa in a beautiful park area. For lunch we visited a local *agriturismo* country house for a special Tuscan Fare lunch. It was on a farm and we enjoyed a traditional Tuscan homemade meal (the cheese dumplings were tasty), and we sampled vintages from the family's vineyard. I felt great, but I don't know if it was because of the miracle water I tasted at the spa or the wine I had at the farmhouse!

One day during our stay in Montecatini, we had a tour of Pisa and Lucca. You know about Pisa and the leaning tower, which is the bell tower for the cathedral. Construction began in 1173 and continued for 200 years. The area is highly commercialized, with an entire street filled with souvenir shops. Lucca is the only Italian city that is totally enclosed, ringed by a high bulwark built between 1554 and 1645. It has many churches dating from the 11th to the 14th century. Another day involved an all day trip to Florence, on the Arno River, and one of the most beautiful cities in Italy. Home to many artists, including Dante, Boccaccio, Donatello, Leonardo da Vinci, and Michelangelo, the city is renowned for its art and architecture. Perhaps the most famous single piece of art is Michelangelo's statue of David. Since we had seen it on an earlier trip, we passed up the opportunity to stand in line for a few hours to see it again!

The next day was very interesting, enjoyable and special (most of them were). On our way to visit an old medieval hill-top town of San Gimignano, Ann, our tour guide made a surprise stop out in the country at a huge, beautiful cemetery: an American cemetery where 4,400 American warriors from World War II are buried. Every blade of grass was manicured and standing at attention. The 4,400 gleaming white crosses were perfectly aligned. It was immaculate and beautiful. I was immediately reminded of the American cemetery in Coleville, France on the Normandy Coast. As in France, the caretakers are AMERICANS! Seeing these cemeteries will make you feel so proud to be an American. As we got back on the bus, I noticed that quite a few of our travelers seemed to have gotten something in their eyes---particles of dust perhaps, although I didn't see any dust. I'll chase a rabbit here: I will always remember my visit to the American cemetery in Normandy. It was a time when we were not very popular in France (does anybody remember when we *were?*), and the French newspapers and propaganda sheets were loudly proclaiming, "Yankee go Home, Yankee Go Home!" A U.S. newspaper somewhere published an article about this, and accompanied it with a picture of the Coleville American cemetery, with the caption underneath that read: "These Yankees can't go home!" WOW!

Our visit to San Gimignano was great---I enjoy the visits to small, old towns more that the cities---after all, I'm just a country boy from Pitkin! We enjoyed the narrow, cobblestone street(s), the medieval towers, small wineries, and the many shops on "main" street, in this old walled town. Our tour director surprised us with a sample of wild boar she was carrying in her picnic basket. After we departed Gimignano, we drove through the Tuscan countryside, past endless stretches of grape vineyards in Chianti wine country to Castle Oliveto. We had a guided tour through the Castle, and enjoyed a wine tasting and a delicious lunch. We had a couple of days of leisure in Montecatini, then traveled back to Rome, for one night, then flew to Niceville. As usual, we thoroughly enjoyed being with Dick and Ann Noack, for this whole trip.

CHINA. On 1 June 2006 we began a 21-day trip to China with Grand Circle Travel, our third trip with this company. This was arguably the most educational and enjoyable trip we ever made, and clearly the most physically demanding. In 21 days we had 13 separate flights and walked through 20 airports! We arrived in Beijing, the capital city, and were escorted to our 5-star hotel, the Jing Guang New World in the center of the city, where we met our tour director, Peng (pronounced Pong). Beijing is built around Tiananmen Square and the Forbidden City. We visited the square, which covers 98 acres. It is infamous because of the pro-democracy demonstrations by students in 1989, which were violently squashed. Surrounding the square are large buildings housing a museum, banquet hall and the entrance to Forbidden City. (On my business trip to Beijing earlier, we were hosted to a dinner in the huge banquet hall, which seats 5,000 people.) We were escorted through the Forbidden City, named as such because for 500 years common people could not enter. It held palaces for the Emperors and their concubines from 1368 until 1911. If a commoner was caught looking at an Emperor, he was immediately beheaded. Forbidden City covers 200 acres, and has 800 ceremonial buildings, containing 9,999 rooms (and I think we walked through every one of them). A 35-foot high wall circles the City. The next day (Sunday) we visited a huge park, and the Temple of Heaven. There were *many* Chinese folks in the park, playing games and exercising. Their favorite exercise is dancing. We were watching the dancing at a very large outdoor tile floor under the trees, and listening to recorded music when a Chinese man came over to Katherine, took her by the hand on to the dance floor and danced. Afterward, another Chinese gent took her for a dance---they aren't bashful. I took pictures, so we could prove to our Sunday School Class that we did attend church that Sunday! That afternoon we visited the Summer Palace, 13 square miles of pavilions, temples, palaces, and a huge lake. It is now China's largest and best-preserved royal garden. Our tour group was conveniently sized, with 35 gringos fitting nicely into one busload.

During the next several days we took rickshaw rides through a section of Beijing known as the Hutongs (narrow alleys) and had tea with a local family. We visited the Great Wall and climbed a portion of it. Sections of the wall were built during the period 403-221 BC. Along the wall, towers were built at a distance of two bowshots apart---meaning that the archers within it could defend the entire wall. The wall snakes along a winding path---Chinese mythology maintains that demons and evil spirits can only travel in a straight line, and the undulating wall effectively keeps them out.

We toured the Ming tombs, where the remains of 13 emperors are buried. On our last night in Beijing, we attended the Beijing Opera----UGH! During our stay in Beijing, we did not see much of the sun. Most of the energy production in China is from coal and it is dirty—lots of smog and air pollution everywhere. We visited a Kung Fu school and a jade factory before leaving for the airport for our flight to Shanghai. Beijing is home to 13 million people and I think we saw every one of them!

Shanghai is the most beautiful modern city I have ever seen!! I had not visited it before. It was awesome---the modern building architecture, the skyscrapers, the elevated maze of highway interchanges, the amount of green space---grass, flowers, trees everywhere, even "downtown" in the city was awesome. The first evening we ate at a local restaurant and then attended an acrobatics show. A word about meals: 43 meals were included on the tour. A western style breakfast was always included at our hotel. The other meals were Chinese style and always served on a large lazy Suzan on a large round table—so you had to turn the lazy Suzan and arm-wrestle your tablemates for your food. Beer, wine, and bottled water were served---nobody drinks tap water, not even the Chinese, and not even in the 5 star hotels. The Chinese beer was almost alcohol free and tasted very good—Katherine even liked it. We visited the Museum of Art and History, containing artifacts from the Song to Qing Dynasties, and we stopped at a carpet factory, where Katherine invested a few Rubles---no, Yuan. After a traditional Mongolian barbeque lunch, we stopped to see the Jade Buddha Temple, and then strolled the famous Bund, a riverfront promenade, with street performers and vendors sharing the boulevard with pedestrians.

On another day, we took a train for a 45-minute ride to 500 year old Suzhou in China's fabled Silk Region. Called the Venice of the East, we traveled several canals (streets) by boat, including the Grand Canal, built 2,400 years ago. A highlight of the visit to Suzhou was the tour of a silk factory, to see how silk is made, from the mulberry-munching silkworms to thread to fine cloth. Suzhou is considered a small town since it only had a population of 400,000!

On other days in Shanghai, we visited a large local market, then a kindergarten school where the kids sang and danced for us, and drew pictures for us (and we sang for them). In the evening we had a riverboat cruise on the Huangpu River, known as the "mother river" of Shanghai, enjoying the architecture of the skyline, resplendent with lights. On our day of departure from Shanghai, we visited a Buddhist temple, and then a senior center in an area where 95,000 people live, about 30% of these are seniors in retirement. The ladies, some quite elderly, put on a fashion show just for us, with dancing and singing. They were so cute, but you know how I feel about little *old* ladies. After these visits, we were divided into small groups and enjoyed a home-hosted lunch, then departed for the airport for our flight to Wuhon. Shanghai is a very prosperous, modern city, and is a base for industry, trade, commerce, science and technology, banking, culture and education. It has more than 8,300 factories and enterprises and it is not nearly as polluted as Beijing. It is home for over 17 million Chinese!

After arriving at the airport in Wuhon, population 9 million, we drove through a part of the city to the dock on the Yangtze River and boarded our "home" for the next six days, the Princess Jeanie. The Yangtze River is the third largest in the world, after the Amazon and Nile. It flows 3,900 miles through China and empties into the East China Sea near Shanghai. We would be sailing from east to west, upstream. There is so much to write about here, but I feel I must *try* to summarize or possibly lose my audience. So…the boat was great, the staff were great, the scenery was great, the tour of the largest hydro-electric power plant in the world was great, the visit to the largest city in the world was great, the panda bears were great, my acupuncture and cupping treatment was great (and it worked), so are there any questions?? Naw, I must add a *little* bit to this---maybe I tweaked your interest just enough to finish reading it---I hope so.

Initially, we headed up stream in relatively flat terrain that changed dramatically as we got into the Gorges area. The Three Gorges Dam is a phenomenal project having been worked on for many years and is nearing completion. When finished, it will be the largest hydroelectric power plant in the world and will displace 1.25 million people and will submerge countless archaeological sites, 13 cities, 140 towns, and 1,352 villages, creating a reservoir equal in size to the country of Singapore! Many of these cities and towns have already been evacuated and are under water and many people have been displaced and resettled. We visited one of these families in Wanxian. The government has compensated the families for their displacement. Incidentally, Chinese citizens can now own property---homes, farms, etc. but the land is owned by "the people", meaning the government. Individuals have a 72-year lease on the land. I don't know what's going to happen at the end of the 72 years!

Most of the terrain through several hundred miles of our river cruise was extremely rugged and scenic, with steep cliffs on both sides of the boat. The food on the boat was excellent, and the lectures and entertainment educational and enjoyable. Most of the food servers, bartenders, cooks, etc. were the entertainers, so it became obvious these young people were not just hired for their daytime jobs, and not at all surprising, they were the friendliest and most polite folks on the planet earth, as most Chinese are.

I need to chase a rabbit here---On the way over to China, actually before we left home, I had a sudden case of (I think the official name of it is "gettin' old and hurtin' for no apparent reason and can't git rid of it") hip "going out". Actually this was a mixed blessing. I discovered that if you asked for a wheel chair to get you through airports, the airlines would furnish you one for every flight, meeting you at your arrival gate, and taking you to your departure gate, including a nice person to push you in it. It gets better---you do not stand in line with the other 1,000 passengers going through immigration, passport control, customs, with screaming, puking babies, etc.---the nice push-person takes you through a separate line (read NO line) with the aircraft *crew!* WOW! You remember I said that we "walked" through 20 airports on this trip? Well, to be more truthful, *Katherine* walked through 20 airports. I rode through most of them. There is a God, and he is looking out for me!

But, my conscience got the better of me (but my hip *really* did hurt). On board the Yangtze River cruise, two cute little lady Chinese Doctors gave a talk and demonstration on acupuncture. Afterward, I figured what could I lose, so I made an appointment for a treatment. These two little sweethearts examined me and recommended an acupuncture *and cupping* treatment (whatever that is). I said OK. They stuck about a dozen acupuncture needles in my left hip and left them there for about 20 minutes (no pain at all). Then they removed them and placed about 10 small glass bottles with small round necks (that had been heated) on my hip. The warm bottles formed a strong vacuum and the bottles readily stuck to my hip. After about 20 minutes with the *cupping* treatment, I returned to my cabin (and life) with not a single pain in my hip until this day in 2007! My family doctor here was not surprised! He agreed with me---whatever works!

After a great six days cruising the Yangtze, we docked and disembarked in Chongqing, the largest city in the world, with a population of more than 33 million! It's true. OK, awhile back, the city expanded its boundaries to include what we would call a county, but can you imagine 33 million folks in Okaloosa County, or Vernon Parish? And we saw them all on the streets and in the parks. Chongqing was the capital of China during WW II. There were at least two highlights of our visit to Chongqing. The first, of course, is the Zoo and the Pandas. They are trying to breed the Pandas, because their population is decreasing and they are on the endangered species list. They are beautiful animals, and you want to go in to pet them, but they are not pets. They respond to theirs handlers and feeders and play with them, but they are wild animals and must be treated as such. There is about one male to every eight females in the park. The male we saw was eating bamboo and resting. With the male/female ratio of Pandas in the park, he was probably tired and *needed* the rest!

A most interesting visit in Chongqing was to the Stilwell Museum. General "Vinegar Joe" Stilwell was the Commander of American forces in China, Burma, and India during WW II. The museum was built in his honor on the site of his headquarters. It was also the headquarters of General Chenault, commander of the "Flying Tigers". These two are honored and revered by the Chinese people---they are heroes. I found it interesting that even during Mao's revolution, these sites were preserved. They credit these two as responsible for defeating the Japanese and evicting the Japanese from China. It is also interesting that wherever we went, the Chinese never referred to WW II, as World War Two. It is The Japanese War.

Time to chase a rabbit. With all the modesty I can muster, I *must* relate that General Chenault is a member of my University Hall of Fame, Northwestern State University's Long Purple Line, where I joined his ranks and was inducted in October 2006, heh, heh. Sorry. More about that event later.

We took an early evening flight to Xian, and were transferred to our hotel. The next day we toured the site of the famous Terra Cotta Army. In 1974, just a few years ago, a couple of farmers were digging a water well on their farm and discovered pieces of terra cotta soldiers. Since then, three large pits have been uncovered, and are now on view to the public. So far, more than 6,000 soldiers and horses have been excavated and the pieces put back together and excavation continues at night when the museum is closed to the public---it is truly one of the wonders of the world.

We also visited a lacquer ware factory, and purchased a large folding oriental screen for shipment to our home in Florida. Then we had lunch in a local restaurant, saw a demonstration on the preparation of the region's famous noodles and then got to sample them. In the evening we returned to the days of the Tang Dynasty with a dinner and spectacular cultural show. The next day we visited the 14th century City Wall and the Wild Goose Pagoda, one of the oldest in China. In the afternoon, we flew to the city of Guilin, a semi-tropical mountainous region. While in Guilin, we cruised the Li River through some of the most scenic and picturesque landscapes in China. The misty limestone mountains and rivers are the celebrated scenes often seen in Chinese watercolors and scroll paintings. Lunch on the boat.

On another day in Guilin, we visited the Yao Shan Tea Garden and Farm, where we learned everything that we wanted to know about tea and *more!* We were given Coolie hats and even picked tea leaves in the field. This completed our cruise/tour to Mainland China and we were transferred to the airport in Guilin for our flight to Hong Kong.

We had visited Hong Kong a couple of times before, but it is a beautiful city, and it is never boring. We went up on top of Victoria Peak for spectacular views of the Hong Kong skyline and harbor. We visited Repulse Bay, Deep Water Bay, and the floating village of Aberdeen, which may soon become only a memory as the houseboats are moved to other harbors. We did lots of shopping and increased their economy considerably! We joined our other travelers for a farewell dinner in the hotel, and the next day departed for our long trip back to our home in Florida.

I cannot overemphasize how educational and enjoyable this trip has been. It was also our last overseas trip, to date. I have about 3 hours of movies that we can view to remind us of how fortunate we are that we could visit China, but live here in the good ole USA! Final observations about our trip to China: It is huge; the size of the country is awesome. I hope we never have to fight them---there are far too many of them---China's population is over 1 billion, 300 million! We are 300 million! By the way, the current strict rule of only one child per family seems to be working with not too much disagreement. They still have a lot of folks to feed. China has been a sleeping giant; she has been awakened. With the current rate of modernization, computerization of machinery, and in particular, the increase in productivity that I attribute to more freedom and ownership of the people in the enterprises (much more incentives to produce---capitalization), I am convinced that in years to come, China will be a major power, possibly *the* world major superpower.

Toward the end of our tour I asked our tour director, Peng, where was China right now, politically and ideologically. He said he could best describe it by relating a story: He said that there was a crossroad with stop signs, and President Bush approached the intersection and turned *right* toward capitalism and democracy without even stopping. Then the Russian leader, Gorbachev, approached the intersection and stopped for a long time, looking left toward socialism and communism, but finally turning right. He said the Premier of China then came along and stopped at the intersection. He told his driver to put on the left turn signal, and then turn right! My own observation is that they (having the benefit of witnessing the Soviet collapse) are headed 100 miles per hour toward capitalism, but they certainly will not call it that. It is the "socialist market economy."

CALIFORNIA. Although California is not, by most people's standards, a foreign country (really?), I will make a few comments about our trip to the left, uh, west coast. Tom and Sheila Kerr had visited Napa Valley before, and they had a great time, so they invited us to go back with them, and visit both of the major wine producing valleys, Napa and Sonoma. Tom planned the whole trip. We were to meet the Carnival Cruise Ship, Paradise in Miami, cruise for 16 days through the Panama Canal, and dock in Los Angeles after several stops on the Mexico coast. We were then going to rent a van and drive to Petaluma, where the Napa and Sonoma valleys go north with a mountain range between them. We were to stay in Petaluma one week and visit the beautiful wineries and grape vineyards in both valleys. Problem: That September ('04) a *few* hurricanes changed our plans at the last minute. We could not get to Miami via either the east or west coast of Florida. We thought we could fly to Miami from New Orleans (the Airlines said we could), so we went over to Slidell where Tom and Sheila's daughter, Jackie lives. We stayed the night and Jackie drove us to the New Orleans airport early the next morning. But all the airplanes were grounded in Miami. We said some bad words, and drove back to Niceville. About 15 days later, we drove to Jackie's house again and she graciously took us in and drove us to the airport. We flew to Los Angeles and timed it so we arrived about the same time on the same day the ship was supposed to dock, so all the remaining travel plans (rental van, motel in Petaluma, AMTRAC train trip back to Florida, etc. did not have to be changed (Tom *is* a magician) and a very good travel agent!

The trip was fantastic. The vineyards in both valleys were beautiful, and the wineries were spectacular. We visited about 5-to 7 wineries each day for a week, and the only thing that saved us, was that they only pour about a thimble sized sample of each wine. And, bless her heart, Sheila volunteered to be the designated driver! We spent one day touring San Francisco, then drove back to Los Angeles, turned in the rental van, and caught the Sunset Limited AMTRAC train for home. This was the Hoglans first experience with AMTRAC. It was a two-day train trip, and we had sleeper cars, *very small* sleeper cars with no bathrooms. The ones with lavatories and commodes in the rooms are very expensive! You had a choice; either get into your fold-down bunk and then undress, or change in the hallway where people were always walking through to the dining car and lounge. In the morning you had the same choice in reverse. The food, however, was really great. Jackie met us in New Orleans at midnight (6 hours late), and put us up for the night. AMTRAC does not own the tracks they run on. It runs on tracks owned by the rail freight companies, like Southern Pacific, CSX, etc. So when a freight train is on a segment of track, it will call AMTRAC and request the AMTRAC train pull off on the next siding and wait for the freight train to pass. Moral of this story; don't go AMTRAC if you are on a tight schedule. It is also usually more expensive than flying, but on a long trip you are also paying for a "motel" night or two on the train and several meals.

We love Jackie. I think she is going to list us on her IRS forms as dependents. Thanks Babe!

In addition to these international trips and cruises we have taken during the last 12 years of retirement, we have also enjoyed visiting closer to home, including the following trips:

1. Montreal, Quebec and Eastern Canada

2. Salt Lake City, Yellowstone National Park, and the Grand Tetons

3. Las Vegas, The Grand Canyon, Zion and Bryce Canyon Parks

4. New England Fall Foliage (Massachusetts, New Hampshire, Vermont, Rhode Island, Connecticut, and Maine)

5. Two vacations in Maine (with the 'Fab 5')

6. Branson, Missouri

7. St. Simon Island, Georgia

8. Austin, Horseshoe Bay, Boerne, Salado, Luckenbach, and San Antonio, Texas

9. San Francisco, Napa and Sonoma Valleys, California Wine country

10. Three visits to Disneyworld

11. 20th & 30th Year Reunions of the Army War College Class of 1976, Carlisle Barracks, PA

I made several comments regarding a couple of the above trips, and I think that a few brief observations about several others would be in order.

Regarding the Texas trip, Katherine had said for a while that she wanted to see the Texas Bluebonnets in bloom---in that regard, we struck it rich. We started the trip by visiting our son Steve in Lafayette, LA, and then spent a couple of days with our cousins, the Bray family in Lake Charles. Nate and Glo took us touring in south Louisiana to the Gulf of Mexico, where they have a beach house. We got together that evening for dinner at their son's house. Nathan, Jr. and his sweet wife Carol invited his sister, Karen and her husband, Darrell and all of us for a great evening. I already mentioned that Nathan, Sr. has since passed away, and was a perfect example of courage and attitude worthy of emulation for all of us.

We continued on to Texas for a week, visiting with great Army friends; Gene & Mary Lou Williams in Salado, Don & Janet Campbell in Austin, Dick & Ann Noack in Horseshoe Bay, Tex and Ann Wilson in Boerne, and Chuck & Kaye Arnecke in San Antonio.

A quick rabbit chase is required here: My Dad, from a radio advertisement by station XERF, Del Rio, Texas in the 1940s, bought a ranch just outside of Bandera, Texas, near San Antonio. Well, sort of a ranch. Actually two small lots from a ranch, that was being subdivided and sold as a future major resort, with an airport, golf courses, country clubs, hotels, shopping centers, etc. This was a serious investment—he paid $86 for each of these two lots! We had visited our "ranch" once, several years before, and by the way, spent the night in a room above the Purple Cow Saloon, where the good ole boys were having a hoedown. The area was noted for Dude Ranches and we were anxious to see our Dude Ranch. Well, when we finally found it, there was only one old hermit living on the entire future resort, in a camping trailer. When we asked him what went wrong with the resort, he said they could not find water---they drilled "water" wells five miles deep and only struck rocks. This accounted for the 55-gallon drums outside his trailer—he hauled water from Bandera. We asked a local real estate firm what these two lots were worth currently. The guy smiled and said, about $86 per lot. Needless to say, we were delighted to hear that the lots had held their value over these 55 or so years!! Another rabbit: One year we got a tax notice saying that they went out to do the annual tax assessment, (we had been paying around $3 a year in property taxes) and could not get to our lots because a dog was threatening them. I replied that it was not my dog—he was obvious an illegal squatter.

Well, on this visit, Tex Wilson and Ann drove us out to Bandera to check on our ranch. After considerable time and effort, we located the property. A Mexican family lived in a small house nearby. We spoke to them and I didn't want Tex to drive down the narrow, dirt road overgrown with briars in his new Lexus, so the young Mexican lad volunteered to drive us the two blocks to our ranch in his old pickup truck. He instructed Katherine and I to get in the *back* of the truck. We did. After touring our 'ranch', we left. When we returned to Florida, our young Mexican friend called and said his Dad wanted to buy our 'ranch'. We, not too reluctantly, said OK. We are no longer big ranchers in Texas.

The remainder of our trip to Texas was wonderful, mainly because we were visiting some of our very best Army friends. The Williams

(Mary Lou) showed Katherine around Salado---a very interesting town and Gene took me out to Ft. Hood, a huge Army Fort (I think it is the largest in the Army.) The Campbells took us into Austin to visit the capitol (we saw the legislature in session) and they took us to the hospital where I think I was born (and all this time I thought I was hatched under a rock). We went to church with Dick and Ann Noack and Dick arranged a great lunch with his children and their kids. Chuck and Kaye Arnecke also attended the lunch and then we spent several enjoyable days with them, to include a visit to the Riverwalk in San Antonio which is always fun. This trip reinforced my belief that the best things in life are friends. Oh yes, Katherine got to enjoy lots of Bluebonnets and Indian Paint Brushes, growing wild along highways and at a flower farm we visited.

On the first trip to Disneyworld, we took our granddaughters and everybody enjoyed it. We reasoned that we had better do it before they got older and would be ashamed to be squired around by two old fogy grandparents! The other two visits to Disneyworld were for almost a week each with the Kerrs. If you are going to see it all, you need a week. These were in December 2005 and 2006, when the Christmas lights and decorations are unbelievable. The Christmas Cantata with a huge composite choir and orchestra were worth the whole trip. We walked many miles during our visits—the walking in December 2005 was particularly good for me, because it was just over a month after my triple bypass, open-heart surgery. More later.

Before we moved to Florida we also enjoyed visits to Bermuda, Nassau, Hong Kong, Thailand, Singapore, Taiwan, Cancun, and Isla Mujares, Mexico. (I'll save the summaries of these visits for the next book!)

Mercifully, the last trip I will summarize is the attendance at our Army War College Class of 1976, 30th year reunion held in Carlisle Barracks, Pennsylvania in October 2006. We graduated in the Bicentennial Class (1976), and attended our 10th reunion in 1986 at Bowling Air Force Base in Washington, D.C. We also attended our 20th year reunion in 1996 at Carlisle Barracks. I was the Master of Ceremonies and our Commandant, Major General DeWitt Smith attended both of these reunions. We were a tight and especially close class. We all had enormous admiration and respect for General Smith. When we were students in 1976 General Smith liked to hear me play Dixieland when the Service Bands visited the War College and humored me by allowing me to sit in with them. He asked me if I would play "Do You Know What it Means to Miss News Orleans" at his funeral. I told him I would if I was still around. At our 10th and 20th reunions, he reminded me of this commitment. Unfortunately, shortly before our 30th reunion, General Smith passed away. I did not find out about it until several weeks later. At our 30th reunion in October 2006, we held a memorial service for "our" General. We were all excited that Mrs. (Betty) Smith attended this reunion, with her grown children. We dedicated a monument and planted a tree in his honor, and I finally got to play "Do You Know What it Means to Miss New Orleans" for him. It was great to see so many classmates and spouses. This is my all time favorite group of people that I was privileged to be a part of. I enjoyed being the MC for these reunions and we all owe a debt of gratitude to our classmate, Jack King for organizing and putting them all together. I told the group that the committee had not yet decided where we would hold our 40th year AWC reunion in 2016, but for our 50th in 2026, Katherine and I wanted to invite everybody (both of them) down to Niceville, FL, and the whole class could stay at our house and we would feed them, and Moses would be the guest speaker!

We particularly enjoyed staying in the same hotel and visiting a couple of extra days with classmates Tom and Carol Lightner, Buddy and Charlotte Beck, and Don and Norma Jean Infanti. I never had any brothers (or sisters), but if I did, these would be them! We also got to visit and spend some time with my "ole" Deputy and Chief of Staff of V Corps Artillery, Mike Daley, now living in Carlisle. Then we visited Hershey, PA., and got our *fix* of chocolate candy. Fortunately, they now have sugar free!

This is an appropriate time and place to announce our retirement from overseas traveling. The main reason is that we have been very fortunate to have traveled to everywhere in the world that we really wanted to! And my body has been trying to get my attention for a while now, saying, "Hokay GI, isn't it time to kool it? My feet are killin' me, and I can't jump as high as I used to!" So we are going to do more "rocking on our back porch, and going to the Gulf of Mexico's beautiful snow white sandy beaches 11 minutes from here, and listening to the waves come in, and then looking at all these hundreds of hours of movies I made of our travels!"

Y'all come. We'll even furnish the popcorn!

"Anything worth doing well, is worth doing s-l-o-w-l-y!"

Mae West

FIVE

Retired, Retired, Retired

I alluded to some health issues that have slowed me down---nothing too big. I'll just summarize these quickly---not to dwell on things unpleasant. Bad foot infection in 2004, and the Doc threatened to cut off my foot, but my foot and I prevailed. I had a heart attack in October 2005, and underwent triple bypass open-heart surgery. After that, I went into congestive heart failure several times, atrial fibrillation (A-fib) with rapid ventricular response several times, was hospitalized 5 times in 4 months, had a pacemaker installed in January 2007, then enjoyed a hard case of Shingles for 3 months. Other than that, I'm in great shape!

There are a lot of people who we met since moving here 12 years ago, that I want to thank for being such great lifesavers, friends, and neighbors, even at the risk of forgetting somebody. I have mentioned some already. Chiefly among the lifesavers are my all time favorite heart surgeon, Dr. Mike Sheridan, his PA Eric Majors, and the greatest nurse on Planet Earth, Rhonda Mitchell (I love her with all of my (new) heart), and all the folks at the Fort Walton Beach Medical Center. We have the finest family Doctor, Greg Turner, and his wife and Nurse Practitioner, Bobbi, who live in Bluewater Bay and have their office here. Thanks to Jim Brown at the re-hab center at Twin Cities. For three months he strapped me into those ominous exercise machines. I didn't get into shape but I confessed to 20 crimes!

Thanks to the greatest neighbors in the world, Keith and Ginny Seago, Jan and Nadine Edeburn, and Bob and Nancy Garcia. Keith is a retired Army Colonel and long time friend and comrade—he is a 'redleg'(Artilleryman) and we served together at Ft. Bragg. Jan is a retired Air Force Colonel and a super friend and neighbor. Bob is our token Marine, a retired Colonel, and the only Marine on the block---so we have him clearly outnumbered; he says it's about even. Bob is a great neighbor and is our computer whiz---he teaches it at the local college and trouble-shoots the neighborhood computers, mine in particular! The eight of us have a lil tradition---we gather every evening about 5 PM at a concrete table with four benches that we bought and placed just outside our corner yard next to the lake. We have been known to have a sip of the Sherry. We catch up on the neighborhood gossip and have solved many of the world's problems! Also, in our neighborhood lives Jack White (a War College classmate) and his sweet wife Bobbie, my ole golfing partner, Gary and Sylva Flora, Cort and Lona Proctor, Bibb and Diana Huffstutler, Tom and Lynn Whitmore, Ginny Meeker, Charlie and Carol Morris, Tony and Hilda Agosta, Joe and Linda Testa, Peter and Eva (Miss Berlin) Kueth, and Mark and Lynn Watson. We all live on Glenlake Circle, around a small lake and have lived here about the same length of time, charter members if you will, because the neighborhood opened up for building about that time 12 years ago. We are all good friends---we already chased off the unfriendly ones!

I want to thank our church members for being such good friends. Our Pastor at Bluewater Baptist Church, Dr. Haywood Day is an outstanding preacher, Sunday School teacher, and Biblical Scholar. He married way over his head—Gail is a Sunday School teacher, gives the children's' sermon, and is a sweet lady. My choir mates are an outstanding group of folks, especially our choir director, Randy (also marrying over his head) Jones and his wife (and my sweetie) June. The Dier girls, Mom Pat, and daughters, Mary and Becky are musically talented friends, and so are Kelly and (Deacon) Martie Courington. Friends and fellow singers, Nancy Buckellew, Faye Smith, Raleigh Langley, Clayton Solomon, and Ken Posey round out the choir. It sounds like a big choir for a little church and it would be if everybody showed up at the same time! Other good friends in church are Allyson and George Gordon, Gail Weaver, Sue Langley, Mary-Anne Childs-Jordan, Carol Hamm, Barbara Posey, Jeff Smith, Wendell and Rhonda Culbreth, Lorene Bass, Anne Sisk, Howard Francis, Brad and Anita Metcalfe, Pansy Prichard, Jimmie Russell, Wallace and Gloria Weeks, Bill and Betty Phillips, and Anita Halupowski. Gail Weaver is a special friend. She and her husband Billy Don were Charter Members of our Sunday School Class when our Pastor started it for just six of us. Billy Don was a great friend, and sadly lost his battle with cancer. I appreciate all these folks' friendship and their thoughts, prayers, and visits when I was in hospital.

Also living in Bluewater Bay are friends that we served with previously, Generals John (and Flo Ann) Crosby, Doug (and Karen) Smith, Gary (and Margie) Turner, and one other 'redleg' that we met when we arrived, Hank (and Suzie) Hagwood, and good friends Bill and Dot Barber. For several years I played golf in a regular foursome every week at the Eglin AFB Golf Club. Mike Spigelmire, who you know now, Gary Flora, my neighbor I mentioned earlier and Charlie McDonald, were the other three golfers in our foursome. I had met General McDonald at a retired General Officers' annual briefing conducted every year at Eglin AFB, by the Eglin Commander and his staff. He lived in our neighborhood in Bluewater Bay. Charlie's last assignment in the Air Force before he retired was Commander of the Air Force Logistics Command, as a 4-star General. He had a distinguished career, was a bomber pilot and held many responsible positions in the Air Force. Charlie and his sweet wife, Lucille, were accomplished sailors and owned a 37 foot sailboat, moored at the Bluewater Marina. On one of their sailing trips, they were on their way to the Caribbean, and Charlie scraped his legs on an anchor. To make a long and unpleasant story short, an infection set in and they went to a hospital in Panama City. We got a call that both his legs, far above the knees, had been amputated. We visited him twice in the ICU, and later in the hospital. I have the utmost admiration and respect for this man. Before this accident we would talk and discuss the 'world' situation and I admired and appreciated his insights and judgment. He has more than his share of courage and determination. He has handled his situation better than I could have, but I know it has not been easy. We see them and play bridge with Charlie and Lucille once a month. He is one of my heroes.

For those folks who like them, pets can play an important role in family life. I grew up on a farm and we always had dogs and cats. In our nomadic, Army life, cats were more convenient pets than dogs. Cats travel better than dogs and are lower maintenance. We had one dog, Senator Beagle of Canterbury Woods in Virginia. He had more personality than most people we knew. We were known in the neighborhood as Senator's parents. We took him to Ft Benning and Katherine spent a lot of time retrieving him from D-cell (jail). He chased cars until one day he caught one! But cats have personalities also, and they are smart. We also learned that cats have several other advantages over dogs (from an owners standpoint): They don't bark, they don't require taking them for a walk, and you don't have to train them to "go on the paper"! That is a major advantage. You put the sand-box down and they know exactly what it is for, when they are about one day old. I am like I am today (crazy) from having to teach Senator to "go on the paper". We had several cats as pets during our lifetime. Goldwater, Peaches, Sagebrush, Tiger and Missy to name a few. Missy was with us for 18 years, longer than the kids were at home. We had to have the Vet put her down 3 years ago and that is the hardest thing I ever had to do! She was smarter than several bosses I worked for. She was a very important member of the family. Katherine promised me that when we finished our overseas traveling, we could have another pet. In January of this year, '07, Smoky and Sugar made the scene. They are brother and sister, "kool kats", and entertain us constantly. They filled a big void in my life---you pet lovers will understand.

One *last* little travel episode. I promise. Last July '06, I received a letter from Dr. Randall J. Webb, President of Northwestern State University of Louisiana, informing me that I had been selected for induction into the University's Hall of Fame, The Long Purple Line. I immediately called Dr. Chris Maggio, Director of Alumni Affairs, and told him there must have been a mistake. He double-checked and said no, that is was for real. I guessed they were just having a slow year. The ceremony was held on 27 October '06, at a banquet during homecoming weekend. Chris assigned his Assistant Director of Alumni Affairs, Janay Matt, to shepherd me through this experience. Her assistance was absolutely essential and outstanding in every respect. I made one advance trip back to Northwestern for a filmed interview, pictures, etc. I immediately discovered that not only was Janay totally professional, she could have easily been Ms. Universe---what a beautiful and sweet lady!!

We had met Chris two years earlier, when we attended our 50th graduation reunions (Katherine's in 2004, and mine in 2005). Chris and his troops do a fantastic job with ceremonies, planned activities, etc. Everything was first class.

They mailed invitations to the Hall of Fame banquet and ceremony, including my guest list. I was truly honored by the presence of 39 cousins (from far and near) and friends. I'm sure they just wanted to make sure it was true and that I didn't just dream this up.

We were guests for the homecoming football game the next day and sat in the President's Box. We even won the ball game. The President's wife, Brenda, was the hostess for all the food and goodies in the box. I can relate to the fact that President Webb married way over his head. Several of us did. Brenda is a sweetheart and perfect complement to Dr. Webb---we get two for the price of one with this couple of great folks. Dr. Webb's track record relative to his accomplishments as President of Northwestern is awesome. We are all very proud of him. Thanks again to Chris Maggio and to sweet Janay.

I *had originally* intended to give you an ear full (eye full) of my feelings about our current war. I *do* have very strong feelings about it and about our great country. In wars since WW II, we have fought on behalf of somebody else, hopefully an ally. In Korea, Viet Nam, Grenada, Bosnia, etc., our very existence was never at stake. None of them attacked us. In the final analysis, it didn't really matter very much that we did not win them; our way of life didn't change at all. Viet Nam is a very good example---*Our country lost that war!* Not the U.S. military, but the national leadership, the congress, and the American people lost it!!! It is fascinating (and disgusting) to me that we had 50,000 Americans killed in that war, and for what?? Because of politics, we snatched defeat from the jaws of victory! And now we want to surrender to a ruthless, brutal enemy who *attacked us,* after 3,700 Americans have given their lives to defend *our freedom, way of life, and our very existence!!* We are *not* fighting to defend South Korea, or South Viet Nam, or Kuwait, or even Iraq. We are fighting to defend *our country and our way of life.* Our enemies want to *kill all of us.* I want to kill *them* over there---not over here!!! We don't even realize we are at war! I guarantee you that the Army and the Marines know we are at war. And most Americans (and congress) don't even know who the real enemy is---they think that if we just get together, hold hands, and sing Kumbaya everything will be OK. I don't understand why so many of our citizens are saying, I support the troops (but we should pull out now, or it's Bush's war, or I don't support their mission). That is like saying, I love my basketball team, but I don't want them to win. So many people are blaming the war on President Bush—he didn't start it!!!. I tend to blame the terrorists and radical islamabastards! The overwhelming majority of the troops support their mission and are risking their lives daily to accomplish it. If you don't support the mission that our brave soldiers are willingly fighting and dying for, then I don't think you support the troops! Another trite expression I am sick of hearing is "we never should have invaded Iraq; it's all our fault". Whether we should have or should not have, is now *completely irrelevant!* The fact is, we are there, and you cannot just wish it would go away. We have people serving in our congress that hate President Bush so much, that they *want us to lose this war!* I believe that with all my heart. It is disgusting, traitorous, and sad. They publicly call the President a liar and a terrorist, and every day it emboldens the enemy and causes more casualties to our forces. Why not complete the act of defeat or surrender by giving the enemy our imminent schedule of departure? I support our troops. I support their mission, and pray every day that they will be safe but that they *will win!* And in this war, I support our President and Commander in Chief. I would do the same if our President were a liberal Democrat!!! Yes, I might have to hold my nose, but I would not give aid and comfort to the enemy. You didn't hear me blasting President Clinton and calling him a liar and a terrorist when he sent combat troops to Bosnia. By the way, they didn't attack us either! I am totally disgusted with how most politicians are politicizing the war. When will we learn that being united is a prescription for winning, and being totally and viciously divided is almost a guarantee for failure and losing?? I realize that some of you will disagree with me. Well, fine. Write your own damn book! At the beginning of this paragraph, I said that I *had originally intended* to tell you how I felt about this war. I changed my mind—call me if you *really* want to know how I *really* feel. But, I totally agree with General Norm Schwarzkofp, that retired Generals should never pass up the opportunity to keep their mouths shut. So my mouth is shut.........starting tomorrow!

"Patriotic dissent is a luxury of those protected by better men than they!"

(Author unknown, but I wish I had said it!)

"History does not entrust the care of freedom to the weak or timid."

D.D. Eisenhower

"Congressmen who willfully take actions during wartime that damage morale, and undermine the military are saboteurs and should be arrested, exiled or hanged."

President Abraham Lincoln

Curt and "Happy" with Friends

Sonja & Kevin Duggar

Hoglan's home in Florida

The Sultan and his Lady in Istanbul, Turkey

Curt & Katherine in Tiananmen Square, Beijing, China

S.C. Gov. Campbell and Curt receiving award

Curt & R.O.T.C. Hall of Fame, NSU

Curt & NSU Hall of Fame, The Long Purple Line

Curt Hoglan

Curt and Katherine

Curt and Katherine Toured China

Induction Ceremony

Our House in the Springtime!

THE HOGLAN
FAMILY ALBUM
2006

Jennifer and Michael get married

Jennifer and Julie

Steve, Janet and Curt

The Long Purple Line

EPILOGUE

WOW! What a ride! Even if I never published this book, it's been a blast, just remembering and reliving so many experiences. And it has been a great reminder of how lucky I am. The Lord has been so good to me, better than I deserve. It has also refocused me on the really important things in life-----family and friends----those are what have made this journey so special. I have mentioned and thanked quite a number of friends and kinfolk, but I know that I have not included everyone who has helped me along the way.

I want to give an update on my immediate family. Our daughter, Sonja, lives in Americus, Georgia with her husband Kevin Duggar. They have two beautiful daughters, Jennifer, 26, and Julie, 23. Sonja and Kevin both graduated from Georgia Southwestern University in Americus, and except for living several years in Plains, GA, they have been in Americus ever since their University days. Sonja worked for 10½ years in Children and Family Services, a State agency. She was a social worker in Sumpter Regional Hospital for 8 years. She worked in Mental Flint Behavioral Health Care for 5½ years supervising activities in 7 Counties. She currently works for a Doctor in Americus. After working for a construction company in Americus, Kevin worked for several years as a research assistant at the University of Georgia Agricultural Experiment Station in Plains, and they lived on the Station's grounds. That is where we met President and Mrs. Carter. It is also where our oldest Granddaughter, Jennifer, on one of the Carters' visits, pulled up her dress, baring her tummy and said to the President of the United States, "See my skeeter bites?" After they moved back to Americus, Kevin began teaching physical education and health at Macon County

Elementary School where he still teaches today after 18 years. He is also an accomplished taxidermist, and has won trophies and many awards in the State of Georgia. Jennifer and Julie graduated from Southland Academy. Jennifer graduated fromValdosta State College and is in her 4th year teaching high school English. She taught 3 years in Brantley County High School and on 22 July 2006, she married the high school baseball coach, Michael Dougherty. In June 2007 they were recruited to Rome, Georgia, Michael's hometown, where they both teach in Rome High School. Julie attended Georgia Southwestern University and South Georgia Technical College, and is working at the Regional Eye Center in Americus.

Our son, Steve, lives near Lafayette, Louisiana, in Youngsville. He attended Murray State College in Kentucky, and LSU, and graduated from Francis Marion College in Florence, South Carolina in Business Administration. He is a Department Head in a building supply store in Lafayette. Steve's girlfriend for the last 8 years, Janet Parrish lives in Lafayette. She is a sweetheart. We love Janet, and she loves us and likes to come visit us often. Steve has fond memories of Hawaii where he graduated from Moanalua High School, and has returned several times for visits.

We love all of our family and we are so thankful that they are all healthy and happy. We think they are all wonderful, but I'll admit that we are not the most objective people to ask about that.

All four of our parents are deceased. I have already bragged about them earlier in the book. They are Saints and there are not enough words to describe what they did for us and how we will be forever indebted to them. And it is very comforting to us that we know exactly where they are, right now!

Katherine's brother, "Happy", lives in Glenmora, Louisiana. I have also bragged about him earlier in the book. Happy and Katherine have always been close and I think he is the best brother-in-law in the world. He stays very busy with his hardware store and several charities and volunteer work. He continues to so some Forestry work. He just won't slow down.

Well, I saved the best till last--------The Wind Beneath My Wings! Katherine, Kay Kay, Mommy, Honey, it is just impossible to adequately describe what you mean to me! I have already said that you were beautiful, smart, and talented-----I guess the only thing left to talk about is how you had the incredibly good judgment to marry me!! ***Everybody*** knows that's a joke. I just hope I haven't been too much of a handicap to you! There are lots of men out there better than I, but you could never find one in the entire world and outer space that could possibly love you more than I, appreciate you more than I, respect you more than I, admire you more than I, want you more than I, cherish you more than I, or need you more than I. We have had a wonderful 53 years together---I hope you agree. I'm looking forward to 53 more! I love you with all my heart!

Well folks, it is finally time to wrap this up. I started writing this epistle almost 2 years ago, had a few interruptions, and I can't believe the AMEN is finally in sight. I said at the outset that this would never make anybody's bestseller list. I'm not going to market it. It is for my family, my cousins, my friends, and my Army comrades. For you that read all of it, thanks for indulging me, and I hope you found it at least interesting. It has been very interesting for me, but what do I know?! I have always been, and I will always be, just A Country Boy From Pitkin!

APPENDICES

APPENDIX A

Education and Training

CIVILIAN

Graduated Glenmora High School, LA, 1951
Graduated Northwestern State College, LA, 1955, BA Degree, Music Ed.
ROTC, 4 Year Program, at NSC, Commissioned 2d Lieutenant, 1955
Graduated Shippensburg University of Pennsylvania, 1976, MS Degree,
    Public Administration
Private Pilot Ground School, Barber's Point Naval Air Station, Hawaii
Flight Training—Hickam/Wheeler AFB and Barbers Point NAS, Hawaii,
    Private & Commercial Pilot License, Instrument Rated

MILITARY—ARMY

Anti-aircraft Artillery Basic Course, 1955, Ft. Bliss, TX
Arctic Warfare Course, 1957, Ft. Greely, Alaska
Associate Field Artillery Battery Officer Course, 1960, Ft. Sill, OK
Jungle Warfare School, 1960, Ft. Sherman, Panama Canal Zone
Artillery Officer Advanced Course, 1961, Ft. Sill, OK & Ft. Bliss, TX
Instructor Training Course, 1964, Ft. Benning, GA
Infantry Officer Advanced Course, 1967, Ft. Benning, GA
Command & General Staff College, 1968, Ft. Leavenworth, KS
Army War College, 1976, Carlisle Barracks, PA
Plus Many Short Courses

CIVILIAN—OCCUPATIONAL

Economic Development Basic Course, 1985, University of South Florida
Economic Development Executive Program (3 Summers at Univ. of
  Oklahoma) Certified Economic Development Executive
Plus Many Short Courses

COAST GUARD AUXILIARY

Boating Skills and Seamanship Course
Instructor Training Course
Auxilliary Administrative Procedures Course
Auxilliary Leadership Course
Advanced Coastal Navigation Course
Communications Course
Search and Rescue Course
Patrols Course
Weather Course
Seamanship Course
Hazardous Materials Course

APPENDIX B

Awards & Decorations

ARMY

Distinguished Service Medal
Defense Meritorious Service Medal
2 Bronze Stars
Purple Heart
2 Army Meritorious Service Medals
Air Medal
Army Commendation Medal
National Defense Service Medal
Viet Nam Service Medal
Army Service Ribbon
Overseas Service Ribbon
Viet Nam Campaign Medal
Viet Nam cross of Gallantry With Palm
Meritorious Unit Commendation
Aircraft Crewman Badge
Jungle Expert Badge
Army General Staff Identification Badge
Order of Saint Barbara (Artillery)
Honorary Doughboy (Infantry)

CIVILIAN

Northwestern State University Hall of Fame, "The Long Purple Line"
Northwestern State University ROTC Hall of Fame
Economic Development Professional of the Year for the State of South Carolina
South Carolina Governor's Job Creator Award

COAST GUARD AUXILIARY

Auxiliary Achievement Medal

4 Auxiliary Public Education Medals

5 Sustained Auxiliary Service Medals

4 Auxiliary Operations Service Medals

3 Operations Program Medals

Coast Guard Unit Commendation

4 Auxiliary Commendation Medals

Coast Guard Meritorious Team Commendation

Examiner Program Medal

Coxswain Badge

Master Instructor Program Medal

Operational Auxiliarist Badge

Auxiliary Membership Service Medal

Best Auxiliarist in Division One Award

4 Auxiliary Vessel Examination Medals

5 Specialty Training Awards

APPENDIX C

Countries, Territories, & Islands Visited

Continental United States (All But 6 States)	Canada
Alaska	Hawaii
Mexico	Bahamas
Haiti	Jamaica
Cayman Islands	Puerto Rico
St. Thomas	St. John
St. Croix	St. Kitts
Dominica	Martinique
Barbados	Grenada
Trinidad	Venezuela
Curacao	Bermuda
Panama	England
Netherlands	Belgium
Luxembourg	France
Switzerland	Okinawa
Liechtenstein	Austria
Russia	Italy
Greece	Turkey
Crete (Greece)	Spain
Rhodes (Greece)	Portugal
Cyprus (Greece/turkey)	Morocco

Mallorca (Balearic Islands)	Azores
Menorca (Balearic Islands)	Monaco
Gibraltar	Israel
Thailand	Guam
Wake Island	Philippines
Singapore	Vietnam
Japan	China (Prc)
Korea	Taiwan (Roc)
Australia	Hong Kong
Tasmania (Australia)	New Zealand
Isla Mujares (Mexico)	Cozumel (Mex)
West Germany	East Germany
Columbia	Costa Rica
Margarita Island, Venezuela	St. Lucia
Bonaire	Aruba
Belize	Guatemala
Poland	Czech Republic
Slovakia	Hungary
St. Maarten	Tortola, Bvi
Vatican State	Isle of Capri
Recap: 82	

APPENDIX D

Membership—Clubs, Organizations, Activities

Sigma Tau Gamma Fraternity, Northwestern State College

Phi Mu Alpha-Sinfonia Fraternity, Northwestern State College

"Demonaires", Official Dance Band of Northwestern State (Leader, 1953-55)

"Modernaires" Jazz Combo, Ft. Benning, GA (Leader, 1966-67)

Masonic Lodge, Ft. Benning, GA

"Anacosta River Ramblers" Dixieland Combo, Northern Virginia

"Dixie 5-0" Combo, Northern Virginia

Potomac River Jazz Club

Hickam/Wheeler Air Force Base Aero Club (Hawaii)

Barber's Point Navy Flying Club (Hawaii) (President—1977-78)

German-American Club, Wertheim, Germany

Florence County Economic Development Commission (Director—1985-89)

Rotary Club, Florence, South Carolina

South Carolina Economic Development Association

Board Member, Southern Industrial Development Council (15 States)

Lafayette Economic Development Authority (Pres & Ceo—1989-95)

Board Member, Louisiana Industrial Development Executives Association

Louisiana Governor's Military Advisory Committee

Coast Guard Auxilliary, Niceville, Florida (Flotilla Commander, 2003-04)

Association of the U.S. Army (Frankfurt Germany Chapter President, 1980-1982)

Retired Officers' Association
Lifetime Member, Marne Association (3d Div)
Honorary Member, Non-Commissioned Officers Association
Vice Commander, American Legion Chapter in South Carolina

OTHER QUALIFICATIONS

Private Pilot License
Instrument Rated Pilot
Commercial Pilot License
Aircraft Flown and Certified in: C-150, C-152, C-172, T-34b, T-41,
    Beach Sierra
Certified Economic Development Executive
    3-year (Summer Sessions) Program at the Univ. of Oklahoma

APPENDIX E

Places We Have Lived

YEARS	MONTHS	ADDRESS
1934	20 June	Austin, Texas (BORN)
1934-1938		Nacogdoches, Texas
1938-1944		Box 15, Pitkin, Louisiana
1944-1945		Acadia Baptist Academy, Eunice, Louisiana
1946		Monroe, Louisiana
1947-1949		Kinder, Louisiana
1949-1951		Pitkin, Louisiana
1951-1954		Natchitoches, Louisiana
1954	Jan-Aug	103 Behan, Natchitoches, Louisiana (Married)
1954-1955	Sep-Jun	General Delivery, Montgomery, Louisiana
1955	Jul-Nov	Fillmore, El Paso, Texas
1955-1956	Dec-Jul	109 Shore Acres, SW, Tacoma, Washington
1956	Jul-Sep	Mountain View Apts, Anchorage, Alaska
1956-1959	Sep-Apr	Qtrs 431-E, Fort Richardson, Alaska
1959	May-Nov	2705 Denver, Lawton, Oklahoma
1959-1961	Nov-Mar	56, South 45th Street, Lawton, Oklahoma
1961	Apr-Jun	1001-f Catalina Way, El Paso, Texas
1961-1963	Jul-May	404 Pine Valley Drive, Warner Robins, Georgia
1963-1964	Jun-Jul	(Curt) HQ 8th Army, Seoul, Korea

1963-1964	Jun-Jul	(Katherine) Pawnee Road, Glenmora, Louisiana
1964-1965	Aug-Jun	215 Munson, Columbus, Georgia
1965-1967	Jul-Jun	111-B Butts Street, Fort Benning, Georgia
1967-1968	Jul-Jun	1001 Kickapoo Street, Leavenworth, Kansas
1968-1969	Aug-Aug	(Curt) Dong Ha Combat Base, Dong Ha, Viet Nam
1968-1969	Aug-Aug	(Katherine) 56, So. 45th St., Lawton, Oklahoma
1969-1972	Aug-Jan	4911 Andrea Ave, Annandale, Virginia
1972-1974	Jan-Apr	315 Lumpkin Road, Fort Benning, Georgia
1974-1975	Apr-Jul	8309 Ramsgate Court, Alexandria, Virginia
1975-1976	Jul-Jul	Qtrs 1-B Young Hall, Carlisle Barracks, Penn
1976-1978	Jul-Sep	1335 Parks Place, Fort Shafter, Hawaii
1978-1980	Sep-Jul	Cdr Qtrs, Peden Barracks, Wertheim, Germany
1980-1982	Jul-Jul	213 Uhlandstrasse, Bad Vilbel, Germany
1982-1985	Jul-Jun	Hoyle, Fort Bragg, North Carolina
1985-1989	Aug-Nov	2488 W. Keswick Rd, Florence, South Carolina
1989-1995	Nov-May	114 Hawthorne Rd, Lafayette, Louisiana
1995	Jun-Nov	800 Bay Drive #3, Niceville, Florida
1995-200?	Nov-???	1517 Glenlake Circle, Niceville, Florida

EL GRANDE TOTAL = 37

The Hoglan Family

Printed in the United States
102052LV00003B/91-99/A